# TODAY IN
# CATHEDRAL FRANCE

### by SYDNEY A. CLARK

To know the cathedrals of France means knowing something infiniately more French than Paris' celebrated Rue de la Paix. The spirit of France dwells forever in the inspiring edifices to which several generations gave unstintingly in labor, money and devotion. Well aware of these facts, and drawing on personal observations in pre-war and post-war France, Sydney Clark has approached his subject in an entirely fresh and stimulating manner. The personal, human side of the cathedrals and the cathedral builders and the character of the towns which sprang up about them are stressed, and the book is enlivened by engaging anecdote and enriched with legendary lore and fascinating bits of history.

By avoiding the technicalities which detract from so many volumes about cathedrals, Mr. Clark has spared the lay reader much weariness of spirit and given him a fair chance to enjoy their real splendor and charm. utifully illustrated, this volume will pro- hours of fascinating reading for the planning a vacation in France as well e person who makes his journeys ously in his favorite armchair.

# TODAY IN CATHEDRAL FRANCE

SYDNEY CLARK

ROBERT M. McBRIDE & COMPANY

NEW YORK

*Published simultaneously in Canada*
BY GEORGE J. MC LEOD, LIMITED
TORONTO

PRELIMINARY

## Some Facts of War and Survival

THIS book is a consequence of the author's half-dozen long periods of living and traveling in France during the past twenty years, including two extensive journeys made in the second and third years following victory in World War II.

Two points need immediate emphasis. First, Cathedral France, as distinct from urban and industrial France, has sustained relatively little war damage. Second, the great medieval stained glass was almost all saved by quick removal and underground storage, and is returning to the cathedrals at a gratifying pace.

The survival of the old cathedrals, irreplaceable by money and modern engineering science, is an unsung wonder of the war. How did it happen? How *could* it happen in cities desolated by repeated bombing raids and in some cases almost blotted out by artillery battles? That they did survive is a fact, not merely a claim. In many towns of northern France they

v

loom up nearly or quite intact from large surrounding quarters absolutely flattened by the hurricane of war and now faltering toward new life in temporary wooden shacks.

Two reasons for this basic fact present themselves. The Allied airmen were very carefully briefed to avoid demolishing such monuments of the past within Hitler's Fortress Europa, and to their aim and their bombsights goes much of the credit, but at least an equal amount must go to the tremendous physical strength of the structures themselves. With their towns tumbling to rubble all around them, they withstood the shocks of near hits, glancing hits, even direct hits. One may hope devoutly that these marvels of a lost age need never test their strength against The Bomb.

Let us be specific as to the present condition of the cathedrals and churches. Some sixty of them, in forty-two cities and towns, are viewed in this book. Of that company only one, the Church of Notre-Dame in St. Lô, may seem to be a total loss, though it is quite possible that even that grotesque ruin may somehow revive. If it cannot it will be recognized as a martyr to the cause of liberty, for it was in St. Lô that the American forces made their famous and decisive breakthrough in the Liberation Campaign of 1944, a few weeks after D-Day. Other towns whose celebrated fanes, whether of technical cathedral status or otherwise, suffered severely but not disastrously are Rouen, Abbeville, Evreux, Coutances, St. Malo, Orléans, totaling (with St. Lô) seven out of our forty-two. Of the remainder, many *towns*, in addition to the seven above, suffered enormous damage, chiefly Caen, Amiens, Laon, Lisieux, Beauvais, Tours, Poitiers, Angoulême and Blois—but their most important churches pulled through without serious wounds or even very noticeable scars. In some cases, especially

Amiens and Beauvais, the cathedrals are completely visible for the first time in centuries. The jungle of old growths around them has been cut down by bombs and shells. The tragedy of war brought that slight touch of recompense. Chartres, Reims, Bayeux and Bourges (and most towns in central and southern France) were luckily spared in the latest war, as was Paris—a phenomenon whose cause is still debated by Frenchmen. Reims, a major victim in the earlier war and by chance the surrender city of the later one, has seen its "National Cathedral" recover much of its old glory, thanks to intelligent restoration made possible by Mr. Rockefeller's gifts.

Strasbourg is not included in this book, although its cathedral is barely less than the very greatest in France. The reason is that that superb church, the color of a sunset's afterglow, was built and brought to completion when Strasbourg was a city of the Holy Roman Empire. It is thus Germanic in origin, more akin to Cologne and Freiburg than to Reims and Chartres.

A word about the glass of Cathedral France. It is the greatest in existence and the most abundant. The amount of it restored on my second postwar visit, as against my first, was surprising and reassuring. A pessimistic verger of York Minster has told me that fifteen years will be needed to restore the medieval glass to that English cathedral. I think he was in a dark mood at the moment, but at any rate the job is going ahead very much faster in France. One might argue that glass could wait, indefinitely, while a lacerated nation binds up its other wounds and seeks security; but without glass these mighty structures would hardly be cathedrals, and without cathedrals France would hardly be France. A recovery plan that gives a place to beauty may be more realistic in such a land than one of colder calculations.

# *Where Angels Fear to Tread*

THIS is not an architects' book about architecture. It is a traveler's book about one of the strangest and most exciting things the human race has done.

The *incidental* approach is used, each town, with the people who made it, serving as the mordant to fix in our minds the color of its great church or churches. We shall not be hampered by the tourist conscience like, for instance, that harassed American mother outside the choir grating of the Abbaye aux Hommes in Caen. She was reading aloud to her daughter, who was not listening.

"The tympana of the choir triforium arches are filled with plate tracery, quatrefoil and cusped—" Then she broke off to exclaim, "Oh dear, that's not Caen at all. It's Lisieux. I have the wrong chapter."

I do not believe that it is very difficult to acquire enough of the jargon of cathedral architecture to talk or write it smoothly,

but it is a useless art except for those who have the time and will
to carry it to the point of scholarship. A few great scholars have
written extensively on the French cathedrals, notably that
warm French Catholic, Emile Mâle; the colder, more critical
English scholar, G. G. Coulton; the Dutch-French specialist
on Chartres, J. K. Huysmans; and of course the encyclopedic
Viollet-le-Duc, whose name threatens to weary us as the name
of Aristides the Just wearied the Athenian voter. Many lesser
scholars have echoed the great ones, and still more and smaller
scholars have echoed the echoes. In all except the supremely
gifted this facile writing takes on a dryness as of tinder. We
may, with clear conscience, touch a match to it and walk away.
The original miracle will be unhurt by the flames.

What is this miracle? It appears that the supreme Gothic
cathedrals of France are the offspring of Faith and Energy
wedded for the span of a human life, seventy years, from 1180
to about 1250 during the reigns of Philippe Auguste and Louis
IX, who was the Saint. Of course there was no sharp action for
divorce brought by either mate, nor did either die at once,
but Faith declined and Energy relaxed. They slowly lost interest in each other and in a sense passed away, but they left
the greatest family of churches—as a family—to be found on
this earth.

I have used the word Cathedral as an adjective in the title
of this book, for it is as an attribute of a distinct period, a miraculous fusion of faith and energy, that we may most profit-
ably regard the separate churches. Even the greatest and loftiest
of them we may think of as chapels of *The French Cathedral*.
As we wander through the aisles and around the ambulatory
looking with awe but not with trumped-up solemnity at the
Chartres chapel, the Laon chapel, the Rouen chapel, we may

always keep in our minds *the* Cathedral. A too literal application of this thought would lead us into clumsy artificialities and absurdities of contour. We will not attempt it. Yet we may recall that many of France's noble cathedrals are a little absurd and out of plumb, though all the better loved, in some cases, because of their deformity. Magnificent Beauvais has only choir and transepts. Saint-Martin in Tulle has neither choir nor transepts, but only nave. St. Maurice in Angers has no aisles, but St. Hilaire in Poitiers has seven aisles. St. Cyr in Nevers has no west front, but instead two apses, with two high altars; while St. Etienne, the cathedral of Toulouse, is a strange monster with nothing right about it.

It will help our picture if we understand the elementary facts that the typical Gothic cathedral is supposed to represent the cross; that the altar is the head of Jesus on the Cross, with the apsidal chapels His crown; that the inclination of the choir axis, an irregularity noticed in many churches, is supposed (though not by Mâle and certain other scholars) to indicate the bowed head of Jesus in His agony. Beyond this and the simple knowledge that practically all the cruciform churches of the Middle Ages were oriented from east to west, one's architectural knowledge need not go at the beginning.

This matter of cathedral orientation is so very obvious to those who write of cathedrals that they can hardly conceive of its being a discovery to any adult. They almost never explain it. Yet there is no reason why every American should be supposed to know it by instinct. More than once I have seen tourists hurrying here and there outside a cathedral, peering first into their books, then furtively up at the sky. They were trying to determine which was the north transept and which the south, and were too timid to ask. If they had known that the altar is almost invariably at the eastern end of the cathedral, the direction toward which the early Christians always bowed in prayer, they would have had no such awkward moments.

This subject of ours is one where angels fear to tread, yet we do not quite admit that we are fools for rushing in. Coulton condemns Henry Adams, whose *Mont St. Michel and Chartres* has charmed tens of thousands, as a superficial student, concealing a frequent ignorance "under a style which implies a vast reserve of learning from which the writer is drawing almost at random." Fortunately for our peace of mind, we imply no reserve of critical learning, but are only seeing what anybody can see, enjoying what anybody can enjoy. If this book succeeds in bringing the French cathedral and its varied "chapels" nearer to those who do not aim at architectural expertness, if it makes the subject happier and more intimate, I shall indeed rejoice.

# Contents

*St. pierre*

# Illustrations

# TODAY IN CATHEDRAL FRANCE

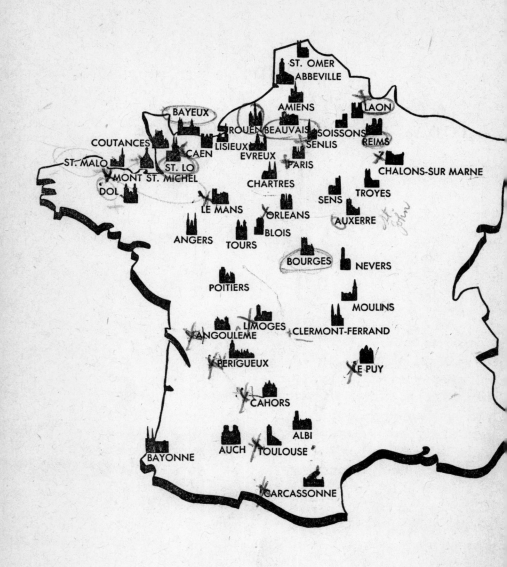

C A T H E D R A L   F R A N C E

## CHAPTER I

## The Spirit of Twelve Hundred

"THAT old serpent, which is the devil and Satan" was bound by an Angel in the bottomless pit, there to rest for a thousand full years. When the time came for him to be loosed men looked for strange and terrible events which should involve, presently, nothing less than the end of the world. It was all clearly set forth in the Book of Revelation. One thing only was not quite clear. Did the Angel incarcerate Satan at the time of Christ's birth or His death? Confusion on this point kept Christendom in a state of panicky suspense for a period of thirty-two years.

The horrors came, no doubt of that, and profoundly impressed mankind. "Vulcan's Caldron" says an ancient chronicler referring to Mount Vesuvius, "gaped far more often than was his wont and belched forth a multitude of vast stones mingled with sulphurous flames; and thus by the stench of his breath he began to make all the surrounding province uninhabitable."

Simultaneously nearly every important town of Italy and France was ravaged by fire and worse still many human beings were consumed by a mysterious plague called St. Anthony's Fire which seemed to race through the victim's tortured body like the flames of hell. (Modern science has diagnosed this disease as poison from impure rye-bread.)

The climax of all these horrors and many more which the chronicler spins out to their limit came in a mighty famine, the like of which had never visited Europe. In the three years 1030-31-32 corresponding to the ministry and crucifixion of Christ the seasons seemed to go topsy-turvy as "that old serpent" struggled to break his bonds. There was no seed-time and no harvest. Hunger-crazed people descended, and this fact is well attested in a few cases, to grim cannibalism. Human flesh was even offered for sale in at least one market-place, that of Tournus, and an innkeeper of Macon decoyed within his hostelry no less than forty-eight victims whom he killed and devoured. Famished wolves invaded many a town and grew ever bolder as the weakened inhabitants shrank in terror.

But Antichrist did not, despite the prophecy, escape his prison. The harvest of 1033 was exceedingly good. It gradually became evident that things were not finished quite yet. Legal charters dropped the portentous preamble, "The End of the World Being at Hand," with which they had been wont to open. Christendom began to breathe naturally once more.

France, being at that time mightily concerned with the things of religion, took all this harder than most nations. Even if we allow for gross exaggerations on the part of medieval chroniclers, whose example it is hard not to follow, it is apparent that the opening years of the eleventh century were years of terrible stress. France was dazed and exhausted and in a very low state. She seemed to devote about a century to rubbing her eyes in order to see if life was a thing worth looking at.

Then gradually there gathered a great wave of driving faith. The crusades were one manifestation of it but fortunately the immense force of this wave was not shattered on the hard rocks of infidel opposition in distant lands. It rebounded from these rocks, formidable though they were, and spent itself on seven or eight decades of magnificent church building in the home land. There is really no accounting for this wave of faith. All explanations are heavy-footed and unsatisfying but this much we know, it required for its formation and growth an object capable of inspiring unlimited devotion. God would not do at all, nor yet His Son Jesus Christ, sublime and just. The Holy Ghost was beyond grasp, too tenuous and meaningless by all odds. But there was MARY.

The character of Mary in the year 1200, by which date the cathedral building fervor had attained its maximum force, is something which we must try to grasp if we would come anywhere near to understanding the Gothic cathedrals. This Queen of Heaven was not a majestic, impeccable goddess, to be viewed afar with awe. She was a warm, understandable, very feminine personage as full of faults, or at least of unreasonable whims, as any queen of France. She was afraid of nobody, not even her powerful Son, whom she could cajole as she pleased. The Trinity she set at naught when it suited her caprice. Humanity clutched at Mary since she alone had power to overrule the strict legal decisions of the Deity. No religious phenomenon in history has ever compared in intensity and spread with this thirteenth century devotion to Mary. The boldest scoffers and skeptics took her seriously. Whatever sinful man might do he was not given overmuch to worrying about the pains of hell, so long as he had the Mother of God on his side.

Henry Adams (Coulton or no Coulton) grasped and reflected rather marvelously this curious medieval veneration of Mary. "In no well-regulated community, under a proper system of police," he says, "could the Vidgin feel at home." . . . The people loved Mary because she trampled on conventions; not merely because she could do it but because she liked to do what shocked every authority. Her pity had no limit. She was the highest of the feudal ladies and therefore could do exactly what she wished. She was the perfect patroness and *her* sinner —*son pecheor*, to use the delightful phrase of an old chronicler —had a much better chance at the bar of heaven than an otherwise righteous man who had committed the one sin of neglecting her.

It is well worth while, I think, to examine briefly a few of the stories about this medieval Virgin, for whom France erected in one burst of enthusiasm some twenty-five great cathedrals. By so doing we may come to know her far better than by merely reading modern analyses of her character.

Her compassion was boundless. When once a sick monk appealed to her she bade him draw milk from her *douce mamelle*, which he did and promptly recovered. Again when a robber who had been accustomed to pray to her before each robbery finally met his just desert, the gibbet, she put her white hands under his arms and held him up for three days and nights so that the rope could not destroy him. Every one saw the miracle and it won pardon for this robber, who was *her sinner*.

She was more than a little given to coquetry. A knight finding himself rejected by his lady love took the advice of a friendly abbot and appealed to the Virgin. For a year he shut himself up and prayed to her. This was a tactical blunder for Mary came gradually to enjoy this devotion. When the knight prepared to attack once more the citadel of his lady's heart, trusting in the Virgin's aid, Mary "came from heaven quickly down" to discuss the affair with him.

> *She who has caused you thus to sigh,*
> *And has brought you to this end,—*
> *Said Our Lady,—Tell me, friend,*
> *Is she handsomer than I?*

The knight was dazzled and frightened and knew not what to say. What *could* he say? This was indeed a terrible poser. The Virgin pitied him but would not let him go without this final warning:

> *Take good care what you shall do!*
> *She you shall love most faithfully*
> *Of us two, shall your mistress be.*

The poor knight dared not flout the Queen of Heaven and decided in her favor.

Another incident related by the poet, Gaultier de Coincy, and translated by Adams, shows in high colors the very feminine character of the Virgin. She was terribly irritated by the defection of a devotee who quitted his preparations for the priesthood in order to marry.

> *With anger flashing in her eyes*
> *Answers the Queen of Paradise:*
> *"Tell me, tell me! you of old*
> *Loved me once with love untold;*

*Why now throw me aside*
*Tell me, tell me! where a bride*
*Kinder or fairer have you won?*
*Wherefore, wherefore, wretched one*
*Deceived, betrayed, misled, undone,*
*Leave me for a creature mean,*
*Me, who am of Heaven the Queen?*
*Can you make a worse exchange*
*You that for a woman strange,*
*Leave me who with perfect love,*
*Waiting you in heaven above*
*Had in my chamber richly dressed*
*A bed of bliss your soul to rest?*
*Terrible is your mistake!*
*Unless you better council take,*
*In heaven your bed shall be unmade*
*And in the flames of hell be spread."*

There is no need to inquire as to the young man's choice. Obviously he had no choice. All this seems infantile to us but to millions of men in the year 1200 it was very real. Men loved the Virgin not less but rather more for her quite understandable faults.

She was nothing of a prude and occasionally her language, when she was irritated, bore resemblance to that of a tavern lounger. She cared little for dignity and would sometimes engage in domestic service or any lowly task, as when she mended Thomas à Becket's hair shirt in order to shame him for having displeased her by dismissing a favored priest. She sometimes enjoyed baiting powerful bishops and on one occasion forced the great Bishop of Chartres to reinstate an utterly worthless priest who had been farsighted enough to establish himself as her man. She spoke sharply to the bishop:

> *Now know you this for sure and true,*
> *Unless tomorrow this you do,*
> *—And do it very early too,—*
> *Restore my chaplain to his due*
> *A much worse fate remains for you!*
> *Within a month your soul shall go*
> *To suffer in the flames below.*

How the common people, in recounting this legend, must have chortled with glee. They cared nothing for the priest nor for abstract justice, but that their dearly beloved Lady should berate a proud bishop as though he were a naughty schoolboy was altogether delightful.

The devils complained bitterly and, one must admit, justly of Mary. They once brought suit to obtain the soul of a certain monk of Cologne who was befriended by Saint Peter. The holder of the keys of heaven could not save him for his case was utterly hopeless, his whole life having been one long scandal. Peter appealed to Mary and she, in a trice, upset the judgment of the Court of Heaven and saved the wretched monk. The devils, raging with chagrin, chorused thus:

> *In heaven and earth she makes more laws*
> *By far than God himself can do,*
> *He loves her so, and trusts her so,*
> *There's nothing she can do or say*
> *That He'll refuse or say her nay.*
> *Whatever she may want is right,*

*Though she say that black is white,*
*And dirty water clear as snow:—*
*My Mother says it and it's so!*

Naive and unquestioning love for this spirited Mother of God was the foundation on which all the really great French Gothic cathedrals were built and as long as this love really swayed men's hearts there was no difficulty about raising the huge sums of money needed. Every one gave for this one cause with an eagerness that we cannot comprehend today. Our modern giving, our church-building drives and community drives and tag days, are utterly insipid by comparison. Many of those who had no money gave themselves and toiled at the humblest tasks without pay. Part of this giving was, of course, a form of selfishness, based on a desire to buy personal salvation, but a much greater part unquestionably, during the Great Era, was based on an almost hysterical affection for the Virgin.

As this affection waned and the need for money continued all sorts of expedients were contrived. Some of these were noble in origin, others of very dubious character. Wealthy bishops not infrequently impoverished themselves to finish what the people had begun. Cathedral chapters worked with a will to raise money, somewhat in the modern style. Seigneurial revenues were often applied to cathedral building and it became the expected thing for rich persons to leave, when they died, a considerable portion of their wealth to the church. Obviously this action gave the departing soul an excellent start on its journey to paradise.

The less respectable ways of raising money were principally the sale of indulgences and the parading all over the country of saintly bones, true or false, and miracle-working relics. The business of indulgences became an open scandal long before Luther's day. Priests bought at a bargain, paying cash to the "fabric" or building fund, the right to lay penances on the people of their flock. Often, through the familiar threats of hell, they wrung large sums from their parishioners and made a very neat personal profit out of the transaction. A churchman writing in 1450, some seventy years before Luther nailed his ninety-five theses on the door of the castle church at Wittenberg, gave expression to this bitter complaint: "Sinners nowadays say, 'I care not what and how many sins I commit before God's face; for I can get at once, with the greatest ease, plenary remission of any guilt and penalty by means of an absolution and indulgence granted to me by the pope.' For these indulgence-mongers scour the country giving a letter of pardon sometimes for two pence, sometimes for a good draught of wine or beer, sometimes as a stake at tennis, sometimes for hire of a prostitute, sometimes for carnal love." This is a dark picture and we may assume that the business was generally conducted on a higher plane but it was a tawdry business at best and its ramifications were tremendous. The indulgence peddler was a familiar and unsavoury figure in the medieval picture.

"Relaxations" were another fruitful source of church income. This generally took the form of permission to eat meat on Mardi Gras and the day previous and to enjoy butter and milk during Lent. For this privilege the faithful paid well, witness the celebrated Butter Tower of Notre-Dame-de-Rouen and many another bit of noble architecture.

The fining of priests for unchastity and application of this money to the fabric fund was a much more startling means of raising money. Obviously the oftener the priests broke their vows the quicker would the cathedral rise. It would be going much too far to claim that unchastity was encouraged by the bishops and sin put on a paying basis, but there must have been many intelligent clerics who saw this shoddy practice for what it was.

The parading of relics started as a highly colorful and fairly respectable means of securing money. The possessors of sacred relics generally believed in their genuineness and their efficacy and it was legitimate, perhaps, that those who felt themselves benefited by gazing, for example, on a tooth of John the Baptist or by touching the shin-bone of one of the Apostles, should pay for value received. But sometimes, inevitably, fraud and corruption crept in. The cathedral chapter of Laon, very enterprising in this matter, sent abroad a glib high-powered preacher-salesman, who boldly used as buttress the learned Abbot of Nogent. Behold what the troubled abbot says of this affair. (He was not too much troubled to see it through.)

"This man [the preacher-salesman], after a long and exaggerated discourse on his relics, brought forth a little reliquary and said in my presence, 'Know ye that there is within this little vessel some of that very bread which our Lord pressed with His own teeth; and if we believe not, here is this great man'—this he said of me—'here is this great man, to whose renown in learning ye may bear witness, and who will rise from his place, if need be, to corroborate my words.' I confess that I blushed for shame to hear this; and but for my reverence of those persons who seemed to be his patrons, which compelled me to act after their wishes rather than mine, I should have discovered the forger."

One is brought back again and again, when considering the Miracle of the French Cathedral, to the Spirit of Twelve Hundred. Very little abuse had at that time crept into the church-building program. The peddling of indulgences had not commenced. Faith burned with a clear and brilliant flame. Within reach of every human being was MARY. Let us not forget her. They of twelve hundred *never* did, waking or sleeping.

# CHAPTER II

## *Beards and a Creea*

ENTHUSIASM and faith alone could not have produced the cathedrals of France. Technical skill of the highest quality was called for and thousands upon thousands of expert workers were needed, as the professional architect of today can appreciate far better than the layman. Summer tourists take the great cathedrals more or less for granted. They are marvelous, of course, and must have meant a lot of work. Beyond that tourist inquiry rarely goes, yet the subject is fascinating if only as a sort of puzzle. Whence came, for instance, the profound mathematical learning that made the cathedrals possible and how was such learning compatible with the infantile piety which accepted without question all the naive Mary legends? Scholars have only half answered these stupendous questions.

The Bearded Brothers (*Barbati Fratres*) of the eleventh- and twelfth-century abbeys were, in general, the nurturers of this enormous garden of technical knowledge and they acquired the seeds of it unquestionably from the Spanish Arabs—

the Moors. "The only version of Euclid obtainable," writes
the scholar George F. Fort, "had been translated from the
Arabic tongue into Latin by a European monk named Adel-
hard." Pope Sylvester II and a certain Peter, Superior of Cluny,
traveled extensively in Spain for the sole purpose of gathering
the mathematical culture of the Moslem savants, which they
then took eagerly to the monasteries. Cluny, Hirsau and other
monastic centers became in part technical schools of incredible
proficiency. The Bearded Brothers, who were the conventual
builders, threw themselves with utmost zeal into the study of
geometry and applied mathematics and raised architecture to
a lonely height, deservedly far above the level of other skilled
crafts. This continued until long after the conventual builders
had merged into the guild system.

The beards of the Bearded Brothers must be taken very seriously. Of enormous size, stretching to the waist if the Brother
was anything of a man, they were a badge of profession and
an object of the greatest pride to their possessors. But they were
against all ordinary monastic regulations of the time, which
held that beards were of the earth earthy rather than in any
way spiritual. They indicated pomp and gay social splendors
and even hinted at dissipation. The clean-shaven face, on the
other hand, indicated that the world had been cast aside, that
the treasured growth had been sacrificed to a God who liked
asceticism. One strongly suspects that the Virgin, out of pure
capriciousness, slyly encouraged the Bearded Brothers, despite
the raging of the abbots. She must have admired those rich and
ornamental forests.

This controversy developed, in more than one monastic
community, into a small war. The abbots were determined that

Notre-Dame-de-Paris, best known of all French cathedrals, gains much of its majesty from its location on the island in the Seine, which is the oldest part of Paris. The cathedral was begun in 1163 and the first stone was laid by Pope Alexander III. *Commissariat Général au Tourisme, Photo by Touring Club de France.*

At Mont-Saint-Michel, man enhanced nature as nowhere else in France. At spring tides "the Mount" is completely surrounded by water, which races in for a distance of ten miles over the flats at the speed of a trotting horse. Chartres (right) has the best and the most stained glass of any church in the world. The glass was removed and hidden during the second World War and is now gradually being returned.

these Brother Masons should conform to the regular discipline. The masons were determined to keep their beards. In 1230 the powerful Abbot of Premontré issued a stern order commanding the immediate removal of the offensive beards. The masons flatly refused to obey *and the order was rescinded.* Nothing could show more clearly than this the vast power which the masons had acquired. The abbeys were on the decline but the building wave was at its height and on its crest rode the all-powerful *Barbati Fratres.*

We feel no desire to follow in any heavy way the gradual shift of power which took place in connection with the great cathedral building wave but the fact of this shift we should understand clearly since it is one of the basic causes of the wave itself. The feudal barons were losing their grasp and the crown was gaining strength at their expense. The abbots and monasteries lost first place in power to the bishops and the towns, which were supporters of the king. The masons lost interest in their beards, since they found that they could wear them as they pleased, and developed interest in the masonic lodges which grew up in close proximity to each cathedral. The cathedrals themselves were a direct manifestation of this change. Each one was the nucleus of a *town* and most of them were intended theoretically to be capable of sheltering the entire population in case of need.

The craft guilds and especially the masons' guild sprang into being and thus opened a most colorful chapter in medieval history. Around each monster cathedral grew a considerable family of masons' lodges and these lodges became the repository of that mass of technical knowledge which the Bearded Brothers had got from the Moors of Spain and so zealously developed. Often these lodges became so numerous around an important cathedral that they gave the appearance of a small village.

The mason, with or without the beard, was almost necessarily a nomad. Occasionally he worked for his whole lifetime on one cathedral and his son and son's son after him, but generally he was forced to wander from town to town in search of work. The Wander-Years which were a temporary feature of most craft guilds, a means whereby the *journeyman*, be he goldsmith, armorer, or wood-carver, won his spurs and prepared himself for mastership, were necessarily chronic in the case of masons. A group of them would finish a "job" or their particular part of it and then perforce disperse to seek employment elsewhere.

There is a colorful tradition that whole bands of masons and architects customarily migrated *en masse* from one cathedral town to another, but Coulton, who is an earnest scholar and tests his colors before applying them to his writing, does not at all credit this tradition. He paints a rather doleful picture of these recurrent dispersals and doleful they must often have been. Pierre, a stone-carver, has worked for ten, fifteen, twenty years with Guibert and Regnault on the same cathedral. They are close friends and have developed a philosophy, a religion, a grand set of jokes. They agree that they will stick together always. Their work is finished. They take the road together and go to the next town. There they find work, alas, not for three but for one. They go on to the next town where there is no work at all. In the third town again there is a chance for one good stone-carver but not for three. Regnault drops out and bitter are the lamentations of all three. Perhaps Pierre and Guibert are lucky enough to find work together but the work languishes for lack of money and one must go on. Pierre goes and never again does he see either Guibert or Regnault.

The mason seldom owned even the tools of his trade, much less a home, so it was absolutely essential that he should establish himself under the protection of some local lodge in whatever town he secured work. To guard against fraud and false pretense a system of passwords, greetings and hand-grips was developed. These the mason had solemnly to pledge himself never to reveal to an outsider. He presented himself at a lodge door where he sought work, went through the rigmarole and concluded: "Honorable Master! I beg thee heartily for God's sake, to give me honorable employment," to which the Master replied, if he could, "With God's help thou shalt have it." A few rounds of cheering drinks put every one in a jovial frame of mind and the newcomer, perhaps the lonely Pierre who had been lately grieving for his lost comrades, feels very happy.

The fraternal life of these expert masons must have been often a most delightful one. They worked together in their atelier or unafraid high up on some lofty cornice. The lodge rules were a bit severe in various ways but the Virgin, whom every man genuinely loved, was not too censorious. She wanted her men to enjoy life. She did not quiver at a few round oaths if the chisel slipped nor condemn a man for enjoying the wine cup of an evening.

The work was driven on unquestionably by an earnest, ardent enthusiasm. The "building game" was good. But there was time, at that, for fun. When a workman spoiled a stone he was jeered mercilessly. The spoiled stone was christened Bernard (I know not why) and a funeral service for it was organized on the spot. The stone was taken on a bier to the "charnel house," the cemetery of dead stones, and a group of mourners followed the bier, led by the chief mourner, the unfortunate "lithocide" who had committed the murder. After this ceremony the culprit was put through a very rigorous "hot oven" by his comrades and he took good care not to spoil another stone. Some of these "charnel houses" have been found with the bones of the murdered stones unravaged by grave robbers or the passage of seven centuries of time.

If the masons built the cathedral, the glaziers *made* it. One may almost say that. What would Chartres or Notre-Dame of Paris or any other cathedral be without stained glass? Who would go to see it? And stained glass *belongs* to the thirteenth century. Then the glassworker's art reached its zenith and in the matter of coloring no subsequent century has equaled the thirteenth. Certainly the twentieth falls far short of it. This is not easy to explain except, in part, by recognizing that while technical perfection was and is necessary to masonry work it has proved something of a handicap in the fine art of coloring glass. The very crudeness of the primitive method of manufacture was a part of the secret of its success. Irregularities often produced wonderful if accidental colors.

But this is unsatisfying and far-fetched. Crudeness could certainly be duplicated today if necessary. There must have been formulae which have been totally lost and never recovered. Further than this, and more important, there was a creed. The glaziers of old held, says Henry Adams, "that the first point in color-decoration was color, and they never hesitated to put their color where they wanted it, or cared whether a green camel or a pink lion looked like a dog or a donkey provided they got their harmony or value. Everything except color was sacrificed— So we laugh—and probably the artist laughed too, but he was a colorist and never sacrificed his color for a laugh."

Adams points out too that the marvelous color effect of old windows is simplified by a complete absence of perspective in the scenes portrayed. A flat surface was invariably implied. "The twelfth-century glassworker would sooner have worn a landscape on his back than have costumed his church with it; he would as soon have decorated his floor with painted holes as his walls. He wanted to keep the colored window flat like a rug hung on the wall."

One other secret of old glass the author gives on the authority and roughly in the translated words of Viollet-le-Duc. It is too vital to omit. "One might maintain that the first condition for an artist in glass is to know how to manage *blue*. The blue is the light in windows, and light has value only by opposition. But also it is that luminous color which gives value to all others. If you compose a window in which there shall be no blue, you will get a dirty or dull or crude surface which the eye will instantly avoid; but if you put a few touches of blue among all these tones, you will immediately get striking effects if not skilfully conceived harmony. So the composition of blue glass singularly preoccupied the glassworkers of the twelfth and thirteenth centuries. If there is only one red, two yellows, two or three purples, and two or three greens at the most, there are infinite shades of blue,—and these blues are placed with a very delicate observation of the effects they should produce on other tones and other tones on them."

Any cathedral whose glass is great will be more enjoyed by those who have learned the three chief tenets of the medieval glassworker's creed:

*I believe in color.*
*Blue is the key to color.*
*My windows shall hang as a rug on the wall.*

CHAPTER III

# Paris, the Junction of the Cross

ONE hundred and fifty-one towns of France are listed by Mil-
toun in one of his books as Cathedral Towns in the broad sense.
Eighty-four of them are such in a strict Roman Catholic sense
today, being each the seat of a bishop or an archbishop. The
others were all so honored at some time in their history but
have lost the cherished distinction for one reason or another.
Many of the sixty-seven which are now without the fold
are more interesting—even architecturally—than many of the
eighty-four lucky ones, so we shall of course use the term in
its broad and not its narrow sense. But do not, I beg, be appalled at the number of these towns and hustle this book
roughly into oblivion. About a third of the one hundred and
fifty-one are worth seeing and one-sixth simply must be seen.
It is these latter to which we shall turn our attention, casting
only an occasional apologetic glance at the others.

By our plan of attack Paris must be the pivot, the central
point of our cruciform structure, which we call The French

Cathedral. At Paris the transepts meet the nave and the choir. Reims, "the National Cathedral," must be the altar, though we could wish it a few miles farther south on the map. The rest of the structure must take care of itself as best it can, leaving many widely-separated towns of southern France to a rambling *évêché*.

It is most fortunate for our convenience that Paris and the Ile-de-France, where the Gothic art was cradled, may sensibly serve as pivot. The French government has focused its *routes nationales* and its railroads in the capital to such a degree that any other pivotal point would be almost impossible. Ten or a dozen of the most essential of our chapels group themselves in a brilliant crown about the capital and can be easily visited from there in one-day sorties.

Neither Paris itself nor Notre-Dame of Paris quite fits into our scheme except as pivot. The city is a subject too colossal and the cathedral alone would call for a more purely architectural consideration than we can give it, yet we must not push it unceremoniously aside. I well recall my son's small-boy reaction to Notre-Dame. At the age of eight he and his sister, being that year in a Brussels school, spent a Christmas vacation with their mother and myself in Paris. On the very first day the boy wanted to climb the tower of Notre-Dame, so we all did. He was thrilled beyond measure and wanted to rush back almost immediately to the hotel to write to his grandmother about it. The letter, which he penned with trembling hand, opened thus:

"Dear Grandma:

"We climbed Notre-Dame today. There were 376 steps. I never saw a better thing than that at Paris."

Many an adult after a lifetime in the French capital has made in effect the same comment (though failing, perhaps, to record the number of steps). What experience can possibly be more wonderful than to gaze endlessly and from every angle, within and without, at this church of the Virgin in Paris? I suppose it is the one most familiar "sight" in Europe yet it never seems to cloy, perhaps because of the somber effect of its interior, which seems to be struggling to emerge from its Roman chrysalis to its Gothic mothhood. One mingles with the milling tourists inside the edifice to stare at the three great roses of the transepts and the west façade. One clatters with the crowd around the ambulatory. Outside, on the *parvis*, one stands where Esmeralda danced and where the poet, Pierre Gringoire, held chairs in his teeth to earn a few sous from the gaping populace. From this point, from the little park behind the cathedral, whence the ancient morgue has happily been effaced, from the Ile St. Louis, from the quays of the left bank, from the *mouches* steaming up and down the Seine, from anywhere and everywhere our eyes are drawn to glorious Notre-Dame.

This cathedral "needs no introduction" and therefore, following the time-honored tradition of the toastmaster, I shall introduce it—but very briefly. Notre-Dame-de-Paris is essentially one of the very early churches. It was consecrated, although far from finished, almost at the beginning of the Seven Great Decades, Philippe Auguste being a youth of seventeen but very much the king of France, for all his tender age. Cathedral and king grew in power, and money was lavished on this church as on few others in France. Much of it was spent undoing work that was scarcely "cool," for the Romanesque was going out and the Gothic coming in. The unknown architect who first built it, commencing two years before Philippe Au-

guste was born, would scarcely have recognized it when this king died.

A sister church to the original edifice exists today in the town of Mantes, north of Paris, a sort of Missing Link discovered, a Cro-magnon church in architectural evolution, if one may be, by implication, so disrespectful to the primitive Romanesque. At Mantes one may see, perhaps one-half life size, the Notre-Dame-de-Paris that was. The evolved structure, familiar to all the world, has been more or less reproduced in many localities and with varying materials—in Uppsala, for example, the university town of Sweden, where it took the form of a brick church, and in Nicosia on the island of Cyprus, where it is of dignified stone, to say nothing of Hollywood, California, where it bloomed for a season in humble plaster.

The main façade of Notre-Dame is its greatest glory, less rich and intricate, perhaps, than that of Reims, but more unified. Victor Hugo loved this façade with a passion that clarified his sometimes wordy style. He calls it "the colossal work of a man and a people." The people we know more or less, those interesting child-men who fought and loved and sinned and prayed so hard, but the man, that is the architect, we do not know. Like him who first designed the cathedral under the powerful Bishop de Sully, the man who built this façade— for Philippe Auguste—left the master work unsigned. Nor is there any slightest record of his name. When cathedral architects were really great, in the early twelve hundreds, they rarely left any record of their names. The later and littler men, on the other hand, were very careful to leave their signatures. But the incomparable façade of Notre-Dame glows like an unquenchable flame in tribute to the Unknown Architect who designed it.

The cleverness as well as the genius of the architect is discernible if one studies carefully the north and south towers. Nine tourists out of ten would say that they are twins but the south tower is, as a matter of fact, slenderer in all its proportions. The arches and windows are a trifle more pointed. If an argument arises on this point, as is very possible, it can be settled by the simple expedient of counting the kings in the band of kings above the three portals. There are eight on the north side and seven on the south.

The towers were built to be surmounted by two spires but these were never added and even when Viollet-le-Duc, that arch restorer of all time, had a free hand, in the middle of the last century, to erect a pair of them he did *not* do so. Let those who deplore his immense activity at Carcassonne and elsewhere put a gold star on his card for this noble abstention. One rather trembles to think of nineteenth-century spires on thirteenth-century towers. Almost everything else about the cathedral Viollet-le-Duc did restore and the lead spire over the central crossing, detested by some and admired by others, he built. On the whole the restorer's work on Notre-Dame was effective and one must be a dyed-in-the-wool "ruinist" to work up a rage, as some do, over the present state of this church.

The menagerie of Notre-Dame is one of the cathedral's most charming and distinctive features. Beasts and birds such as never were on land or sea abound on the stone parapets of this Gothic church. No doubt the restorer created some of them but he certainly did so in the true Gothic spirit. We call them all carelessly gargoyles, but this word means really a spout or throat and is a cousin to the word gargle. Many of these strange beasts do of course use the rain as a mouth wash and lean far out from the coping to gargle and eject it, but others by the score merely look out over the roofs of Paris, brooding, sorrowing, snarling, grinning, according to their nature.

One may of course climb the towers and "meet" these strange creatures. They are fascinating and generally hideous. My children enjoyed trying to imitate or even outdo their grimaces but what chance has a normal child with two eyes, a nose and a mouth against a chimera, a basilisk, a griffin, a phoenix or a *charadrius?* This last is a bird "to whom it is given to know whether or not the sick will escape death. Placed near a sick man, if the sickness is unto death the bird turns away its head; if the man will live it fixes its eyes on him and with open beak absorbs the illness. Then it flies away into the rays of the sun, the evil absorbed streams out of it like a sweat and the sick man recovers."

The question of the symbolic meaning of church beasts has absorbed the attention of many scholars and some have been determined to read a meaning into every bit of sculpture to be found. Take two of countless examples, the elephant and the unicorn.

The elephant was thought by the ancients to be the least amorous of all beasts. He could only be interested in feminine society by eating of the mandrake, a plant with a semi-human form that gives forth a shriek (or used to) when pulled from the ground. The female elephant used to gather mandrakes and present a nice meal of them to her sluggish lord who thereupon looked at her with sparkling eyes and commenced his amatory approaches. Because of this quaint belief, whenever an elephant is pictured in the sculpture of a Gothic church we are supposed to see in it a symbolical representation of the story of Adam and Eve and the Apple.

The unicorn, a favorite figure in church sculpture, is supposed to represent the Incarnation. This is what Honorius of Autun said of it: "The unicorn is a beast so savage that it can only be caught by the help of a young maiden. When he sees her the creature comes and lies down in her lap, and yields to capture. The unicorn is Christ, and the horn in the midst of its forehead is a symbol of the invincible might of the Son of God. He took refuge with a Virgin and was taken by the huntsmen, that is to say, He took on human form in the womb of Mary and surrendered willingly to those who sought Him." Because of this statement in a labored book of sermons written in twelve hundred and something we are to see the symbol of the Incarnation whenever we come across a charming unicorn on a Gothic parapet.

Emile Mâle, by far the greatest scholar on medieval church symbolism, throws upon the junk heap three-quarters of all this nonsense. Men chiseled these amazing beasties, especially the gargoyles and *chimères*, because they enjoyed doing it and doubtless they cared little what meaning theologians might choose to attach to them. Saint Bernard, "the great mystic, the interpreter of the Song of Songs, the preacher who spoke only in symbols," said boldly and a little angrily, "What is the meaning of these unclean monkeys, these savage lions, and monstrous centaurs? To what purpose are here placed these creatures, half-beast, half-man, or these spotted tigers?—Surely if we do not blush for such absurdities we should at least regret what we have spent on them!" If Saint Bernard could see no meaning in them, why should we, questions Mâle with point. But we need not, on the other hand, share the saint's petulant anger over the waste of money. We are very glad these beasts are here for they help to usher us into a quaint and marvelous lost world.

The personal history of Notre-Dame (not the architectural history) is more immense than that of any other cathedral in France save possibly Reims—our altar. Suppose we allow some of the more colorful events of this history to flit in rapid review before our eyes. Think of Raymond VII, the powerful Count of Toulouse, being led down this aisle "naked save for his shirt" to beg absolution for his sin in having sustained the heretics of Albi. Think of Saint Louis, of whom Voltaire said, "It is not given to man to carry virtue to a higher point," setting out from Notre-Dame on one of his crusades. Then think of James de Molay, Grand Master of the Templars in the year 1313. The wealth of his order had stirred his greedy sovereign, Philip the Fair, and even the holy father in Rome, Clement IV, to great and ignoble effort. De Molay and other officers had been accused, along with the whole order of Templars, of heinous crimes and had long been languishing in prison. From them "confessions" had been extracted by the most frightful torture. Now, on March 18 of the year 1313, the Grand Master was led to a scaffold erected in the *parvis* of Notre-Dame and bidden to tell the multitude what he had already told the torturers. Before confiscating the wealth of the powerful Templars King Philip wished to clear himself with the people. De Molay, emaciated from suffering but buoyed up by a sudden inner strength, raised his chained hands as best he could to heaven and made this plea of guilt:

"I do confess my guilt, which consists in having, to my shame and dishonor, through the pain of torture and the fear of death, suffered myself to give utterance to falsehoods, imputing scandalous sins and iniquities to an illustrious Order which hath nobly served the cause of Christianity. I disdain to seek a wretched and disgraceful existence by engrafting another lie upon the original falsehood."

The Papal Legate and the king's provost gnashed their teeth in rage. The Grand Master and with him Guy, the Grand Precentor, were snatched down from the scaffold. That very day as dusk descended they were burned to death in lingering agony over little charcoal fires kindled on an island in the Seine. King Philip confiscated the Templars' wealth and then, letting the people think what they would, attempted to square himself with the Virgin by building with some of this money a portion of the north wall of Notre-Dame as it now stands.

Not all the stirring events which Notre-Dame has witnessed were as tense and tragic as this crime against the Templars. There was a bit of the theatrical when Philippe de Valois, after a successful battle, clattered into the cathedral on his horse and deposited his armor at the Virgin's feet. There was an element of comedy when Henry VI of England, a child of ten years, was here crowned King of France in 1431, six months after the condemnation and burning of Jeanne d'Arc. I suppose he wondered vaguely what it was all about and why people were making such a fuss about him. Five years later the boy was unceremoniously robbed of his paper kingship by the French troops, and later—in the cathedral—the Maid of Orléans was rehabilitated.

Many interesting marriages have taken place in Notre-Dame. Mary, Queen of Scots, here married Francis, the Dauphin of France. In the next year Philip II of Spain here married the French princess Elizabeth. The Duke of Alva, one of the best hated personages of history, was proxy for the Spanish monarch. Thirteen years later Henry of Navarre here married Marguerite de Valois but the ceremony took place at the portals, for Henry had not then abjured Protestantism so the wedding could not take place within the cathedral. After the ceremony the bride went in to attend mass while Henry, wandering about the cloister, "gaped and kicked his heels against the coping." I imagine that without knowing it he longed for a cigarette at that moment.

Napoleon III married Eugénie in Notre-Dame, and this was perhaps the last royal wedding which that great cathedral will ever see. In 1930 I happened to be in Paris when Miss Anne Tyrell, the daughter of the British ambassador, was wedded—in Notre-Dame—to the second secretary of the embassy. It was an enormous "event" of the social world and all the papers played it up. Miss Tyrell was the first British girl in three hundred and seventy-two years, the first, in short, since Mary Stuart, to be married in this cathedral. Three thousand guests were invited and were thus classified by one of the "snappy" American periodicals:

"The suave gentlemen of the Corps Diplomatique, the dowdy but invincible aristocrats of the Faubourg St. Germain, the most presentable of the Nouveaux Riches, a sprinkling of tail-coated French statesmen, a dash of the long-haired Boul' Mich (for the Baroness Tyrell gave literary suppers), these along with the most eminent Roman Catholics of the English and U. S. colonies jammed vast Notre-Dame-de-Paris."

I, being neither suave nor aristocratically dowdy, being not even long-haired and Boul' Michy, fitted nicely into the dramatic picture as a member of the crowd outside.

On a still greater occasion and one of a very different type I was also a member of the crowd outside Notre-Dame. I refer to the funeral of Ferdinand Foch on March 26, 1929. Never have I witnessed anything more solemnly impressive than that ceremony. The day was dull and damp. From the *parvis* I could dimly see through the cathedral's main portal the heavily shrouded nave with the marshal's bier resting on an enormous black-draped catafalque. France's great soldier had lain for two days and a night beside the unknown poilu under the Arc de Triomphe and now after the ceremony in Notre-Dame he was to be borne to his final resting place beside Napoleon in the Invalides. Sixteen years later another notable soldier of France, hero of another war, entered Notre-Dame in solemn triumph at the time of the Allied liberation of Paris on August 26, 1945. General Charles de Gaulle, *le grand Charley*, was the embodiment of France Unbowed and he received the tribute of bullets fired by still-lurking Nazis or collaborationists but they did not touch him.

Of course we note many omissions in our hasty survey of the cathedral's personal history. We have no time to bother with Mademoiselle Maillard, the Goddess of Reason, who was enthroned here by the Revolutionists, with Napoleon and his gaudy coronation show, with dozens of other incidents that would interest us more than these two. Even the mythical Quasimodo, immortalized for early picturegoers everywhere by Lon Chaney, we must rather slight. I have recently re-read Hugo's famous novel, including the very lengthy dissertations on architecture which have no bearing whatever on the story. Whatever its faults as a novel it leaves the reader with a very intimate affection for the mighty cathedral. One cannot look at the bell tower without thinking of the ugly little bellringer who was wont to leap upon his largest bell in a frenzy of adoration and ride back and forth as it clanged its message to the populace. One cannot gaze at the sculptured west façade without wondering just which bit of carving caught and held the body of the archdeacon's hapless brother when Quasimodo threw him from the parapet. As for the heroine, Esmeralda, whom Hugo, in the fashion of the time, depicts as a very paragon of saintly loveliness, she certainly should be canonized as the Gypsy Saint and given her niche in the sculptured façade.

Notre-Dame of Paris is peculiarly the church of the Virgin, as Mâle points out. To her four of the church's six portals are dedicated. She is the central theme of two of the great rose windows. She is indeed "the center of all things. Never weary, the centuries sang her praises turn by turn, the twelfth century in the Porte Sainte-Anne, the thirteenth in the Porte de la Vierge, the fourteenth in the bas-reliefs on the north side. Nowhere was she more beloved."

In the Paris of today this soaring Christian monument rises, as it always has, like an island of peace in the midst of the maelstrom of life. Most travelers who have visited the French capital will agree with my small son's profound comment and will say with him, "I never saw a better thing than that at Paris."

CHAPTER IV

# Chartres, the Chosen Citadel of Mary

THE first jeweled shrine in our Chain of Chapels surrounding Paris must be Chartres. There is every reason for this and not the least of them is our own convenience. Our attention shall swing counter-clockwise around our pivot from Chartres, which is southwest of Paris, to Rouen, which is northwest. This is the ambulatory of The French Cathedral, the semi-public passage around the apse that separates the Virgin's throneroom from her boudoir. By sheer chance the town of Chartres is not only convenient but also the one logical gateway to an understanding of the spirit which produced the really great cathedrals of France.

"The First Town of Our Lady!" With this picturesque title as well as with a variant of the one I have used, Cecil Headlam characterizes Chartres, and a medieval chronicler goes still farther in picturing for us by a single phrase the intimate yet reverent love which people of the Middle Ages held for the Mother of God, who had taken up her abode in the plain of

La Beauce. The chronicler calls Chartres Cathedral "the very couch and chamber of Our Lady," and a truly regal couch and chamber it made.

There was nothing cheap about the thirteenth-century Queen of Heaven and we must be sure that we understand that. She insisted upon the best that money could buy and devotion could build. Fortunately both money and devotion were available. It was estimated nearly a century ago that the eighty cathedrals and five hundred churches which France built during the Great Decades would have cost if then replaced (in 1840) five billion francs or one billion dollars. We must certainly multiply that sum by five to figure it in mid-twentieth-century dollars, and if we compare the population and national wealth of medieval France and of present-day America we are bowled over by the most conservative estimate of what America would have to do in order to duplicate that money-effort. She would have to inaugurate, I suppose, at least a fifty-billion-dollar church-building program. Call that a wild guess, if you like. It is probably less than the reality. To modern business men it would not seem too great a price if they believed without cavil that Mary would give them eternal bliss.

Of course there was this definite investment idea back of the enormous outlay, back of the devotion to the Virgin. The intensity of conviction which led to this investment has never again been reached, believe many authorities, "by any passion, whether of religion, of loyalty, of patriotism or of wealth," and it was all touchingly simple. Since Mary could and would help the investor over the difficult threshold of heaven no price was exorbitant. The business side of this was rarely sordid, as any setting of it into words must be. Mary was not a glorified indulgence peddler. She merely demanded as her due the utmost that humanity could give her and in return she was prepared to give humanity the utmost gift in her power, eternal happiness. Had the money side of the bargain been dominant the Miracle of the Cathedral would never have been achieved. Rather the personal side was dominant. Mary stood beside each architect and sometimes directed his quill. She stood beside each mason and sometimes directed his chisel. She was not the Mary of theology, not the Mary of the Roman Catholic Church, but the Mary of the people, their Queen of Queens. Nearly all the cathedrals of the Great Decades were dedicated to her rather than to any saint. It was only when men began to doubt her, to question whether she could or would keep her side of the bargain, to try even to repossess themselves of the money their fathers had invested that cathedral building fell with increasing swiftness into confusion and then oblivion.

The Virgin of Chartres is Heaven's Queen at her best and most potent but she was none the less feminine for that. She demanded lofty spaciousness and light and these the builders set themselves to give her. It involved new and tremendous problems. The heavy round arch would no longer do and the pointed, climbing arch must be perfected. The mean little windows of Romanesque churches were inadequate and the cathedral walls must yield more—far more—to satisfy the Virgin's desire for light. All the builders' problems and especially that of the windows were rather staggering, and the supreme skill with which they were solved persuaded all France and, what is more noteworthy, the builders themselves, that Mary and not human brains and hands had solved them. The greatest wonder that the Virgin of Chartres ever wrought was the building of her own home. It had unimagined graciousness and elegance yet it was strong and virile too. With Chartres the heavy Romanesque was done forever and the Gothic established.

The arrangement and decoration of the Virgin's home absorbed her attention as fully as its construction. The choir, as I have said, was her throne-room, the nave and transepts her public reception hall and the apse her real chamber. Here she *lived*, emerging to acknowledge the obeisance of her subjects, to support a saint whose hold on the people was weak, to display her faultless robes. Her tastes were exquisite and expensive. She scorned anything less than the best and the very thought of housewifely economy was repugnant to her. She laughed at it in earthly queens and would have despised herself for selecting the less expensive of two proffered gowns. Her public ceremonies were more glittering than those of any French queen but the glitter was never, in the great days, tinsel. Her presence was radiant, overpowering, worthy of her sumptuous home. In the matter of interior decoration of this home one need only look at Chartres Cathedral today to be convinced of the Virgin's excellence of taste. It is the supreme monument of her genius when unhampered by the rising tide of human doubt.

Chartres is the most visited cathedral town of France. There is no doubt whatever of that. It is the tourist's darling and nearly everyone, whether architect or artist, whether writer or chance traveler, selects it as the one indispensable place of pilgrimage. I should enjoy being original, proclaiming the all around superiority of some out-of-the-way place, Coutances for example or Cahors, but I too find Chartres on the whole the very finest of all the glories of churchly France. It is "my favorite."

Public taste is only following in this matter the lead of the Queen of Heaven who selected for her special abode—more special, by far, than even Paris—this little Roman town originally named Autricum. Why did the Virgin make this choice? It is an interesting story. Here there existed, according to one of the most firmly established of ancient traditions, a Druid altar with a statue of the "Virgin who Shall Bear a Son." Scholars as well as theologians have discussed this tradition interminably and all agree to this much, that it is not impossible that the messianic prophecy of Isaiah *"Ecce Virgo pariet"* (Behold, a Virgin shall be with child) had somehow found its way to the Druids as it had to the Romans. If one is able to concede this, then what is more natural than to conceive of the Druid priests "playing safe" by erecting an altar to this Unknown Virgin as the Athenians of Paul's day did to the Unknown God? It is an absorbing speculation. Even if the tradition is only a trumped up story it served at a very early date to establish Autricum (Chartres) as the western center of Christian worship and especially of veneration for the Virgin. Missionaries from Sens built a little church over the Druidical grotto which thus became the crypt, and from this beginning came the cathedral of Chartres.

The original statue, or what purported to be the original, was burned in a fire in 1020. The replica of it was burned in 1793 by the Revolutionists. A copy of the copy, now set up in the crypt, serves as Notre-Dame-de-Sous-Terre and draws, together with the cathedral's other great relic, the Virgin's Veil, an enormous number of pilgrims from all over the world. One notes a curious fact about this Madonna and child. The mother's eyes are closed, the baby's open. This is supposed by those who can believe it, to represent the idea of the Druid priests that the new faith was yet in darkness but that faith's eyes should be opened by the miraculous birth of the child.

The Virgin's Veil has been even more potent than the Druid's statue in spreading the fame of Chartres. Formerly this precious piece of raw silk was thought to be the chemise of the Virgin but when the Revolutionists sacrilegiously broke open the chest in which it was contained, it proved to be a veil five and a half yards in length. They cut it into pieces and less than half of it ever found its way back to the shrine. The history of the two pieces that now remain can be traced with certainty back to the Byzantine Emperor Constantine Porphyrogenetus, which title means Born-in-the-Purple. He gave it to Charlemagne whose grandson, Charles the Bald, gave it into the keeping of Chartres as being the most ancient and august stronghold of Christianity.

A third object of veneration in Chartres Cathedral is the black Virgin of the Pillar but this, while very popular nowadays, is a mere upstart, scarcely five hundred years old, and we may dismiss it from our thoughts almost immediately. The Underground Virgin and the Sacred Veil we may not dismiss for it is impossible to understand this cathedral or any medieval cathedral without giving such venerated objects as these their just due. They were the immediate motivating force, more powerful by far than any modern machinery, which built many of the finest and most colossal churches.

Imagine yourself for a moment to be an ordinary medieval toiler, not a monk or a churchman. The hope of heaven and the fear of hell are strong upon you all the time. You believe profoundly, as everyone you know believes, that God once came to the earth miraculously from the womb of a Virgin. You hear that an intimate garment which once graced the actual body of God's Mother is guarded in a strong chest in the church of Chartres. Would you laugh at this story? Would you achieve a witty bit of scoffery? Would you apply the scornful medieval equivalent of the word "bunk"? I hardly think you would unless you were quite prepared to be struck dead on the spot. It is much more probable that a queer mist would fill your eyes, that your heart would thump with excitement, that you would cast about to see what little part you could take in housing this very precious garment properly.

That, at any rate, was the reaction of hundreds of thousands in medieval France. In great waves of fervor bands of workers came from Orléans, from Paris, from Dreux, even from distant Rouen. Sometimes a thousand of them, says the letter of an old abbot of Dives, attached themselves to one heavy load of stone to drag it from the quarry which was seven miles distant from Chartres.

"Who has ever seen or who heard in all the ages of the past that kings, princes and lords, mighty in their generation, swollen with riches and honors, that men and women, I say, of noble birth have bowed their haughty necks to the yoke and harnessed themselves to carts like beasts of burden, and drawn them, laden with wine, corn, oil, stone, wood and other things needful for the maintenance of life or the construction of the church, even to the doors of the asylum of Christ?"

The story goes on, not only in the abbot's enthusiastic letter but in the words of innumerable other witnesses. It was a veritable "crusade of chisel and trowel," says Headlam. Those who were qualified as artisans worked at the actual construction. Those who could not help directly were content to do the most menial tasks. They prayed also and sang hymns. They brought the sick to be healed and Chartres became a medieval

Lourdes. Like a vast camp the workers' wagons and temporary shelters surrounded the town and the companies from the various parts of France organized their own sectional headquarters.

It was specifically in the year 1144, before the Gothic era was in full swing, that the greatest wave of building fervor burst upon Chartres, and yet, when, exactly fifty years later, a terrible fire ravaged the cathedral, another wave of almost equal power formed itself and swept all obstacles before it. The Virgin's Veil and the Druid statue were saved by what seemed to the people a miracle. Nothing was so important as this one thing, that the Virgin's chosen home should be restored. The glorious cathedral that we now have was then erected with incredible swiftness. Numerous other fires have attacked it; lightning has darted down its towers; the cannon balls of Henry IV smashed some of its statuary and windows; horrible "restorations" were effected in the eighteenth century and made visible (Oh, crowning irony!) by the removal of eight priceless stained glass windows, dating from St. Louis's time; the Revolutionists held their obscene orgies in its nave; and yet the structure which we see is essentially that which was dedicated a few decades after the fire of 1190. "It is a world to explore," said Walter Pater, "as if one explored the entire Middle Ages."

Two events in the cathedral's hectic career are of especial interest, the coronation of Henry IV which took place within its walls, and its hairbreadth escape from complete destruction at the hands of the Revolutionists. The mention of Henry IV for the second or third time seems to require an interpolation in the manner of Victor Hugo. I feel that any one would enjoy this book or any book about France's cathedrals the more for having recently refreshed his memory on the main events and personages of the history of France herself. I personally find it convenient to hang my historical memories on a very few pegs whatever the country. In the case of France the pegs are mostly kings. One need feel really familiar with only these few: Philippe Auguste, that hard but very successful king who consolidated France and under whom cathedral building reached its climax; Louis IX the Saint; Charles VII, the weakling who was bolstered up by two women, Joan his military captain, and Agnès Sorel his lovely and ambitious mistress; Louis XI, one of the strangest men that ever lived, a genius in statecraft and a veritable fool in his crafty dealings with the saints; Francis I, the dazzling monarch who met England's Henry VIII on the Field of the Cloth of Gold; Henry IV, the Huguenot king of Navarre who became the Catholic king of France; the fourteenth, fifteenth and sixteenth Louis. From then on French history is plain sailing, reasonably familiar to everyone without special reviewing.

Henry IV, "the most lovable of kings," attacked and finally subdued the town of Chartres in 1591. He was then king of Navarre but determined to be king of France. He fought furiously yet even in battle he sought to be a gentleman. One day during the siege he heard the pealing of many bells and especially the booming tones of "Marie" and "Gabrielle" in the *Clocher Vieux*, stout bronze girls weighing, between them, twenty-five tons. He learned that Chartres was celebrating the anniversary of its delivery from a former siege and was imploring the Virgin to deliver it on this occasion. Henry was touched and ordered that all his guns should be silent for the entire day lest he should spoil the celebration. The next day he resumed the attack and eventually subdued the town. The mayor presented him with the keys of the city and said with what grace he could summon, "Sire, we are obliged to obey you both by human law and divine law." The king, dreading a long harangue, cut in with this quip: "You might add by *canon* law."

The capture of Chartres was the prelude to an epochal event in French history. Chartres became Henry's seat of government and here, a little later, he took the "perilous leap" by deciding to become a Catholic. He abjured his "errors" in the basilica of St. Denis and then returned to Chartres for his coronation. Never before or since has this cathedral witnessed a ceremony of such pomp. Henry, preceded by heralds, Knights of the Holy Spirit, Swiss Guards, Scots Guards and archers of the Grand Provost, entered the cathedral by the Royal Portal. He wore a tunic of crimson satin and over this a cloth of silver robe. The climax of the ceremony came when Henry concluded his formal oath with these words:

"Further, I will strive to my uttermost, in good faith, to chase from my jurisdiction and lands all heretics denounced by the church, promising on oath to observe all that has been said, so may God and His holy Gospel help me!"

The Bishop of Chartres anointed Henry with holy oil and the air was rent with the enthusiastic cry *Vive le Roi!*

The concluding words of Henry's oath had convinced all Chartres and presently convinced all France that his conversion was sincere. We know now that it was a political conversion pure and simple, that Henry was profoundly indifferent to religion in general and in particular, but the travesty was of inestimable benefit to France, ranking hardly lower in this respect than the conversion of Clovis from paganism to Christianity.

This coronation was the only one which ever took place at Chartres. Practically all the other kings from Philippe Auguste in 1179 to Charles X in 1824 were crowned at Reims but that city was not available for Henry, since it was at the moment stoutly held by his enemy, the Duke of Mayenne. France was in those days at the crossroads. A feather's weight might swing the balance toward development as a strong nation or toward complete and hopeless disruption. Henry's nominal conversion was that feather's weight. Let ethical societies debate the righteousness or unrighteousness of it. France exists.

Two centuries later Notre-Dame-de-Chartres faced a very great peril. The idiots of the Revolution, led by the Paris fanatics, were determined to wipe out all trace of the old order. It was solemnly voted that this cathedral should be torn down. A start was promptly made on the north porch but then an unexpected difficulty arose. No *citoyen* of Chartres was willing to allow his property to be encumbered with the débris. To haul it away would involve an enormous expense, so in the end France's most glorious cathedral remained intact for one reason only, that it had "no place to go."

It was, however, profaned in a way that was both ludicrous and disgusting. The statue of the Virgin in the choir was adorned with a red cap and a pike was placed in her hands. A mountain of earth was built in the middle of the choir and on this a statue of Reason was erected. Plays were enacted and half-baked sermons delivered to teach the populace that liberty had at last replaced the bonds of superstition. Dances, which degenerated into licentious orgies, were held in the nave every tenth day, the Revolutionists' Sunday. Over the great white and gray labyrinth on the floor of the nave where thirty generations of the devout had painfully hitched along on their knees, praying their way to Jerusalem, men and women, youths and maidens danced to the strains of an orchestra ensconced in the pulpit. The dancers had been assured that they were children of nature and needless to say they behaved accordingly. The wittier of them brought off many a good jibe at the old defeated God and His mother, who had imagined themselves so secure in their big cathedral.

In spite of these insanities Chartres cathedral remains for us. It is difficult to know what aspect of it to admire most. Henry James went into raptures over the "endless upward reach of the great west front (and) the clear silvery tone of its surface." Lowell was carried away with the beauty of the south tower, the *Clocher Vieux,*

> *"molten now in driving mist*
> *Now lulled with the incommunicable blue,"*

while other writers have devoted equally ardent words to the graceful *Clocher Neuf,* or north tower, the young sister of the other "smiling through the lace of a wedding veil, comely as a bride, fair as the spouse of Christ." I personally felt obliged to cast my ballot for this New Tower because I once put up for a few days at a small hotel named for the builder of it, Jehan de Beauce. He completed this wonderful structure only the other day, in 1513 to be precise.

The two towers together are commonly considered to form the most perfect ensemble in France, but the remembrance of them is somewhat dimmed in the minds of most visitors by the still greater glory of the cathedral's interior. And the chief glory of this glory is *glass.* Chartres has the most glass and the best in France. For once statistics alone are eloquent. Listen to these figures presented with forceful introductory remarks by

Cecil Headlam. "Consider the list of windows as they have come down to us across the ages, in spite of fires and sieges, artists and vandals, cleansing and restoring, in spite of the winds that sweep across La Beauce, in spite even of the eighteenth century architects and their eagerness to throw daylight upon their abominable deeds. This is the reckoning:— One hundred and twenty-four great windows, three great roses, thirty-five lesser roses and twelve small ones! And in these are painted[1] 3,889 figures.—This is the national portrait gallery of medieval France!"

As a rule I am quite content to let cathedral glass make upon my mind a general rather than a detailed impression but on a prewar visit to Chartres when all the glass was in I once bumbled around the church with Clerval's excellent guide in my hand. I felt that I was marvelously well rewarded. Instead of oh-ing and ah-ing only over the great roses, over that celebrated miracle of blue, the Jesse Tree window, and over the window called Notre-Dame-de-la-belle-Verrière I ran down many of the obscurer windows, especially those presented by the different guilds. The modest "signatures" of these latter interested me immensely. The butchers' window was identifiable by an ox hanging from a hook, the innkeepers' window by a customer paying a bill. (Perhaps this was a subtle hint to some of the faithful.) The blacksmiths signed their window by means of an anvil, the druggists by counters, the money-changers by scales.

In the lancets under the rose of the south transept there is a delightful curiosity in the representation of the four evangelists riding pick-a-back on the shoulders of the four prophets.

---

[1] This word is broadly used. For comment on painted glass, as against stained glass, see Chapter XX.

Matthew sits on Isaiah; Mark on Daniel; Luke on Jeremiah; John on Ezekiel. This is symbolical of the New Dispensation resting upon the Old, but it gives irreverent moderns the inevitable idea that these dignitaries are playing some sort of a game.

Still more curious appears the color of the faces in these windows. Early glaziers had rather little range outside the primary colors. Beards, for instance, they often portrayed in blue, and faces in a purplish brown. The flesh tints in these lancets of the south transept are most extraordinary. I noted them with care. Matthew is dark brown, Mark and Luke are white, John almost black. Daniel and Isaiah are white but Ezekiel is swarthy and Jeremiah of absolutely African blackness. In the central lancet of the north transept, across the way, Saint Anne is shown carrying in her arms the Virgin, and the faces of both are extremely swarthy. There are many explanations, aside from the narrow range of the glazier's palette, to account for the black Christs and Virgins and saints to be found in the various cathedral windows of France. The most sensible seems to be that the medieval artist vaguely thought of all persons of the east as swarthy to the point of blackness, and being capable of reproducing no true flesh tints thought it safe to resort to dark browns.

There are numberless other things about Notre-Dame-de-Chartres that attract and interest everyone. Among these the "frozen lace" of the choir screen is notable. One tires of this phrase but does not tire of the unique stone screen, begun under the direction of Jehan de Beauce who built the *Clocher Neuf*. The prominence of Saint Anne, the mother of Mary, is an unusual feature of the cathedral. This is due to the fact that Anne's head was sent to Chartres by the Count of Blois in 1205.

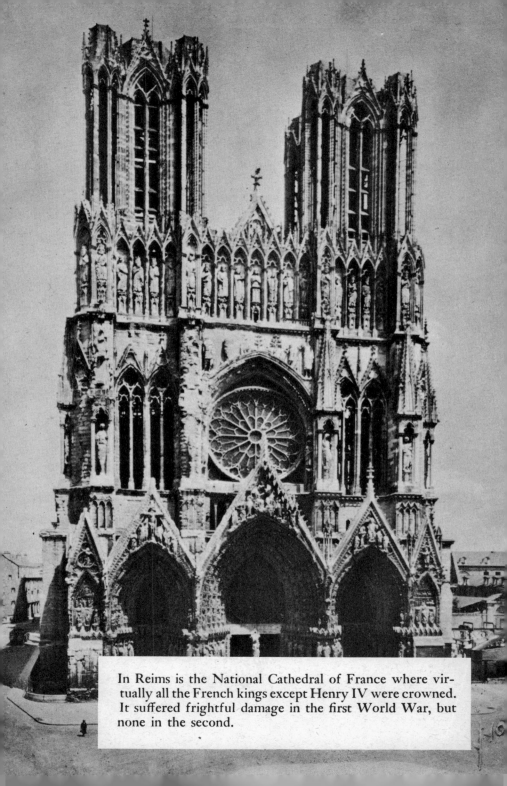

In Reims is the National Cathedral of France where virtually all the French kings except Henry IV were crowned. It suffered frightful damage in the first World War, but none in the second.

Châlons-sur-Marne has been a battleground for 1500 years. In 451 a battle here saved Europe from Attila. The city suffered in both World Wars but substantially survived. Its large cathedral is not of the first rank. *Air France.*

"The head of the mother," says an old manuscript, "was received with great joy in the church of the daughter." This gift was received during the building of the present cathedral and furnished an enormous stimulus to the builders. Fortunately they did not know that Mainz on the Rhine possessed at that time *another* head of Saint Anne or if they did they doubtless reviled the people of Mainz as cheats and liars.

The labyrinth of this cathedral is the only one now to be seen in France except that of St. Quentin and the restoration of the ancient one at Amiens. It is a maze built into the pavement of the floor in the center of the nave and measures just under a thousand feet in length. Its intricate pattern is outlined in white on large gray slabs of stone quarried at near-by Berchères. Along this tortuous thousand-foot white path pilgrims made their miniature pilgrimage to Jerusalem on their knees, as I have said. It took a good hour for the fast ones and must have ruined many a pious dress and many a pious pair of breeches, to say nothing of bare knees. Anyone who is willing to spend five minutes walking on his knees on a rough stone floor can gain some faint idea of what an hour of this self-torture would be.

The town of Chartres climbing sharply from the banks of the slumberous Eure is unusually quaint and yet, in spite of my boldly announced plan that each town shall serve to fix in our minds its great church, we have no time whatever to devote to it. In the case of Chartres as in a very few other cases the cathedral *is* the town. Without it Chartres would be nothing at all but a sleepy little town lost in the waving grain fields of La Beauce.

I remember loitering on a beautiful summer evening, in the garden of the *évêché* back of the church, a glorious sequestered park where priests were pacing back and forth, fingering the pages of their breviaries and thinking whatever thoughts priests think on such occasions. The park overhangs the three-branched Eure which has cut deeply into the plain, and a half-mile or so distant the upper levels of La Beauce continue endlessly into the distance. As I loafed in this priestly park dusk came on and with it the red lights of an airplane hangar across the way. Two planes whirred restlessly overhead and then another taxied to the hangar. Then I had a thought, too late, like most of my first-rate thoughts. Why, oh why had I not brought Lowell's poem, "A Day in Chartres" (called also "The Cathedral"), and read the whole of it in this garden? Why had I not secured it, at whatever trouble, in Paris and spent a twilight hour with it here? The airplanes really made this too-late suggestion for they recalled almost inevitably the words Lowell puts into the mouths of the sculptured saints and kings:

> "*Ye come and go incessant; we remain*
> *Safe in the hallowed quiets of the past.*"

An attentive reading of this brilliant, reverent poem discloses any number of lines that make the reader warm to the warm heart of Lowell. He tells how the cathedral was built

> "*By suffrage universal . . .*
> *. . . for all the country came*
> *From far as Rouen, to give votes for God,*
> *Each vote a block of stone securely laid*
> *Obedient to the master's deep-mused plan.*"

He pictures quaintly and aptly the medieval faith which produced the miracle.

> *" 'Tis irrecoverable, that ancient faith,*
> *Homely and wholesome, suited to the time,*
> *With rod or candy for child-minded men."*

He seems to condense his whole bundle of impressions, and ours, into a dozen words when he writes of the Cathedral's

> *. . . "vast repose.*
> *Silent and gray as forest-leaguered cliff*
> *Left inland by the ocean's slow retreat."*

Ruskin pecked away at this poem, objected to the word "rote" to describe the ocean's roar, objected to Lowell's use of "whiff," "downshod," "misgave" and so forth. The poet stood his ground, genial, unruffled. One day he wrote to the editor of the *Atlantic Monthly*, "I can't tell yet how the poem will stand. Already I am beginning to—to—you know what I mean—to taste my champagne next morning."

Perhaps you and I will have the same experience when we return from Chartres to Paris, particularly if the day is too hot or too cold or if the exit at the Gare Montparnasse is tedious because of the crowds, but nevertheless we would not have missed for anything in the world the intoxicating thrill of the party.

## CHAPTER V

# Three Towns on Three Rivers:
## Sens—Troyes—Châlons-sur-Marne

SENS is on the Yonne. Troyes is on the Seine. Châlons—not to be confounded with Chalon—is on the Marne. All three rivers have become one before their waters reach Paris. If three blocks of wood were to be tossed simultaneously into the three streams at the point where each passes through its famous cathedral town it would perhaps be a close race between them for the capital. I am inclined to guess that since the Marne is a swift, vigorous river the Châlons block would be the first to float past Notre-Dame-de-Paris, though that town is the most distant of the three.

Sens and Troyes are in the ancient department of Brie where cheese is made, but both departments were always in pre-Revolutionary days linked together under the style Champagne-et-Brie. We shall locate our cathedral towns according to the old broad nomenclature rather than the new. It is far more interesting and comprehensible. Champagne, Normandy, Maine, Anjou—these names mean something, but who cares about such provinces as Seine-et-Marne, Loir-et-Cher or any others of the ninety *départements* (beside Alsace and Lorraine) which constitute modern France?

Sens is an exceedingly interesting town historically. In itself, as a modern town, it is rather tame, though cooler, parkier (these words I find in my journal) than many provincial French cities. The name is in great demand among those who are given to punning and to making jingles. I have more than once listened to lengthy tongue-twisters in which this word was tangled up with *sans, son, cent, cense, sont, sang, Saint-Saëns* and I know not how many other words of somewhat similar pronunciation, and of course practically every tourist who visits Sens feels obliged to rid himself of a pun involving the sign so familiar to motorists *Sens Interdit*. In medieval French the word was a variant of *sans* and one wonders seriously if this town may have been nicknamed "Without" and the name stuck. I certainly do not propound this idle speculation as a theory, for in olden times Sens was without very little to which a town might aspire. In the days when religion was uppermost in all men's minds Sens boasted an exceedingly important archbishopric with seven suffragans at Chartres, Auxerre, Meaux, Paris, Orléans, Nevers and Troyes. The first letters of these towns taken together spelled the mystic word *Campont* which was emblazoned everywhere in Sens as the device of the metropolitan church.

The cathedral of Sens is of very primitive style, more Romanesque in many ways than Gothic, as any layman can see for himself. Elise Whitlock Rose lists it first in her early

Gothic studies. The solid, somber round-arched effect of the side aisles, for instance, proclaims the extremely early origin of the church—it was largely completed in 1168—and only here and there does one see a tentative approach to the Gothic. Only the transepts, which were built four centuries later than the body of the church, are Gothic of the Gothic and they make a strange contrast to the rest.

As I first approached the cathedral I could not make it out at all. It seemed as though the nave, strangely low but very beautiful, had been attached in the wrong place with no sensible relation whatever to the west front. This curious effect proved to be due to the linking together of the cathedral and the synodal palace, to the advantage of neither. Viollet-le-Duc was an active restorer of both of these buildings. Sometime we must "look into" Viollet-le-Duc. He must have had one of the most active minds of the nineteenth century. But we shall run across him anywhere, everywhere. There happens to be too much else at Sens to take up our attention. Here Thomas à Becket lived for four years as an exile from the English monarch's wrath. Here Saint Louis was married to his beloved Margaret. Here the abbot Bernard of Clairvaux denounced the monk Abélard, beloved of Héloïse. Here at the Hôtel de l'Ecu Napoleon lunched *au pied levé* on the black day of March 30, 1814 when Paris surrendered to the Allies.

England's martyr-archbishop is enormously admired in Sens cathedral circles. A statue of him adorns the north wall, an elaborate and very famous window in the ambulatory depicts the scenes of his life from his hollow reconciliation with Henry II to his murder in Canterbury cathedral, and in the treasury are the actual vestments worn at Sens by Becket. A souvenir hunter once induced the authorities to cut off for him a portion of Becket's chasuble. We earnestly hope the souvenir brought bad luck.

In the Synodal Hall adjoining the cathedral Saint Louis (IX) took to himself a wife, Margaret of Provence. A ring was placed on his finger with these words engraved upon it:

God, France, and Margaret

The king stated that "beyond this ring" he had no love. Margaret was "about" thirteen years old at the time of the wedding. She presently began to bear children to her saintly lord and did not cease till she had borne eleven. There is something especially engrossing in the thought of a saint's wedding. One wonders if the bridal pair "knelt their way" to Jerusalem on some hard church labyrinth as a honeymoon. One wonders if Louis gave to Margaret a jeweled scourge as wedding gift and if Margaret gave to Louis a wonderfully wrought hair shirt. They did at any rate live together for thirty-six years with whatever earthly comfort a saint might allow. Margaret supported him in all his charitable and religious ventures, one being the purchase of the Crown of Thorns in Constantinople. For five years Louis left this precious relic in Sens while he was building as its shrine the sublime Sainte Chapelle in Paris.

The conflict between Bernard and Abélard antedated both Becket's exile and Saint Louis' marriage but it far outshines both events in interest. Seldom has any cathedral witnessed so dramatic a struggle with such a shameful ending. It was a twelfth-century edition of the modern struggle between the Fundamentalist and the Liberal. Bernard of Clairvaux was the

Fundamentalist, Abélard the Liberal. Bernard was a Cistercian abbot, holy, austere, extremely eloquent, humble in esteeming himself, bold in counsel. He was the prime champion of rigid orthodoxy, the implacable foe of all persons that seemed to him tinctured with heresy. Peter Abélard, a Breton of noble birth, was a profound scholar, a philosopher, a cold dialectitian. It was inevitable that some of his utterances should rouse the wrath of Saint Bernard. In particular it was Abélard's interpretation of the dogma of the Trinity that stirred Bernard. Another heresy of the Breton scholar so picayune that its importance cannot be grasped by modern minds, brought him endless persecution. He insisted that Dionysius the Areopagite had been Bishop of Corinth, not of Athens as the church held, and that Saint-Denis was not identifiable as the Dionysius converted by Paul. Since the church was always right, even this historical heresy must be stamped out. Eventually the scholar was arraigned before a church council at Sens.

Tense excitement filled the very air of the place as the second day of the great council dawned. King Louis VII entered the cathedral with a gorgeous retinue. Archbishop Henry of Sens, heavy, brutal, nicknamed the Wild Boar, ascended the archiepiscopal throne and grouped about him his powerful suffragans, the "Campont" seven. The church was filled with ecclesiastics and lay nobles, while the square outside was packed with people. Bernard of Clairvaux ascended the pulpit, trembling, it is said, for fear the Devil, in the person of Abélard, would plague him. Abélard entered the church, walked slowly down the nave and faced his opponent calmly. Breathless silence reigned as the assembly waited for the opening guns of the abbot.

Slowly, fighting for self-control, Bernard commenced his

charge. Then suddenly, to the utter astonishment of every one, Abélard interrupted with four clearly spoken words: "I appeal to Rome." Swiftly he walked out of the cathedral, leaving saint, king, prelates and nobles stunned and vaguely disappointed. Bernard recovered himself and continued his charge with more confidence. The minutes dragged into hours. What promised to be vastly exciting proved an interminable bore. Then gradually a disgraceful situation developed. An eyewitness has left this description of the later hours of the day:

"The bishops having grown weary, relieved their fatigue with wine. The wine and the weariness brought on sleep. The drowsy assembly sat, some leaning on their elbows, some with cushions under their heads, some with heads dropping on their knees. Still the reader droned on, the assembly snored. When he came to some thorn-bush in Abélard's field he exclaimed to the deaf ears of the bishops, '*Damnatis?* Do you condemn this?' At each pause they murmured sleepily, '*Damnamus*. We condemn,' till at length some cut short the word and faintly breathed '*Namus*.' "

So Peter Abélard was brought low by the mumbling votes of drowsy bishops who made almost no effort to understand the charges. He was never able to secure satisfaction from Rome. His health soon broke down and he died an exemplary monk at Chalon-sur-Saône. Of course the world today knows him not as a scholar but as a martyr to love. The story of his passion for Héloïse, niece of Bishop Fulbert, is too familiar and too lengthy a story to insert here. Never did love travel a thornier path. Now the lovers lie together in peace in the cemetery of Père-la-Chaise at Paris and I, like every honest tourist, have been to gaze upon their monument.

I wandered one day in the cathedral of Sens dreaming about the dramatic happenings of the past, searching in my bungling way for those things which interested me. I was so careless as to stand for some moments, fingering my guide-book, before the chapel containing the tomb of *Ludovicus Delphinus Optimus Princeps*, in other words the Dauphin who was son of Louis XV and father of Louis XVI. Of course I was fair game for the sacristan, who saw me from a distance and bore down upon me like a pirate galley. I had wanted to study this tomb, for a figure of conjugal love had caught my eye and it actually represented this love as a girl, fair and slender, instead of robust and fertile-looking. But I cannot abide sacristans so I pulled myself hastily together and returned my guide-book to my pocket. Nothing daunted, the sacristan started briskly explaining the tomb to me. I interrupted with great firmness and explained to him that I had no time and must be leaving. He *utterly* ignored my remark and went right on, whereupon I turned on my heel and "walked swiftly out of the church" like Peter Abélard. The last words I heard were "*dix-huitième siècle*." They would be. Dates and especially *siècles* are meat and drink to most French sacristans. They roll them around their tongues as the very choicest morsels of speech.

I strolled through the town passing the Maison d'Abraham, where the Virgin's ancestors, from Abraham down, are carved on the corner-post, and reached the beautiful Parc Jehan Cousin where trees, whose like I have noticed only in Rio de Janeiro, waved silvery white leaves in the sun. This Jehan Cousin was a celebrated glazier of Sens and recalled my thoughts at once to the cathedral. I even contemplated purchasing a false mustache so that I might return and enjoy the cathedral further.

Sens has been rather a nursery of church artists and architects. Guillaume of Sens was the designer of a portion of Canterbury cathedral. Martin Chambiges, though really a Parisian, seems almost a Senonois, for he spent years here designing and constructing the cathedral transepts and the north and south façades. The latter is the most beautiful portion of the cathedral and anyone who gazes at it can well understand why Martin Chambiges was the most quarreled-about architect of his time.

To the old town of Troyes I first went by cross-country train, as it seemed simpler than to make the V by way of Paris. Just now I have covered the same exact route, in a spirit of nostalgia, but with some regard for comfort. On that earlier occasion I yielded to the lure of an advertisement and bought a two-months' card giving me the right on all of the six *grandes lignes* of France to purchase tickets at half price. The card was third class and I have ever since admired my courage if not my wisdom. The railway carriages themselves one can endure, though they are not like third class of England or Switzerland, but the French railways long ago managed to devise a series of hurdles for the third-class traveler which are veritable marvels of exasperating ingenuity. I can hardly overstate this case. Practically every important train in France has a joker in its hand capable of taking in the ace of third-class trumps. You pick out in the time-table exactly the train you want and plan for a large day. Oh, but there is a marker referring you to the *Conditions d'Admission* on pages 12 to 16. Experience soon teaches you that these little markers invariably spoil your fun. You cannot travel by that train third class unless you are going a minimum of three hundred kilometers. You cannot even travel second class unless you are going at least one hundred and fifty kilometers, but the town you wish to visit is only seventy kilometers distant. Victor Hugo's characters were always tearing out their hair in handfuls, yet they did not even know this supreme annoyance of modern French civilization. I believe I have never had so thorough and sustained a course in patience as I did by "sticking it out" with my third-class card. On about fifty per cent of the rides I paid for mileage which I could not use in order to take a decent train. On the other rides I *crawled*.

I traveled, then, to Troyes by crawling *omnibus* of the *chemin de fer de l'Est*, and arrived less distraught than my introduction would lead you to suppose. It is a delightful old town, as full of old houses, proportionally, as Rouen, as full of churches as Poitiers. It is full of "past" too. Here St. Loup prevailed upon Attila, the Scourge of God, to spare the episcopal city. Here, by the Treaty of Troyes, France gave Catherine of France to Henry V of England, and the dowry was nothing less than France itself. This was a national disgrace wiped out nine years later by the victorious Maid of Orléans.

Troy weight takes its name from this town rather than from ancient Troy as one may be pardoned for assuming. Great fairs were held here annually, notably under the energetic direction of Count Theobald. Merchants came from all over Europe and from the East. Credit was established. A uniform system of weight—Troy weight—was fixed upon. Customers, even from far lands, were not required to pay cash but interest ran as high as one hundred per cent. We are told that bad debts were very rare, for bands of professional guards, headed by powerful knights, undertook to enforce payment from any purchaser anywhere. One may picture a band of these agents sweeping down on a merchant, say, in Constantinople, presenting the contract sealed with the Seal of the Fairs, demanding payment of goods purchased last year at Troyes, and hinting that their swords and dirks were splendidly sharpened.

I attacked the serried line of Troyes churches with more vigor than success. From the first, St. Nicholas, I was repulsed by a funeral service, which crammed the church with mourners; from the second, St. Pantaléon, by locked doors. Then my luck changed. I enjoyed the church of St. Jean, where Henry of England married his "Kate," and then walked on through some of the quaintest streets I have seen in France to the church of St. Urbain, begun by a man who has become perhaps the most famous of "Trojans," Pope Urban IV. This man was the son of a cobbler and the church which he erected to his patron saint stands directly on the spot where the paternal shop once stood. As a boy he was called Jacques Pantaléon, the second name being doubtless a tribute to that saint whose church stands just around the corner, and I have not been able to find out why he elected to discard the name of that saint and take up the name of Urban.

This church is strongly reminiscent of the Sainte Chapelle at Paris, though of course far less beautiful as to its glass. When Urban founded it St. Louis was alive and had very recently erected the Sainte Chapelle. Pope Urban had many dealings with the king, in most of which the difference between the papal conscience and the royal conscience is obvious, a difference altogether in favor of the king, though Urban was not bad or even very hard in his outlook. He was always trying to persuade Louis that this thing or that, which favored his schemes or the throne's aggrandizement, "didn't matter."

Urban's record is conspicuously posted on the wall of the church and would fit in admirably to a book about self-made men, designed to stimulate youthful ambition. Of course in his day boys looked forward to becoming the Pope as the one glittering, almost unattainable goal. It was far more dazzling than the thought of becoming President in our day and land. To be the Pope was to be just a single stage below God himself. One wonders if the alert Trojan boy who helped his father repair sabots for workingmen ever dared to dream of becoming God's representative for the whole earth. He was made a clerk of the cathedral at ten and advanced by steady strides to become priest, bishop, then Patriarch of Jerusalem and lastly Pope. The crowning honor was a bit of pure luck, the result of bitter jealousies which prevented the election of the more logical candidates.

I was interested in the banners displayed in this church. They seemed typical of the attempt one often notes in French cathedrals to awaken the piety of the faithful by appealing directly to the senses. Consider these texts, which I copied down from two of the banners:

> *Fête Divine et Charmante;*
> *Une Visite à Jésus Ravit de Joie et d'Amour*
> *Que Délicieuse est l'Hostie [the Sacred Host]*
> *de ce Jour!*
> *Que Désirée est celle de Demain!*

Across a canal lies the Cathedral of St. Peter and St. Paul, damaged only slightly in the late war. Each of these saints was to have had a magnificent tower. Peter's, the north one, was finished so late in the Gothic period that it lacks utterly the grace and rich beauty it should have had. Its upper section reminds one of nothing so much as several pairs of slatted wash-room doors. Paul's tower was never built. Even the west façade of the cathedral was never completed. The great Martin Chambiges was commissioned to build it but he was so quarreled for and detained, notably by Beauvais, that the canons of Troyes became restless and finally gave the work to second-rate men who were never able to carry out the ambitious design of Chambiges.

An impression of great width, of solid immensity rather than grace or upward reach, is left upon the mind by this cathedral. Its glass, now being replaced, is extensive and of high quality. The structure was consecrated in 1229 in the presence of Charles VII and the conquering Maid, say the guide-books, but scholars spoil the story by insisting that the ceremony occurred on July 9, the day before Joan entered Troyes. One sees in this town, as in nearly every cathedral town in northeastern France, a bronze tablet recounting Jeanne's entrance or her exploits in the neighborhood. These tablets were all erected by the committee in charge of the five hundredth anniversary of Jeanne's martyrdom, and with the innumerable statues of her erected since her canonization in 1920 testify to the wave of adoration for the Maid which swept France in the decade after World War I.

I have visited so many churches on several occasions in Troyes (only a few of the multitude suffered in World War II) that I do not deserve to have a single clear memory of any of them, but I do, as a matter of fact, remember the little church of Sainte-Madeleine better than almost any other small church in France. It possesses a jube or rood screen which is exquisite beyond anything one could possibly expect in such a drab little structure. It was wrought in an angry "I'll-show-you" mood by one Grant-Jehan Gailde in 1508. This artist, often called Giovanni Gualdo, had been in the employ of the cathedral canons and had submitted to them in 1506 a *pourtraict* (model) for the proposed towers of St. Peter and St. Paul. His model had been rejected in favor of one designed by Martin Chambiges. It is quite possible that the worthy canons had given the preference to Chambiges purely because of the glamor of his great name. They had wanted perhaps to remark in a casual way to the canons of Auxerre or Noyon, "Oh yes. It's quite true that Chambiges is designing our towers." This, at any rate, was Gailde's belief and he was stung to the quick. He resolved to show the cathedral dignitaries what he could do, so he designed for an unimportant church this white gleaming rood screen which is to this day considered one of the marvels of the sculptor's art. It is like heavy lace draped in three loops from an open parapet and surmounted by statues of the Virgin and St. John. One practical thing that I liked especially about its design was that it did not completely shut off the choir as so many jubes do but permitted one to look through and under it to the fine painted windows of the apse.

One incidental service Troyes renders to the Anglo-Saxon tourist, especially to the female of the species. It fixes in the mind a certain French word, *Bonneterie*. The town possesses a large industry and school of *Bonneterie*. It specializes, to come right out with the news, in hosiery and, more broadly speaking, in knitted goods. A hosier is a *bonnetier*. I do sincerely hope that the meaning of this word is an item of news to someone.

Châlons-sur-Marne, the last of our three towns, is the "Aldershot of France," so-called by all travel pamphlets and guidebooks. No doubt Aldershot is also the Châlons-sur-Marne of England. Both towns became great military centers in the middle of the last century. About Châlons there seems to be a veritable aroma as of war. Not only do *casernes* spring up to the right of us and to the left on the outskirts of the town, not only is there a vast Camp de Châlons, founded by Napoleon III, but the history of the place reeks with battle. Here was fought in 451 that mighty battle, "fierce, manifold, huge, stubborn," called by school textbooks, which love such classifications, "one of the ten decisive battles of history," by which Attila was definitely driven away from western Europe. To come down in a single leap to recent times, the town was taken by the Germans in August, 1914, and retaken by Foch on the eleventh of September. The Germans tried to take it again in 1918 but failed. They had to wait until the next war when they swept all France before them in 1940.

But other things than war have made the town celebrated. In Chaucer's day it was widely known for the woolen cloth there produced. In the *Canterbury Tales* the Reeve refers to

*". . . a bed*
*With shetes and with chalons fair y-spred."*

Bernard of Clairvaux was associated with Châlons and more happily than with Sens. Here in the spot now covered by a *jardin*, oddly called *Le Jard*, he mounted a stone chair and passionately preached the Second Crusade. The king of France and Pope Eugenius were among his hearers.

Joan of Arc was here of course. Her quinquecentenary bronze tablet is directly opposite the cathedral. But another woman, still young though twice as old as Joan when she was martyred, spent a night in Châlons—at the Préfecture—which must have been as wretched a night as ever anyone lived through. She was Marie Antoinette, Queen of France. With her husband and children she had just attempted to escape from the Paris mob but everything possible had gone wrong. It must have been like those dreams which everyone has, in which one annoying obstacle is piled on another. You cannot run, you cannot shout, people who should be meeting you are not at the appointed place, you lose your way and with it all hope. The royal family had *almost* escaped but had been recaptured at Varennes and brought back prisoners to Châlons on their way to Paris and eventually the guillotine. Of course Marie Antoinette thought back that night to a previous stay which she had made at Châlons twenty-one years before, when, as a proud Austrian princess of fifteen years, she was on her way to wed a prince of France. On that occasion the people of Châlons had erected a triumphal arch to celebrate her entry.

The cathedral, called St. Etienne, is large but not especially notable. Its classical west façade is quite out of keeping with its general Gothic construction. I was much more interested in a smaller church called Notre-Dame (generally this name is reserved for the major church), and still more in a third, a curious basilica erected for a special purpose in the fifteenth and sixteenth centuries. I refer to Notre-Dame-de-l'Epine, Our Lady of the Thorn, a very beautiful miniature cathedral five miles northeast of the town. The church was built to house a miraculous statue of the Virgin found on the spot in a thorn-bush. We have in this church another evidence of "that ancient faith, homely and wholesome, suited to the time," which produced Notre-Dame-de-Chartres to house the Druid Statue of the Virgin.

At Châlons we are in the heart of the old province of Champagne. This sparkling thought leads us direct to Reims, the ancient and modern capital of the district. Let us make an effort to approach this tremendous spot with open minds. This may not be easy, for the city means very different things to different people. The name fans old angers and slumbering war hates. To use it is the very Altar of The French Cathedral and surely we cannot afford to roil our minds with anything that would detract from our deep and reverent pleasure in it.

## CHAPTER VI

# The Smile of Reims

IN THE sculpture before one of the minor doors of the west portal of Reims Cathedral two angels, one of whom is Gabriel, may be seen conducting St. Nicaise to heaven. The group can be identified by the flat-topped head of the saint which looks as though it had been sliced off by a carving knife. Having found this saint, visitors always (and quite properly) neglect him to gaze at Gabriel who stands at his left hand. Gabriel's smile, every bit as interesting as that of Mona Lisa, is known as "The Smile of Reims." It is alluring, contagious and, when you are not in its presence, haunting. Heaven becomes a really interesting place as foreshadowed by Gabriel. This smile is to me the symbol and cognizance of modern Reims. Gabriel's lip was shot off by one of the German shells in September, 1914. His whole head was shot off by a later shell. His wings and fingers and feet were damaged, his stone robe badly scorched. But courageous and devoted priests gathered up the fragments after every bombardment and took them to a place of safety, and Gabriel, smile and all, was after the war put together again. The smile is possibly less perfect than it was but hardly less beguiling. You cannot look at it without smiling yourself.

Reims too is smiling again. It is a city built between 1919 and 1939, a victim of savagery in the first World War but largely escaping damage in the second (though the monument to heroes of the earlier war was struck by a bomb!). Of its fourteen thousand houses standing in 1914 less than a hundred were habitable in the fall of 1918 and most of those were ruined beyond repair. New houses, new hotels, new business blocks sprang up with what seemed like the rapidity of a movie set yet there is nothing flimsy or temporary about these constructions. They are handsome, solid, civically satisfying. Many of them were built on false hopes, though none the less solid for that. "Les Boches Payeront" was the wishful rallying cry during the better part of a decade following Armistice Day. France then rebuilt her ruined areas with feverish rapidity, expecting that a good turn of the screw and then another and another would invariably squeeze out the money from the defeated foe. The high hopes were inevitably blasted, the bright mirage faded, but gradually the hard readjustment was effected and France accepted facts rather than fancies. After the second World War, in which the nation as a whole (though not Reims) suffered infinitely more hurt, her people entertained no false hopes of substantial reparations. They girded themselves to tackle the great job alone.

Reims enjoyed a special favor from fate, a special gift of balm to her pride, when this city was selected by the Allied High command for the surrender of the Nazis. This took place in the *Collège Moderne et Technique*, which then served as

SHAEF headquarters, and the Salle de Capitulation of this building has become a major tourist attraction though it is located on "the wrong side of the tracks," not too easy to reach from the hotel sector. Visitors see the black-topped surrender table and the very chairs, all tagged with the names of their occupants, at which visitors and vanquished sat to deal with the surrender document. This was finally signed by General Jodl and his associates "at 0241 hour 7 May 1945," as a sign states. Interesting photographs of the great occasion are displayed, along with maps, statistics and assorted data. Included are views of the "welcome" of the Nazi generals and a photostat of the surrender document itself, with the name of the Nazis' principal signer appearing as a bold, angry, humiliated *Jodl*.

In accordance with our announced plan we shall take a little time to see what we can of Reims before directing our attention to its world-famous cathedral. The city is not completely overshadowed by this as in the case of Chartres. It is of unusual interest in itself. It possesses notable Roman ruins. It possesses a piquant suburb unlike anything I have seen elsewhere in Europe. It possesses a Carnegie Library which is the envy of other French cities. It boasts a vast and colorful industry which has spread the name of its district, Champagne, on gay menus and pretentious wine lists the world over.

To the Frenchman there is nothing whatever incongruous in associating the city of Reims with two great leaveners of human life, religion and sparkling wine.

Somehow he knows how to take both cheerfully. He seldom lends himself to morbid introspection in religious matters and almost never to drunkenness in vinous matters. Any American traveler, even the most rabid dry, will testify that he has scarcely ever seen a drunken Frenchman though he has seen plenty of drunken Americans in France.

True champagne comes *only* from the district immediately surrounding Reims, that is from the few square miles within a rough triangle whose three points are Reims, Epernay and Châlons-sur-Marne. The French government is exceedingly strict in supervision and its laws are drastic. Any dealer who sells as champagne a sparkling wine which does not originate here may be and almost surely will be prosecuted. The inner end of the cork in every champagne bottle must be stamped with the word *Champagne* and woe betide any cheat who so stamps corks not destined to seal the true article. He is in the class of the counterfeiter of money. Champagne, for all its renowned golden color, comes from black grapes, the skins of which are very dexterously removed from the pulp. The black grapes are grown on the northern slopes of certain hillsides and develop qualities which differentiate them from all other French grapes. Invariably champagne is a blend of the grapes of several vineyards in different parts of the district and that is the reason why, instead of being marketed under the name of some parish or château, it is marketed always under the name of a dealer. We do not hear of *Verzenay, Mailly* or *Mareuil*, which are among the great *vignobles*, but of *Pommery, Piper-Heidsieck, Moët-et-Chandon, Ruinart*, the great dealers.

The clustering establishments of these dealers at the southeastern edge of Reims remind one of nothing so much as a back drop for a musical comedy. "It is not possible," you say as you gaze at the outlandish turrets and minarets of the Maison Pommery. I applied at the Maison Ruinart for permission to view their cellars and was astounded at the vastness of what I saw. Cut deep into a stratum of damp chalk one hundred feet or more below the surface, three tiers of corridors extend a total distance of five and a half miles (the Pommery *caves* are twelve miles long) and in these dank corridors at the time of my visit were stored a million and a half bottles whose contents were at various stages of fermentation. The smallest bottles contained less than half a pint, the largest just under a gallon. The big bottle of *Ruinart et Cie* is called affectionately the "Jeroboam," and this name I offer as a text to prohibition lecturers in the United States, for it was "Jeroboam, the son of Nebat, who caused Israel to sin."

The various stages of champagne manufacture are of absorbing interest but since this is not, after all, a treatise on wines we must largely neglect the topic. One used to find on the façade of the house (no longer standing) of Veuve Clicquot Ponsardin a series of mosaics picturing the ten stages of manufacture and preparation for the market. He who strolled could read of them in pictures:

| | |
|---|---|
| Vendanges | Dosage |
| Collages | Bouchage |
| Recoupage | Ficelage |
| Remuage | Habillage |
| Dégorgement | Emballage |

I believe I witnessed seven or eight of these operations in the Ruinart establishment. One, *dégorgement*, I know well that I witnessed. This means the removal of the unpleasant sediment which collects after many months on the inside of the cork, the bottles being always tilted upside down. Learned articles on champagne manufacture are apt to state that this sediment is

removed by freezing the contents of the neck of the bottle and
then extracting a lump of dirty ice, but Ruinart's experts do
it by a clever flip of the wrist exactly at the moment when the
cork, to the roar of a fine young explosion, is removed. Once,
while I was watching, the flipper was less clever than usual.
A veritable geyser of champagne flew all over me. My hat,
which had already acquired a cigarette burn in Paris and a delightful purple ink spot in a provincial post office, happened to
bear the brunt of the attack and considered itself from that moment a gone hat.

I noticed that Ruinart had agents in Milan, Toronto, Lima,
most of the world's leading cities, but none in New York.
"Too bad," said my guide mournfully. "It ees so good for ze
illness."

In the first World War the chalk cellars of Reims played
a brilliant, brave, romantic part. The enemy took the city on
September 4, 1914 and looked with gloating eyes on these magnificent stores of the world's most coveted wine. But suddenly, eight days later, D'Esperey's advance guard drove the
invaders out. The cellars were almost untouched and the German army never had another chance at them. Under an incessant bombardment of twenty-eight months the city was reduced to smoking rubble, but some seventeen thousand
intrepid citizens took refuge in the champagne cellars and "carried on" here. Here schools and churches and law courts func-
tioned regularly and the local newspaper, *L'Eclaireur de l'Est*,
was published. A complete underground city was developed,
actually within one mile of the nearest German trenches. Finally after twenty-five thousand shells had, in one week, Easter
week of 1917, raked the surface of what had been Reims, the

citizens of Reims-sous-terre were ordered away by the French authorities.

Almost adjoining the northern boundary of "Champagne Village" is *Le Foyer Rémois,* an experiment in city development which is sure to be followed by other French cities. It is a charming *Cité Jardin* with hundreds of clean attractive ivy-covered little houses which are rented cheaply to *familles nombreuses.* This enterprise, which is a philanthropic one conducted by a group of private individuals, seems to me far more practical in encouraging the increase of the French birth rate than the government's occasional prizes for record families. Any humble Rémois, it would seem, would be more willing to assume the obligations of rearing many children if he could thereby be assured of securing one of these pleasant stucco cottages at a nominal rent. Rose hedges, green lawns, fruit trees, attractive parks make this in a sense the most desirable quarter of the city. The church, named St. Nicaise, is an amazing mosque-like structure. Its ceiling is of dull gold streaked with blue beams, its windows are of a curious lemon color and the domed recess over its high altar is like a "bomb bursting in air."

One may not like this futurist church but upon emerging from it one sees in the distance, straight down the Avenue de la Marne, the chief glory of the city, Notre-Dame-de-Reims. The bombardments made the west front more visible. One should walk up the rue Libergier and its continuation, rue John D. Rockefeller, to let its glory gradually dawn on the senses. Everyone, from Mâle down, proclaims this west façade of Reims one of the supreme masterpieces of French art. It is that still despite the horrible mutilations of the long bombardment. I have struggled against inserting in this book the old French saying which defines the ideal cathedral. It is so hackneyed that it calls forth a groan from writer and reader, yet it would be as absurd to avoid it in a book of this kind as to avoid the use of the word "and." The perfect cathedral, says the dictum, would be composed of the portals of Reims, the towers of Chartres, the nave of Amiens, the choir of Beauvais. I should certainly cast my feeble vote for the first and the last of these four component parts but I am not quite so sure of the other two.

I wish there were four or five good cafés along the edge of the cathedral *parvis* instead of four or five blatant curio shops and an ugly garage. I would like to spend comfortable hours here absorbing with my coffee or apéritif as much as I could of the majesty of the cathedral. This is, however, impossible. The only café on the square, contrary to all French custom, has few sidewalk chairs. Huge buses, loaded with tourists, come thundering into the square every few minutes. Touts for the curio shops make your life a burden, and even while you are studying the quaint *Sourire de Reims* on Gabriel's face you are wondering whether you must give something to each one of the pathetic beggars who are hanging about. But those whose repose of mind is great can forget all these superficial annoyances and lose themselves in contemplation of the great national façade. It is "so rich," writes Mâle, "that on a coronation day it needs no further decoration, for tapestries of stone hang in the porches." In these tapestries of stone there are or were no less than five hundred and thirty sculptured figures. Above the great rose window, utterly destroyed in 1914 but restored, postwar, as well as possible, stretches the gallery of kings, forty-two of them, and each one eighteen feet in height.

These kings with Clovis in the center being baptized by Saint-Remi give the keynote to the cathedral. Clovis had made a bargain with the Christian God that if He would strengthen his arm to win the important battle of Tolbiac he would turn Christian. He did win and like a gentleman he kept his bargain —on Christmas Day of the year 496. There, high in the angle of the gable, we can see him in his little bathtub with his beaming Christian wife Clotilde on one side and the holy bishop on the other. The story of the ampoule of inexhaustible baptismal oil brought by a dove direct from heaven is too familiar to call for repetition here. "Archbishop Hincmar invented this story three centuries after the event," says one cold-blooded authority, but devout French Catholics even today will flare up with resentment if you hint at such a fraud. A fiery Revolutionist named Rhull sharing, by anticipation, the view of the above authority smashed the small phial against the statue of Louis XV. "The people," he shouted, "will never again see the insidious farce of the coronation of a lucky brigand. The Ampoule—this holy bauble of fools—no longer exists." But a brave priest, risking his life, rushed into the fray, scraped together two or three drops of the sacred fluid, and preserved it until a new ampoule could be made to hold it. This meant a great deal to the Bourbon Charles X, some thirty years later. He had himself anointed with it seven times in Reims cathedral, thus symbolizing the complete return of the old order.

The most important and colorful of all the coronations which took place at Reims was of course that of Charles VII who was shepherded to triumph by Jeanne d'Arc. The scene, looked at in retrospect, is one of the most moving in all history. Why, one asks, does not God arrange mighty happenings with a little more care and forethought, as you and I would arrange them? Why does He work a miracle by sending to the sore pressed land of France a girl of Jeanne's incomparable force and spiritual magnetism and at the same time furnish her with such fearfully shoddy material as Charles VII to work on? Have you ever looked at a picture of this king? If not, it will pay to hunt one up, that, for example, painted by Jean Foucquet and reproduced in Malet's *Nouvelle Histoire de France*. He looks like the local half-wit in any coastal village, capable possibly of peddling clams but of nothing more. Yet Foucquet labeled his painting *Le Très Victorieux Roy de France; Charles Septiesme de ce Nom.*

This "very victorious" king of France had been skulking in Bourges. Everyone had called him in derision the "King of Bourges." He was the son of a feeble-minded father and a Bavarian mother whose life as queen of France had been both a national scandal and a national curse. She had brought France to its then low estate. Her weakling son, the new king, looked on with sullen, apathetic glance as his nation crumbled more and more to destruction. Then came Jeanne and prodded him into a little semblance of life, carried him, almost bodily, to victory, and stood beside him at the coronation ceremony in Reims cathedral. As the archbishop prepared to anoint him with oil from the sacred ampoule Jeanne's emotion overcame her. She knelt down, kissed the king's feet, and while hot tears rolled down her cheeks, exclaimed: "O noble king, now is God pleased, Who desired that I should raise the siege of Orléans and that I should lead you to your city of Reims to receive the Holy Sacrament, showing that you are the true king and that to you must belong the crown of France." The ceremony proceeded.

The next year Jeanne was captured by the English at Compiègne. The "very victorious king" looked on with sullen indifference. He might have ransomed her but that would have cost him money.

The interior of Notre-Dame-de-Reims is coming year by year nearer to a semblance of itself. The work was so far advanced even in 1927 that it could be rededicated in the presence of the late beloved Cardinal Luçon who was almost the Mercier of France. Since that time it has gone on steadily except for the years of the latest war. I once overheard an oily guide explain to a group of assorted American tourists, "If zis casedral shall be repair it shall be due to ze grand heart of one of your own fellow-citizens, Mr. G. D. Rockefeller."

"John D.," suggested one of the tourists timidly.

"Yes," said the guide, "G. D."

It is true that Mr. Rockefeller, in the unostentatious spirit that has characterized all his generosity to France, has gone very far to help the stricken city rebuild its cathedral. The roof of the nave is his gift entirely.

The glass of the great roses and lancets is irreplaceable in its former glory but a gradual restoration has been made even in this part of the work and much more successfully, to my untutored view, than in the case, for example, of Soissons. The main rose, forty feet in diameter, has been replaced, then removed for the new war and again restored. It tells, as in *The Golden Legend*, of how the Virgin's soul was carried to heaven in the arms of the blessed and how her body ascended three days later to rejoin the soul. The eight small roses high over the restored double windows of the nave contain the original thirteenth-century glass which was saved from destruction by an extraordinary act of courage and skill. These windows had somehow survived all the bombardments and fires until the winter of 1918. A group of Paris firemen and two glaziers then undertook to remove them. They could not erect a scaffolding as that would have invited a fresh bombardment, so under cover of a particularly dark night they climbed to the dizzy height on ladders and succeeded in accomplishing their difficult task before morning.

The desolation of the church after the great fire of September 19, 1914 must have been appalling. The structure was used then as a hospital for wounded German soldiers and the German authorities had been made fully aware of this by official communications. Nevertheless they fired on the cathedral and one shell ignited the elaborate wooden scaffolding that surrounded the north tower. Soon a terrible fire was raging (one is reminded of the similar fire that once started in the scaffolding of the Sherry-Netherlands Hotel tower in New York) and the fire spread to the roof of the nave. The lead was melted and poured in rivers through the mouths of the gargoyles. The roof succumbed and crashed in. The angel spire with its eight caryatids plunged into the hellish abyss. The great western rose and many other windows flamed up like celluloid for they were made of "chemist's stuff," to use the local guide's phrase. The archiepiscopal palace and thirty-five acres of dwellings were destroyed. Of the German wounded, however, all but twelve were rescued.

I have read with deep interest a booklet by the Abbé Laluyaux on the sufferings of his beloved cathedral during that war. Two hundred and eighty-seven direct hits were recorded during the first two and a half years and in the violent bombardments of 1917 and 1918 the hits were too numerous to count. Yet the great edifice was not utterly destroyed. I have unfortunately lost the abbé's little booklet but I remember very

Senlis, a "sleeping beauty" among French towns is seen from the passenger planes that shuttle between Paris and London. The old Gallo-Roman wall encircles the 12th-century cathedral. *Air France.*

The spire of Notre-Dame-de-Senlis is one of the finest in France. The cathedral, built in 1155-1190, was a pioneer in the Gothic style.

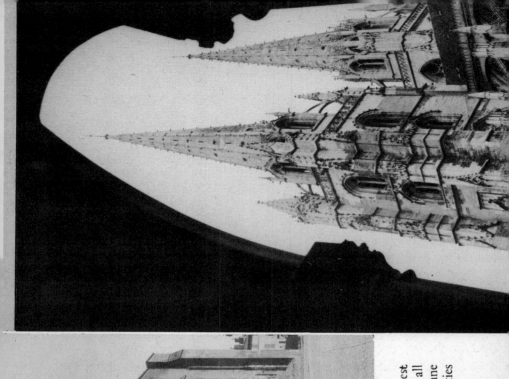

The church of St. Sernin, in Toulouse, has been called the "finest brick building in the world." It is safer to call it the dean of all the Romanesque churches of France. The cathedral of Bayonne (right) is pure and restful Gothic with none of the eccentricities that encumber many churches in the south of France.

well one sentence which rang out like a paean of victory. Speaking of the cathedral he wrote:

*Elle vivra, car aucune de ses blessures n'est mortelle!* How nobly those two first words challenge fate. The abbé can no more conceive of the cathedral dying than he can conceive of God himself dying.

The war-stricken church of St. Remi, whose chief treasure is the reliquary containing, presumably, the bones of him who baptized Clovis, is a gloomy and pitiful reminder of ruthlessness in striking contrast to the now hopeful cathedral. St. Remi I almost fear will not live for its wounds appear mortal. It was once a noble abbey church of great proportions and wide fame but only one sepulchral unlighted portion is now in use. I have rarely seen anything so depressing as a service I witnessed here. The reliquary of the saint made a brave show but it seemed to me that most of the worshipers were quietly weeping. It was with a sense of relief that I escaped to the bright open air and made my way to the sumptuous Carnegie Library in the Place Carnegie. This is a very beautiful building and adds another link to Franco-American friendship. On the left of the façade appears the motto *E Pluribus Unum* with a representation of the American flag. On the right is the motto *Dieu En Soit Garde* with the civic emblem of Reims. The Laird of Skibo, in bronze, surveys the city from a little park at the entrance.

Many things about Reims have changed for the better as a result of its trial by fire. Its streets and public buildings are far finer than in the old days. It has an immense new covered market, the most up-to-date I have seen in France, with four doors named like gates of a city to honor the four rivers of the district, Porte Marne, Porte Aisne, Porte Suippe, Porte Vesle. One thing about Reims has not changed, however, since the days of

Clovis. That is the spelling of its name. I do not understand why Englishmen and Americans feel called upon to spell it Rheims. There is no more sense to it than to spell the capital of Italy Rhome. It can only be justified if, and when, some scholarly etymologist shall prove that the city derives its name from "Rheims, reemz, a post-village of Steuben county, N. Y., 2 miles by rail from Hammondsport. Pop. 100."

In the central part of the elongated Place Drouet d'Erlon, which is really the main business avenue of the new city, a veteran shell-battered fountain still exists. It is a symbolical fountain with the four rivers, whose names adorn the market gates, represented by four female figures. After the big bombardments of 1914-1918 the Marne had lost the lower half of her face, the Aisne had lost her left foot, the Suippe had lost her head and her right arm, the Vesle was almost altogether gone, yet the fountain continued to play. And the city of Reims continued to play, in that sense, pouring out its energy incessantly to replace, so far as was humanly possible, that which had been destroyed, to create new features of civic growth which should blot out, in some measure, the sting of staggering losses.

As I first saw this sorry but still brave fountain in the Place Drouet d'Erlon the paean of Abbé Laluyaux inevitably came to my mind. I found my lips forming, like a comforting refrain, the words of his triumphant dictum: *Elle vivra, car aucune de ses blessures n'est mortelle!*

## CHAPTER VII

# Northward in the Ile de France: Senlis—Soissons—Laon

I SUPPOSE ever so many tourists who embark at New York on the great French liner *Ile de France* are vaguely disturbed by the realization that they do not know what the name of the ship means. They intend to ask somebody sometime if they can bring the question in casually. Some of them undoubtedly visit France and return without finding out. It is not a particularly important bit of information to possess and yet it is of some interest. The people of old France thought of that small north central section of their land which lies between the rivers Seine, Marne, Aisne, Oise and Ourcq as an island. A canal of a few miles length would have made it so. This "island" early outgrew its unresisting boundaries and came to include—politically—all that district which surrounded Paris and was most effectively controlled by the kings. It was the Royal Domain.

Within this irregular and shifting district the cathedral building fever developed early, and "raged" for many decades. For centuries, in fact, the malady reared its beautiful head intermittently. One of the earliest towns to succumb and one which longest felt the recurring symptoms of the fever was Senlis. This was once an important town but has sunk out of sight commercially since the railroads came and the main lines passed it by. It now boasts less than six thousand inhabitants, but the very deadness of the place makes its beautiful cathedral seem to belong all the more intimately to those few persons who take the trouble to hunt it up.

Senlis is far easier to approach by motor than by train but it is almost worth the tedious train trip to use the pleasant little station which is so wonderfully different from most small-town railroad stations in France. The old building was *incendié* by German ruthlessness when the first World War was but a month old, as a conspicuous sign upon the new station relates, but the second World War luckily by-passed station and town.

Before visiting the cathedral, whose marvelous spire I had seen while the train was still miles from the station, I felt called upon to view the ancient Roman amphitheater which is the town's secondary claim to tourist fame. I confess that I was somewhat lacking in enthusiasm for this part of the Senlis venture, but my sight-seeing conscience was unaccountably tender that day and I felt that I ought to do the job and get it over. One sign near the station directed my steps toward it but then all signs ceased. I wandered interminably through the outskirts of the city. Finally I passed the Senlis cemetery and asked the *gardienne* where the amphitheater was. She had never heard of it. I next noted this sign on the door of a high walled enclosure:

T
oot
wice
o
ommie

I was enormously curious to know who Tommie was and why one should toot twice to him but he was obviously interested only in automobilists so I walked on. Presently I found the Hôtel des Arènes which looked hopeful and proved to be the key to the situation. Its proprietress did in fact have the key to the amphitheater, which she said was *tout près*. She took me to see the wondrous sight which included a grass-grown arena, a lions' den, a cell for the victims before eaten and a deep hole to receive the bones after the lions had finished their meal.

The sight is interesting for those who happen to be in an amphitheatrical mood but I was much more interested in the woman's personal story of Senlis in the first World War. She developed a fine and certainly a righteous anger as she talked about the invasion. The cathedral was hit fifty times by shells. The mayor of Senlis was shot. But the climax of her story came in her vivid description of how the Germans took fifty *casseroles de cuivres* from her kitchen, every single one she had, to make bullets with which to shoot her fellow-countrymen.

I finally left the excited lady (heaven knows she had cause enough for her bitterness) and walked past the old ramparts and on into the town. As in every French town, and Paris is no exception, many of the streets are quaintly named. I noticed rue à la Coquille (Shell Street), Place aux Gateaux (Cake Place), rue aux Fromages (Cheeses Street) and rue de Chat-

Haret (Wildcat Street). The stillness everywhere was un-canny. It is a fact that I walked through four streets succes-sively at two-thirty of a fair afternoon without meeting a soul. I find in my journal this statement—"I *never* saw such an Eze-dead town." The reference is to the deserted village of Eze in the hills above Nice, a familiar curiosity to Riviera visi-tors. Senlis is not really in the class with Eze, for it is not shabby or dilapidated and if you walk through enough streets you will presently meet someone.

Notre-Dame-de-Senlis, hidden from view as you traverse the narrow streets, suddenly bursts upon you in all its ancient loveliness. It is not a gigantic overwhelming thing like the greater cathedrals, but rather a gracious and intimate church. No longer is it presided over by a bishop, for it lost this honor at the time of the Revolution. But it makes no business of mourning for the past. Great ambitions no longer cloud its serene brow. It seems content to be admired and loved by those few who still come to pay a visit.

The *flèche* which surmounts the south tower is the cathe-dral's chief glory. Some critical students of architecture con-sider it unsurpassed in the whole of France, not forgetting the more celebrated spires of Chartres. It is at least very lovely, full of originality, endowed with both strength and lightness, a spire to force admiration from the most critical and the most light-minded. How it escaped serious damage in the bombard-ment of September, 1914, is beyond my understanding. I al-most dare to ask myself if the German gunners may not have been so struck with its compelling beauty that they tried *not* to damage it. It would of course be easier to believe such a thing if one could forget Reims.

One other feature of Notre-Dame-de-Senlis besides its spire

fascinated me. It was a seasonal feature, for I was there in the heart of spring. In a score of places on its west façade and elsewhere a riot of orange-yellow flowers touched up the ancient stones like waving sunshine. From many unexpected places the flowers sprang—from the wings of angels, from the broken toes of saints, from the bodies of little beasties. I asked a passerby the name of the flowers and after several moments of deep pondering he said with some firmness that they were called *giroflée ravenelle*. Subsequent study on my part has established the fact that this means in plain Latin *Cheiranthus Cheiri*, of the family *Brassicaceae*, which means (you knew it all along) wallflower of the mustard family, distant cousin to the cauliflower and the turnip. It made one of the most charming effects I have ever seen and I became so enthralled with the wallflower's beauty that I made this bold resolve: When next I should dance with a lady whom I desired to compliment, even if it should be my wife, I would murmur in her ear, "My dear, you're a perfect wallflower tonight!"

Senlis is decidedly a town of the far past. Many of the kings of medieval France delighted in it and spent much time in the royal château here. Judith, the seasoned beauty who had been queen of two English kings and who was the stepmother of Alfred the Great, was living in Senlis when Baldwin-of-the-Iron-Arm came from Flanders and snatched her for his bride as though she had been a slip of a girl. Perhaps he called her his little *giroflée*. Louis XI made frequent visits to Senlis and no doubt closed some of his best bargains with the Virgin here. Senlis is old, sleepy, beautiful, much to be loved. Its little river bears the name Nonette, which seems exactly right for such a river. But we must go on to a larger and livelier town on a real river, the Aisne.

Soissons is not a town where anyone would desire to stay for any length of time. It is too depressing in its combination of ruin and garish newness. The first war ruined it, the second passed it by, but it never had the glamor of Reims and to me at least its reconstruction between wars seems less happily conceived.

The name of Soissons, like that of the district about Reims, has been widely used on menus, but oh the difference in social status of *soissons* and *champagne*. The former means beans, and one buys a plate of them for the equivalent of about twenty cents in any cheap restaurant in Paris. For a bottle of champagne in one of the cabarets one pays perhaps one hundred times as much.

The cathedral of Soissons, which was once a very noble edifice, is a truly pathetic shadow of itself today. Slowly, without a Rockefeller to throw in an occasional judicious million, it is struggling toward rehabilitation. It was mercilessly shelled by the Germans and its entire nave was laid in ruins, though fortunately its curious but admirable south transept was little hurt. This rounded transept, terminating in an apse rather than a door, is Romanesque in origin and outward appearance but most delicate Gothic in its interior effect.

The glass of the renovated portion of the church (transepts and choir) is chiefly responsible, I think, for the utterly depressing effect which Notre-Dame-de-Soissons now makes upon the visitor. It is about what one would expect to see in a small-town Catholic church in America. In short, it is bright and garish. Possibly on a very dark day it would be effective, but as I saw it, with the sun's rays cruelly searching its marrow, it was too shocking for words in a cathedral of such venerable traditions.

Let us close our eyes and recall briefly one scene which this church witnessed at the beginning of the thirteenth century. Philippe Auguste, that sovereign under whom church building started its great forward drive, had married the Danish princess Ingelberga. Apparently he had scarcely seen her but had liked her name, her "long bright hair," her shadowy claim to the English crown. Immediately after the wedding he had suddenly realized that his bride was dull, awkward, utterly impossible as queen of France. He began to loathe her, caused his subservient clergy to annul the marriage, and promptly took to wife a noble lady named Agnès de Meranie. Ingelberga then astounded the king by refusing to be laid aside. She appealed to the Pope and this appeal resulted in one of the famous quarrels of history. Innocent III vigorously championed the ex-queen, for he saw in this a chance to humble the French monarch. Philippe Auguste would not yield and things finally came to this awful pass: the Holy Father placed France under the ban.

Philip tried to laugh this action down but it proved to be anything but a laughing matter. In the words of an eye-witness it was "horrible—pitiable. The doors of the church were watched and Christians driven away from them like dogs. All divine offices ceased—and there was no gathering of people at festivals. The bodies of the dead were not admitted to Christian burial, their stench affected the air, and their loathsome sight appalled the living."

The king held out. He loved Agnès. The ex-queen held out. She was not to be cast aside. The Pope held out. His authority was at stake. France, practically without blame, suffered terribly. At last the King was driven to parleying. Following the tedious ecclesiastical precedent a council was convened six months, six days and six hours after the promulgation of the ban. The appointed time was March 2, 1201. The place was Soissons.

Weeks of wearying eloquence from ten ecclesiastics and ten royal lawyers then left everyone in a state of utter exhaustion. Endless argument was met with endless rebuttal. Suddenly the king electrified the council by yielding. Angrily he seized his former queen, bade her mount his horse behind him and the royal pair "rode off through the wondering streets" without bidding good-by to anyone. Agnès very shortly thereafter died in childbirth. Ingelberga lived on and on—for thirty-seven years. Her angry lord kept her in prison for the first twelve years and took to himself a "*demoiselle d'Arras*," which seems to have worried Pope Innocent not at all since the Holy Father had won his point and shown his power. Ingelberga was patient and not too sensitive. Eventually she wearied the king into re-instating her as the true queen of France.

Laon lies some twenty miles east of Soissons, not on a river but on a most amazing V-shaped hill which rises, for no apparent reason, from the monotonous flatness of the surrounding district. If there is no good reason for this hill, barring the inscrutable whims of nature, there is a very good human reason for the town on it—a feudal reason if you will. In the days of the arquebus and the stone cannonball it was an easy town to defend. Also, within the arms of the V there lay and still lies a huge green bowl which has always been the kitchen garden of Laon. It is called the Cuve St. Vincent and can support the entire town almost indefinitely in case of need. Is it any wonder that the ambitious medieval prelates seized upon this curious hilltop with its fertile *cuve* as an ideal stronghold for God—and, to be quite frank, for themselves, as sub-vicars of God?

Laon was at one time an exceedingly important bishopric. Its bishop was one of the twelve peers of France and he had the still loftier distinction of carrying the sacred ampoule at the coronation ceremonies in Reims cathedral. The fourth and fifth Louis of France who reigned in the tenth century made it virtually their capital, the former called *d'Outremer* because he had been born in England, being actually crowned here. From that high estate Laon has sunk today to the status of a mere parish of Soissons. Its sky-piercing cathedral is not a cathedral but a common church, yet, architecturally speaking, it is often rated with the big six of France (Chartres, Reims, Beauvais, Amiens, Paris, Bourges). The men who built it boasted quite properly that where other great churches stopped theirs began, for being on the highest part of an abrupt four-hundred-foot rock they planned "to double the height of the hill." God had raised this little lump of rock from the vast plain. Man would raise a church (a home for God's mother) an equal distance above the topmost surface of the rock.

The story of the building of this mighty cathedral reads like a romance. Its grandparent, so to speak, was tragically destroyed in the year 1111, a date which I set down only because it is so ridiculously easy to remember. A terrible feud had grown up between the turbulent citizens of Laon, who desired and secured a charter of independence, and their haughty bishop, who bought from the king the revocation of the charter and then had the consummate impudence to try to secure the money which this had cost him from the very people whom he was thereby reducing to bondage. The feud grew to civil war and finally the bishop was captured as he lay cowering in a wine cask. He was murdered and his house set on fire. The fire spread in all directions, destroying the cathedral and thirteen more of the *sixty-three churches* which infested this little rock city.

The succeeding bishop, undaunted, set to work to replace the cathedral with another. His prelates marched through Maine, Anjou and Touraine, then actually through all southern England, exhibiting various holy relics, including the "sacred sponge," that very one which had been filled with vinegar to relieve Jesus on the Cross. Money poured in and in the incredibly short time of two years the new cathedral was built and consecrated. This, however, the parent of the present structure, soon went the way of the other, and then laboriously, but with faith and ardor undiminished, the Laonnais began to build the present structure. It is not necessary to trace the long struggle of this cathedral toward completion. It is sufficient that it was completed—more or less, for no cathedral ever considers itself absolutely completed any more than a city.

I wish I had words adequate to describe the majesty of Notre-Dame-de-Laon. Only five towers of the seven planned were ever built and these no longer double the height of the hill, for their spires were pulled down by the Revolutionists and now rise scarcely two hundred feet above the *parvis*, but for all that the church is overpowering in its effect. Since volleys of superlatives defeat themselves I will content myself with dwelling briefly on the curiosities of the cathedral.

Most celebrated of these curiosities are the sixteen stone oxen which gaze mutely from near the summit of the western towers over the wide-spreading plain. One discovers upon mounting the towers that these beasts are demi-oxen, their hind quarters having been amputated as there was no room for them. One discovers too that each animal has a facial expression of his own almost more human than ox-like. One is wistful, another gloomy, another almost laughing. These statues constitute a fine tribute to the beasts of burden that toiled up the steep slope of Laon innumerable times dragging blocks of stone for the cathedral. I believe the idea is unique in France as all the other cathedral animals—and they would form, in the aggregate, an immense and very curious zoo—were designed either from caprice, like some of the gargoyles, or as an integral part of the book of life sculptured on the cathedral walls. These Laon oxen have been very properly included in the local Roll of Honor because of their invaluable service.

The other curiosities of the church are more in the purely architectural field. The nave gives an extraordinary effect of openness and light because of the square apse, very rare in France and attributed to the influence of an English bishop who held the see of Laon in the late eleven hundreds. There are four columns in this nave that never fail to excite the interest even of the layman, for each consists of a massive pillar flanked as though it were an hour glass by four slender columns. One wishes that the idea had been carried out further. Still another strange feature of Notre-Dame-de-Laon is the square "lantern" built over the central point of the cross. This is a touch of Normandy but seems oddly out of place, though not displeasing, in a church of the Ile de France.

Laon, like all this section of France, has suffered repeatedly from war and invasion. In the war of 1870 at the moment of the town's capitulation to Germany a vengeful and misguided French sapper blew up the powder magazine in the citadel, killing some eighty German soldiers and two or three times as many Frenchmen, including himself. The cathedral, especially its ancient glass, was considerably damaged by the explosion. In the first World War it luckily suffered very little but it was profaned in a manner worthy of the Revolutionists. Some six hundred German army horses were stabled in its luminous nave. The whole edifice resounded with whinnying, with the ring of iron-shod hoofs on ancient stone, and with the guttural curses of soldiers deputed to shovel up the dung. Of course there is no such thing as a "nice war" and yet it is hard to see how any war could have induced a great nation, with fine Gothic cathedrals of its own, to countenance this dreary desecration. The second war wrought havoc with Laon's lower town but did not touch the church.

Laon has had many native sons who have carried its fame to other lands but none interests Americans more than Jacques Marquette, the Jesuit father, who, with Louis Joliet, explored the "Father of Waters." Père Marquette left his name in a goodly number of places on our American map—a river, a bay, two cities, two counties and numerous hamlets.

I wandered completely around the straggling V of Laon both by daylight and by moonlight, both on the outer rim and on the inner. From many vantage points and in many lights I saw the noble five-towered church. One of these vantage points was that selected by John Taylor Arms for his superb etching made in 1929 and included in the volume called *Churches of France*, which he and Dorothy Noyes Arms brought out in that year. It is worth a major effort on the part of anyone who is at all interested in this subject to secure this book from the nearest large library and let the spirit of the Gothic churches of France soak into his soul through the unsurpassed etchings and pencil drawings of this great draftsman. It is even worth, to those whose purse is not too lean, the fifteen dollars which the book costs—if it can still be found in bookstores.

Notre-Dame-de-Laon is worth seeing, whatever it costs.

## CHAPTER VIII

# Beauvais, the Perfect Choir

BEAUVAIS is today almost a cathedral without a town. It is the first place, of several encountered by the geographical plan of this book, where war razed a large part of the community but left the central church almost intact, like an ecclesiastical mountain saved by its own sanctity. Some of the faithful see in this a special miracle, whereas more practical-minded citizens are impressed by the excellent aim of the bombers and by the massive strength of the structure itself. Much of the damage to the town occurred during the invasion by the Germans in 1940, and their sparing of the cathedral, in contrast to their ruthless performance at Reims in 1914, seems to have been based on the Nazis' carefully conceived plan of conquering France in a "friendly" way. At any rate the wonderful edifice, dedicated to St. Peter, stands almost unhurt (though the restoration of its glass will take years), looming up in weird majesty amid hundreds of acres of desolation dotted by a mushroom growth of temporary wooden shacks.

This cathedral is a major curiosity, made doubly conspicuous by war's leveling of the area around it. As has been stated in the introduction, it consists of choir and transepts only; but what a choir and what transepts! I know of but one serious critic who has remained unimpressed by this crippled giant. Mr. James Fergusson, the Scottish expert, found that "notwithstanding its size, it has no majesty," but he is almost alone in such condemnation. Many have condemned the architectural rashness of it, but hardly any one else has failed to be stirred by the majesty of it. Viollet-le-Duc, dean of all critics, so far as France is concerned, even defends the daring plan of the mysterious "master-builder of Beauvais," whose name is not known. "If the architect could have had the proper means," which is to say good hard stone, stronger financial backing, better men to assist him, the work would have stood the test of time. "His calculations were correct; his combinations profoundly learned; his conception admirable." But a bagful of "ifs" is enough to ruin anything, and the story of Beauvais is one long record of tragedy and struggle, which has left us a part of a cathedral.

To complete this today as originally planned would drain the resources of a race of Rockefellers. The actual cost of such a work, taking into account the towers, the intricacies of carving in wood and stone, and the making of all the stained glass windows would be almost beyond computing. Of course, the work could not be completed anyway. The spirit is irrecoverable. St. Pierre of Beauvais will never be finished.

My personal thoughts of Beauvais are tinged with inescapable nostalgia, for many of the incidental wonders which I formerly enjoyed in the town no longer exist or are pitiably battered. They were reduced to ruin in the fighting of 1940 and 1944. Among these victims were the National Tapestry Factory and the church of St. Etienne, but in the hope that they will some day revive I may permit myself some mention of what they were.

The celebrated Beauvais tapestries were made on the appropriately named rue de la Manufacture-Nationale, centering an area utterly destroyed by war but now being rebuilt with one-story structures. The relics of this industry—hardly more than "goodwill"—have been absorbed by the Gobelins plant in Paris. The Beauvais tapestries, however, were made on a wholly different type of loom. The Beauvais looms were of the type called low-warp, in which the warp-threads are horizontal, whereas the Gobelins looms are high-warp and the threads are vertical. The material used at Beauvais consisted largely of wools, but their variety of hue was so great that only years of training could teach the human eye to make the proper selections. There were seven hundred and forty-five *nuances*, said my guide, and to each *nuance* twenty-five grades. He showed me the spindle racks to prove it, and had I taken time to count almost twenty thousand spindles I suppose I might have checked up this statement. I was overwhelmed by the thought of human eyes capable of selecting the right gradation from the right hue among twenty thousand.

I visited the school of weaving as well as the workrooms of the master weavers. The schoolroom, where self-conscious youths were struggling with their first designs, was plastered with sound texts and maxims of business virtue such as those which Polonius gave to Laertes. I remember for example this one:

> *Qui travaille doit être payé*
> *Qui est payé doit travailler*

In the main workrooms I was shown the actual weaving operations as executed by the trained weavers. The finished design was always on the *under* side of the loom so that the workers had to gaze at their product wrong side out. To correct this difficulty mirrors were so placed that each weaver could see both sides of the tapestry he was making. Patiently, all day long, he toiled, achieving, if the design was not too complicated and if he relaxed not at all, perhaps four or five square inches. I remember a double tapestry depicting scenes from the first World War, which the guide said would take ten years to finish (the ten years ran their course before a new war "finished" everything), and I remember a beautiful screen which the guide said was worth a hundred thousand dollars. A third thing I remember—and after all why shouldn't I?—there was one weaveress and only one among the weavers. She was young and comely, a brunette. No, I have not the least idea as to the color of her eyes. She kept them on her weaving.

Feeling that I needed a stepping-stone between the absorbingly interesting tapestry works and the sublimities of the cathedral, I visited the church of St. Etienne (now a pathetic derelict of war but with a small portion open for services only). A mixture of Romanesque nave and Gothic choir, it possessed a rare curiosity, rare in France at any rate, in the person of a venerated female saint with a full beard. She hung on a cross on the south wall of the church and was without doubt one of the oddest saints in the calendar, as indeed she still is, regardless of her war sufferings in this particular church. Her whiskers were exceedingly luxuriant, in the Beauvais representation, yet to prove to all the faithful that this was really a female the swell of her bosom was exaggerated. By the aid of a Catholic reference work I later ran down this fabulous saint.

She was the Christian daughter of a pagan king of Portugal. Fearing lest the young men of Lisbon should rob her of her chastity she prayed to God to disfigure her so that her suitors would be repelled. God thereupon gave her a noble black beard and her virtue was forever safe; but, alas, her father, angry at this folly, crucified her. The lady's name was Wilgefortis, but the faithful have adored her under various *noms de prière*, for example, Uncumber, Kummernis, Komina, Comera, Cumerana, Hulfe, Ontcommene, Dignefortis, Eutropia, Reginfledis, Livrada, Liberta.

The account explains, with admirable frankness, that she is a complete myth, being a distorted copy of a Christ on the Cross at Lucca, in which the figure is clad in a long tunic. Portuguese worshipers, mistaking this because of the tunic for a female figure, developed the quaint story of the much-named saint. In spite of this Catholic "exposé," which seems decidedly official, Wilgefortis continues to be venerated in Beauvais and many another pious town, though much less in France than in Germany and Austria.

The cathedral, St. Pierre, is only three or four hundred yards across the desert of war rubble from St. Etienne. From rue St. Pierre, the slowly reviving street which flanks it on the south, it looms above one at an almost terrifying height. Perhaps Ruskin was a bit frightened when he made the often quoted and often laughed at statement: "There are few rocks, even among the Alps that have a clear vertical fall as high as the Choir of Beauvais." This is strong talk but St. Pierre is at least the world's highest Gothic church. The ridge pole of its roof is two hundred and twenty-three feet above the ground, the equivalent in height of a twenty-story modern office building. It is difficult to conceive of the temerity which led an unknown thirteenth-century architect to hope that he could build a whole cathedral of such proportions. Disaster followed disaster until finally workmen closed the "bleeding wounds of the giant" at the place where the nave should have begun, and Saint Peter's of Beauvais was left as it remains today, a gigantic half-church. Saint Peter himself sits in the south transept—an imposing statue—mutely accepting kisses on his great toe from myriads of the faithful.

Worldly ambition brought about the fall of this cathedral as surely as it did that of Napoleon. In fact the adjective Napoleonic is the only one which seems to fit St. Pierre in its rise and fall. The early bishops, with few exceptions, yearned for a church whose height—for height was the Gothic ideal—should eclipse everything then known in the world and which should eclipse specifically the church of its neighbor Amiens, begun seven years earlier. It did eclipse by some eighteen feet anything that Amiens dared attempt, but no sooner was the choir built than the first crash came. The damage was painfully repaired and the walls strengthened a little, but in a few years there came another and a more terrible crash. Forty years elapsed this time before Guillaume de Roy and Aubert d'Aubigny finally completed the repairs for the second time. It is said that these two repairing efforts cost enough to have completed the whole cathedral, had there been no disasters.

To raise additional money all sorts of measures were adopted. Part of the cathedral treasure was sold. The Pope granted a very special indulgence to those who prayed at the seven altars of Beauvais *and* made a donation. The privilege of eating butter and cheese during Lent without committing a sin was sold to all and sundry who "had the price" and much money rolled in from this source. The canons gave a portion of their yearly stipend. At a later date Francis I gave a portion of his royal revenues from the salt tax. After two and a half centuries the transepts were finally built.

This portion of the church is almost as striking as the choir. Being of a much later period, it is exuberant, flamboyant Gothic. Martin Chambiges, with whom we became acquainted in Sens and Troyes, started this work and his successors, notably Jean Vast senior and junior and Michel Lalye, carried it out, achieving not something graceful and incidental but imposing and magnificent. Nowhere else in France do the transept façades possess such independent grandeur.

Had the Vasts and Lalye rested on their laurels their names would have been handed down to succeeding generations linked imperishably with that of Martin Chambiges, but ambition was their undoing. It so happened that Michelangelo had just sprung into fame by the construction of the great dome of St. Peter's in Rome. Lalye thereupon laid before the canons of Beauvais a scheme for a Gothic spire which should prove that the Gothic was capable of exceeding in height and boldness anything hitherto known in the world, and in particular the dome of the Roman St. Peter's. The canons rubbed their hands at the thought of discomfiting the Italian upstart. Of course this spire was utter folly. The nave was crying to be built. The tower should come later, when and if enough money —not half enough—could be raised. But it was exciting, intoxicating, and the cautious ones who feared further attempts at sheer height and who recalled the two previous catastrophes were laughed down. It was Michel Lalye who laid this plan before the chapter in 1534. It was Jean Vast, *fils*, who completed the tower in 1569.

The chapter's supreme ambition seemed to have been realized. All Europe rang with the news of the tower of St. Peter's of Beauvais, higher and more wonderful than the dome of St. Peter's of Rome. It was the highest structure in the world, exceeding the pyramid of Cheops by twenty feet. And it was as beautiful as it was high.

On feast days a huge lantern was raised within the tower and shed a soft radiance, which penetrated the marvelous stained-glass windows. For four prideful but terribly worried years the bishop and canons of Beauvais experienced the sensations of sated ambition. Repeatedly the supporting pillars of the spire gave warning that the strain was too great for them, at least without any support from the non-existent nave. Nothing was done.

On the eve of Ascension Day in 1573 there was an alarming shower of small stones from somewhere high on the spire. The next day, Ascension Day, just after the celebration of High Mass and while the procession was forming outside the church, a hideous cracking sound rent the air. Then before the eyes of the crowd, too sick with horror to exclaim, the two pillars next to what should have been the nave buckled and began to give way. After a moment a third pillar did likewise. The fourth pillar struggled, wavered, gave up the hopeless task, and five hundred feet of incomparable Gothic stonework crashed violently to the ground. No one was killed. Two priests only were injured. A part of the vaulting fell in, wrecking the newly finished jube and many windows and choir stalls, smashing also a main pillar of the choir roof and seriously endangering the whole edifice. It must have been horrible beyond our power to understand. The loveliest thing man had yet made, the thing that reached nearest to God and the Blessed Virgin, had crumpled into a mass of rubbish.

Then occurred one of those incidents which serve to lighten the blackest disasters. High above the cathedral floor were certain loose and jagged fragments of stone, clinging dangerously to the wall top at points where the roof had been wrenched off. Repairs could not go forward until these fragments were removed, but no one wished to risk life and limb to remove them. Finally some one had an idea. There was a condemned criminal in the local jail. He was to be hanged in a few days. Why not give him a chance to win his life and freedom by undertaking this hazardous task? If he should fall —well, a two-hundred-foot fall, after all, was hardly worse than a noose around one's neck. He eagerly accepted the chance, accomplished the removal of the dangerous stones and finally reached terra firma and liberty.

I have searched in vain for the criminal's name and subsequent record. It stirs my curiosity. Did he go back to his profession—perhaps he was a skilled assassin—or did he, while working at fearsome heights in the cathedral, sense his unwonted nearness to heaven and repent of his sins? I suppose I shall never know.

Within the choir of Beauvais is one curiosity—and it came through the war quite unscathed—which the sacristan delights to show off. I believe he is prouder of it than of the cathedral itself. It is an astronomical clock which exceeds in complicated grandeur the similar ones at Besançon and Strasbourg. It is forty feet high, boasts fifty-two dials, is composed of ninety thousand parts. It tells the time of twenty cities beside Beauvais. It tells the week, month and year, and includes, for good measure, a perpetual tide calendar for the various coasts of France. It tells also the age of the world, proclaiming it now as 5948, "selon Moïse." Cross-checking by reference to a King

James Bible reveals a moderate discrepancy, but one may generously grant that mechanical scholarship must be allowed to disagree with scholarship by royal appointment.

Every hour during the middle of the day this versatile robot depicts the Last Judgment. I have watched the whole rigmarole and wondered how anyone could be seriously impressed with it except as a wondrous mechanical toy. Virtue appears, and while he travels slowly across the ornate face of the structure Christ waves his hands in blessing. An angel choir is heard inside the clock. Vice appears, and sudden tongues of flame dart up in all the miniature windows. Christ mournfully shakes his head twice. There is a peal of thunder. The devil appears, pitchfork in hand, and drives Vice into the flames.

For one of its accomplishments the Beauvais clock has my profound respect. It presents the complete ecclesiastical calendar. What a vast subject is this for one ambitious clock to undertake! The Spanish *Enciclopedia Universal*, drawing its lore from church sources of impeccable authority, attempts to wade through the intricate maze in thirteen large pages. The *Britannica*, a little less wordy and sacerdotal, leaves the ordinary reader in hopeless confusion. Did you suppose that Easter, for example, occurs on the first Sunday after the first full moon after the twenty-first of March? If so, I invite you to investigate this matter, if not on the dials of the Beauvais clock then in some work of reference. You will discover that the ecclesiastical full moon differs from the astronomical full moon and that you must determine the former by first ascertaining the Dominical Letter and the Golden Number. This leads you to the most complex formulae and soon your mind succumbs beneath the accumulating weight of cycles, indic-

tions, epacts and so on. Or perhaps you are a modern Euclid
and find the going easy.

Two prominent churchmen of perennial interest are associated with Beauvais. One is Vincent de Beauvais, the Domini-
can monk who achieved unaided the first compendium of
general knowledge, the famous *Mirrors*. He must have been a
man of powerful intellect and indefatigable industry. Emile
Mâle frankly bases his study of thirteenth-century symbolism
on the plan of Vincent's *Mirrors*. He characterizes him as "the
most comprehensive thinker of the day," a man "whose learning was immense yet it did not overwhelm him." Vincent's
encyclopedic work (80 books; 9,885 chapters) was the standard for six centuries.

The other churchman whose name is inseparably linked with
Beauvais is Bishop Pierre Cauchon, the judge who condemned
Jeanne d'Arc at Rouen, and who has ever since been damned
up and down the land of France. Traitor is the least of the epithets hurled at him. His name, unfortunately for him, is almost
indistinguishable in pronunciation from *cochon*, meaning pig,
an epithet as common in France as *Schweinhund* in Germany,
and this coincidence has helped his memory not at all. He died
while being shaved twelve years after he sent Joan to the
stake. Although he received Christian burial in Lisieux, he was
excommunicated after his death by Pope Calixtus IV. His
body was exhumed and thrown upon the *voirie*, which word
is defined as *le lieu ou l'on-porte les boues, les immondices*,
etc. (the place where they throw dirt, filth and so forth). The
body of the Bishop of Beauvais seems to have constituted the
"and so forth" of the *voirie*.

It is hardly proper to leave this town of distinction with the thought of a bishop on a dump uppermost in our minds, nor should Beauvais's present tragic appearance weigh too heavily upon us. Rebuilding life from what little the war left, the community clusters around its cliff of sanctity, its rock of ages. It finds solace in pride, for it still possesses one of the wonders of the world. Saint-Pierre-de-Beauvais has been likened to a Colossus standing on tiptoe. It is the very utmost that Gothic could do in its reach toward heaven.

## CHAPTER IX

# An Alliterative Wanderweek:
## Amiens—Abbeville—Saint-Omer-on-the-Aa

AMIENS is another notable example of a city whose whole center was blotted out by war but whose cathedral, miraculously spared, looms up from ruin as beautiful as ever and far more conspicuous. The damage to the city, occurring chiefly during the German invasion in 1940, was terrible, but unlike most cities of northern France this one has not waited for state aid. In a prolonged campaign of remarkable vigor it has undertaken to advertise and sell bonds to raise large sums for its own reconstruction from the *sinistres de guerre*. The campaign has been successful and for many months past a din of building sounds has filled the air, as it does now and will for long to come, especially along the central artery, rue des Trois-Cailloux (Street of the Three Flints), and in the neighborhood of the Hôtel de Ville. One cannot hear oneself talk, but one can think, with pride, of the enterprise and courage of this cathedral city, a major victim of both World Wars.

As every realtor in every large American city well knows, a street which leads directly from the office section to the railroad station is not a good shopping street. The suburban commuters are invariably *hurrying* to or from work. The buying power of these commuters may be immense. The stores on this street may be actually the handiest for them, but they rarely enter one for when they pass along the street they are not in a buying mood. They have no time "today." This same psychological phenomenon on a different plane sorely affects the towns of Amiens and Abbeville. They are both on the direct line from Boulogne and Calais to Paris. Nearly all English tourists and many Americans bound for Paris or on their way home from Paris pass through them but they do not stop. Always they intend to do so next time. So Amiens, which would surely be one of the most visited cathedral towns in France if it lay an equal distance from Paris in some other direction, receives only a few thousand Anglo-Saxon visitors yearly, perhaps one-sixth of the number received by Chartres. Abbeville receives only a handful each year.

Notre-Dame-d'Amiens is the largest church in France and one of the finest Gothic edifices in Europe. The city which it guards was the old capital of Picardy and possesses today a very distinctive charm in its *hortillonages* and numerous waterways. Of course it is called "The Venice of Picardy," as Annecy is called the Venice of Savoy and Bruges the Venice of Flanders. Ruskin, who specialized in the study of Amiens and loved it beyond measure, permitted himself a number of other colorful names. "This fountain of rainbows," he called it, and then "a little Frankish maid" who "writes herself the sister of

Venice." Again, she is a "little white-capped soubrette" and "the French River-Queen."

Realizing that he must explain his pleasant fancies to readers who are not yet warmed to his enthusiasm, he says: "But the Venice of Picardy owed her name, not to the beauty of her streams merely, but to their burden. She was a worker, like the Adriatic princess, in gold and glass, in stone, wood and ivory; she was skilled like an Egyptian in the weaving of fine linen, dainty as the maids of Judah in divers colours of needlework." John Ruskin has become unfashionable as an architectural mentor, and yet I doubt if any book written in England or America in fifty years dealing with the French cathedrals has failed to refer to him and few have failed to quote him at length. His "Bible of Amiens," for all its didactic manner, has remained something of a classic.

This "French River-Queen," regardless of her great house of worship, deserves far more attention than she customarily receives. The river Somme divides a few miles above the city into innumerable little branches (*rieux*, fishermen's lines, the Amienois call them), which form again into a single river below the city. Between these numerous twisting rivulets rise the *hortillonages*, this word being an ancient Picard term for marshy gardens. They are accessible only by boat, and on them are raised vast quantities of garden truck. I decided not to risk a sudden bath by trusting myself to one of the flimsy-looking local rowboats, but I did wander long and happily in the Venetian part of the lower city and within sight of the *hortillonages*. Among the Venices of northern Europe (a really large collection of them could be made) I would rate old Amiens rather high for its ill-smelling picturesqueness, but in some of the industrial sections one sorely needs, in spite of the branching waterways, occasional more obvious reminders. These one receives in the form of a *Buvette à la Petite Venise* or a *Restaurant Venitien.*

The "Bible of Amiens" is the west façade of Notre-Dame, so simple for the people of old to read, so arduously and lovingly studied by modern scholars. I asked myself here an old question which every traveler must ask sooner or later. Allowing for the tidal wave of thirteenth-century enthusiasm for the Queen of Heaven, admitting the studiousness of the Bearded Brothers and their lay successors, where—*where* did France find the skilled workers necessary for the simultaneous construction of more than a score of large and elaborate cathedrals? Popular education was non-existent, travel was difficult and full of real danger. The physical and moral exhaustion of the Dark Ages was hardly past. Whence did the architects derive their wonderful taste? Whence did the workers, scores of thousands of them, derive their uncanny skill? There seems to be no answer but the modest one the workers themselves gave. Mary stands in the midst of the work. Here is the power.

The cathedral of Amiens cries for statistics, a thing which this book shall rarely be guilty of giving. It covers an area of 75,000 square feet. It is 470 feet long and the spread of its transepts is 214 feet. The height of its walls is less than the height of the Beauvais walls by only eighteen feet. All in all, it is a "giant in repose." The giant has a heavy appearance from some angles owing to the squatty, unfinished towers, but the interior of the world-famous nave is a marvel of vast perfection, strongly lighted as only a thing of perfection should dare to be lighted. This church was fortunate in being built in one grand burst of energy and with no remains of its four predecessors to hamper the architects, the fourth of the Amiens dynasty having been utterly destroyed by fire two years before the commencement of the present structure.

Of course a prime relic would be indispensable in furnishing the motivating force for such a monster cathedral. The canons of Amiens possessed such a relic in the head, or rather one half of the head, of John the Baptist. Unlike St. Anne, who seems to have had two well-authenticated heads, John the Baptist had but one. The front portion is in Amiens, the rear portion in Rome, in the church of St. John Lateran. A dent in the forehead of the skull, which faithful Amienois are permitted to see on certain festival days, helps to establish the authenticity of the relic, for it was obviously a wound inflicted upon it by the dagger of the vengeful Herodias after the decapitation. An ancient Greek inscription carved on the skull also vouches for its genuineness, though we are left in some doubt as to who made the inscription.

Of all the innumerable sculptures of Ruskin's "Bible," the *Beau Dieu* of Amiens standing against the pier of the western central door is easily the most celebrated. In prewar days this Beautiful God was always compared with the other famous *Beau Dieu* at the north portal of Notre-Dame-de-Reims, but the latter statue, alas, was sadly mutilated in the first World War. It was struck by a German shell and its head, one of the wonders of the sculptor's art, shattered beyond repair.

As one enters the cathedral choir one finds oneself in a veritable shrine of the carver's art, for "there is nothing else so beautiful," says Ruskin, "cut out of the goodly trees of the world," as the Amiens choir stalls. Releasing his enthusiastic pen, and very properly too, from all restraint, the critic goes on:

"Sweet and young-grained wood it is; oak, trained and

chosen for such work, sound now as four hundred years since. Under the carver's hand it seems to cut like clay, to fold like silk, to grow like living branches, to leap like living flame."

A three-page "footnote" to this paragraph gives us the full story, essentially, of the making of the one hundred and twenty stalls, and it is a fascinating one. Six or eight skilled Picard carvers toiled on them for fourteen years with an enthusiasm equal to Ruskin's own. They received as pay the equivalent of two thousand dollars for the *whole* job, or about eighteen dollars a year apiece. It was good pay and they were content. Only one of these men thought it worth while to leave his signature on this incomparable work. One Jhan Trupin left his name and carven face on the elbow rest of the eighty-fifth stall and his name again under the ninety-second stall. We know nothing about him except the obvious fact that he was a good workman and the further fact, culled from the cathedal records, that he drew as wages "three sous a day," which was about equivalent to three American cents, though very much more, of course, in buying power.

The labyrinth on the floor of the nave, though a restoration, is of even more interest than the one at Chartres, for it contains a quaint old verse giving the names of the chief builders and the important dates. I shall quote the first three lines and the last four in the ancient French and in Ruskin's translation.

*"En l'an de Grace mil deux cents*
*et vingt, fu l'oeuvre de cheens*
*Premièrement encomenchie."*

("In the year of Grace, Twelve Hundred
And Twenty, the work, then falling to ruin
Was first begun again.")

The cathedral of Beauvais before and after the second World War. The structure consists of choir and transepts only, but these portions are universally considered the greatest of their kind and are also the loftiest. The tallest spire ever built (nearly 500 feet) rose from this half church; completed in 1569, it crashed in ruins four years later. The town was razed by the Germans in 1940 but the cathedral's great strength saved it. *Office Français d'Information Cinematographique.*

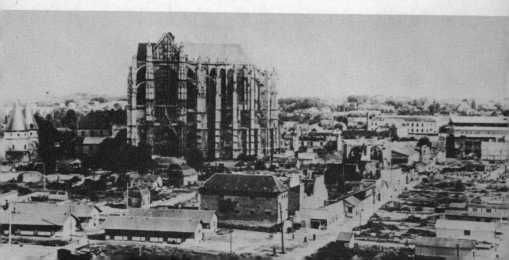

The cathedral of Amiens stands in the city where St. Firmin introduced Christianity in the year 301. One of the most imposing Gothic churches in Europe, it was begun in 1220. The view of the splendid façade with the three lofty recessed portals is unfortunately partly masked by houses.

The ending of the gay rhyme is irresistible in its ancient French spelling. It records the achievement of

> *"Maistre Regnault, qui mestre*
> *Fist a chest point chi cheste lectre*
> *Que l'incarnation valoit*
> *Treize cent, moins douze, en faloit."*

("Master Reginald, who to be put
Made—at this point—this reading
When the Incarnation was of account
Thirteen hundred, less twelve, which it failed of.")

It is a delightful and not too difficult exercise to set the ancient French into modern, though I confess that for my own part the words *"de cheens"* at the end of the second line formed a hurdle which I could not clear. Ruskin translates the phrase "then falling into ruin." I was just becoming thoroughly vexed with it for bothering me and had made up my mind to call it "going to the dogs," when I read on in my Ruskin and found the answer, simple, like all answers, when one is told. It stands for *déchéant*, the present participle of *déchoir*.

Amiens teems with memories of Clovis, who was crowned here when fifteen years old, fifteen years before his Christian crowning at Reims; of Peter the Hermit, preacher of the First Crusade, who was born here; and of Jules Verne, who lies buried here.

Abbeville, some thirty miles down the Somme from Amiens, is not a cathedral town, and furthermore—I may as well confess this now—it never was one. I believe no other complete outsiders except Caen and Mont-Saint-Michel will force their way into this volume, and in dealing with these three I shall be decently brief.

Abbeville was a major center of battle when the Germans invaded France in 1940 and it suffered, in proportion to its size, as much damage as Amiens. Moreover, its chief church, named in honor of St. Vulfran, was not spared like Notre-Dame-d'Amiens. It was terribly but not mortally hurt. Most of the roof fell in and the whole rear portion of the edifice became a mass of broken stones but it has *not* been abandoned. The whole interior is now a *chantier*, forbidden to the public, and restoration goes slowly forward. The main façade was fortunately little hurt.

St. Vulfran, more imposing than many a cathedral, is a tall flamboyant Gothic church with one daring bit of originality. Its "west front" faces north. Its worshipers have always knelt in prayer toward the south. The plan of the town seemed to make this necessary, but had the church been started in the thirteenth century instead of the late fifteenth unquestionably the town and not the church would have been changed, for in the early days the matter of proper orientation was thought to be of paramount importance.

Again in the second war it lay squarely in the path of the German advance in 1940 and was badly "knocked about," to use the British term, by both bombs and shells.

Picturesque intrigue lurks in the memories of one of the dullest streets in this dull town, within the dreary walls of an *Hôpital Militaire* which was once a Jesuit College. In this college Titus Oates, arch-plotter, posed as a Roman Catholic in order to gather "evidence" for the absurd tissue of falsehoods which finally cost him a terrible flogging and three years in jail. Daniel O'Connell, the Irish Liberator, was also—and to better purpose—educated in this college, as was John Carroll, the first Roman Catholic bishop of the United States.

The cathedral, dedicated to the Virgin, is exceptionally interesting in the interior because of the contents rather than the architecture. Among its many tombs is that of St. Omer himself. Among its statues is the "Big God of Thérouanne," a colossal statue of Christ brought by Charles Quint from the cathedral of Thérouanne to that of St. Omer. The figure is seated, and the contrast between its enormous torso and its spindly little dwarf legs is utterly ridiculous, yet the face and head, crowned by the crown of thorns, achieve a certain thirteenth-century dignity.

Charles X visited this church and left a record of his visit under a painting of himself. The record reads:

*CaroLUs X hVIC teMpLo aDfVIt*

I spent more time than it was worth trying to make the capital letters mean something. LUX and VIC seemed hopeful, but MLDVI left me floundering. It looks like a Roman numeral date but fails to work out as such.

Abbeville was and still is in the diocese of Amiens. To it came the Amienois Bishop de la Motte d'Orléans in the year 1766 to view a much talked-of outrage, the mutilation of a sacred crucifix that stood on the town bridge. The prelate was horribly shocked and proceeded to fan the religious passions of the people to such an extent that they demanded a victim. One was presently found in the person of the young Chevalier de la Barre, a wild likable scapegrace who often drank more than was good for him and who laughed at religion. His condemnation came about in a way so tawdry that one blushes for the age which could countenance it. A certain aging judge, Duval de Saucourt, developed an unworthy passion for the chevalier's aunt, who was an abbess. The old satyr had the amazing impudence to *"déclarer sa flamme,"* which means in our harsher language to "make indecent proposals." The abbess spurned him. The young chevalier, hearing the story, heaped endless but well-deserved ridicule on the old judge, who thereupon determined to "get him" by hook or crook.

He spied on the young man and caught him in the act of standing "covered" while a religious procession passed. With this scandal as the chief support, he succeeded in making out a case for the bad character of the young noble and convinced the court that he must have committed the outrage upon the crucifix. La Barre was condemned to have his tongue torn out, his right hand cut off and then to be burned alive. He appealed to the *parlement* of Paris and that august body altered the sentence to require that his head as well as his tongue and his right hand should be struck off before he was burned. That was clemency indeed. The victim was led through the streets of Abbeville in a tumbril bearing this inscription in large letters:

*Impie, Blasphémateur, Sacrilège, Abominable et Exécrable.*

He died heroically, *sans plainte, sans colère, sans ostentation,* fully conscious that his death afforded the multitude keen delight. Voltaire, as shocked by this fiendish execution as the Bishop of Amiens had been by the original sacrilege, took up his pen and fought like a tiger for the rehabilitation of the chevalier's memory. At last the Revolutionists did rehabilitate La Barre and he has gradually become a hero-martyr. Beside a canal in Abbeville, between the station and the church, stands an interesting monument,

*"Erected by the Proletariat to the Full Emancipation of Human Thought in Memory of the Martyrdom of the Chevalier de la Barre, Executed at Abbeville July 1, 1766, at the Age of Nineteen for Having Failed to Salute a Procession."*

How often has France hounded to death those upon whose memory she was destined to heap honor! Generally religion has had a finger in the dirty side of the business if it has not actually whipped up the whole thing, but France has no worse a record than most nations.

The little town of St. Omer, the third of our trio, is within the boundary of old Artois, bordering on French Flanders. It is located upon the river Aa, which means in various old Teutonic tongues "Flowing Water." This name tells a tale, for there is nothing French about it. We know that we must be close to the border line of the Flemish language, and it is a fact that in the marshy suburb of Haut-Pont one hears almost nothing but Flemish. There are nine rivers in Europe named Aa and all have a more or less Teutonic quality, through whatever country they may happen to be flowing.

The Aa of St. Omer is brisk and cheery and one needs some such note as this to enliven one's spirit, for the town is anything but lively and it suffered much from the war, though not as much as Abbeville and Amiens. Its cathedral was scarcely touched.

Prewar Baedekers used to say that many English families

settled here "for purposes of retrenchment," and that is the only good reason I can think of for selecting this morgue-like little town as a residence. But to visit St. Omer for a day or two is a sheer delight. Its ancient abbey church long ago fell to ruins in a most genteel way and Notre-Dame, its former cathedral, has an extraordinary personality, like an attractive old lady whose faculties are unimpaired.

The abbey was founded by a certain Saint Audomare, Bishop of Thérouanne, and it is rather interesting that while his modern name, Omer, is applied to the town his primitive name is applied to the inhabitants, who are known as Audomarois. The towers and the walls of the abbey alone remain standing and the interior, open to the sky, was kept beautifully sodded, making one think of Glastonbury Abbey, until this latest war brought severe damage to the whole ensemble.

Sieges have been, through all the ages, the unpalatable meat and drink of St. Omer. At one of these sieges, laid by Marlborough and the redoubtable Prince Eugene, in 1711, the town was saved by a brave girl, Jacqueline Robins, who brought in a  boatload of provisions on the Aa. In the first World War the town was British "G.H.Q." for a period of eighteen months. Lord Roberts died here in a house on rue Carnot. During the last part of that war St. Omer suffered terribly from shell fire.

In no French church have I seen so many ex-votos and pious inscriptions. Of the multitude of testimonials to the Virgin's power I selected and copied six which interested me especially. How quaint and moving is the picture of "that ancient faith" as it shines through these inscriptions:

Allis de Lioc, Dumb, Speaks 1260
Marguerite, Blind, Sees Clearly 1260
A child of Haut-Pont, Drowned, Returns to Life 1261
A Paralytic Boy of Quelmes, Cured 1210
A Woman, Incurable, of Blendecq, Cured 1219
Baudouin d'Esquelbecq, Suffering in the Fires of Hell, Cured 1231

I was very curious about the case of Baudouin d'Esquelbecq. Was he, perhaps, in the throes of a nervous breakdown? If so, we are glad the Virgin had compassion on him.

By pure chance it happens that St. Omer was the very first cathedral town of France I ever visited. I remember gazing into the swirling waters of the Aa more than twenty years ago and wondering if I should sometime conclude my cathedral wanderings by spending a day or two in some hallowed town on the River Zz. That has not happened, and so I am inclined to think I have not finished these wanderings and never shall.

## CHAPTER X

# *Rouen Survives Her Liberation*

ALLIED bombers, chiefly American, rained such terrible destruction on Rouen in the Liberation Campaign of 1944 that the Rouennais have scarcely yet developed an objective view of that event and perhaps the older citizens never can do so. They are prone to say that the Americans flew too high to make good aim possible, thereby saving a few planes and fliers at the expense of a great city. Many of the younger people, however, view the thing philosophically. Saving planes and fliers is an essential of military strategy. Rouen lay in the path of freedom and was an important port for the Nazis, in fact the first port of France, exceeding even Marseille in annual tonnage handled, though it lies on the River Seine some seventy-five miles from its mouth. This surprising fact of maritime trade was published in France about 1930, until which time Marseille had led.

In bombing the Nazis out of Rouen the Allied fliers not only destroyed the Seine bridges, docks, warehouses and sectors on both sides of the river for a depth of a quarter of a mile, a wide tangent of ruin running into the heart of the city, but they also wrought havoc with the great historic monuments. The cathedral and the lovely little church of St. Maclou were badly damaged and the best portions of the Palais de Justice and the sixteenth-century Hôtel de Bourgtheroulde were virtually razed. All this may have been an inescapable accident of war, or perhaps the airmen's aim was not as good as usual, but the tragedy happened. It may serve to emphasize how very *seldom* such things happened in France in that worst of wars. In general the monuments of the past were ringed about with deadly bomb hits just as an expert knife-thrower's accomplice, standing scatheless, is "outlined" in knives.

Rouen survives and revives. It has not bounced back with the decisiveness of Amiens but it is over the hump of discouragement and now picks up speed in recovery. André Maurois, in tribute to the city's many-sidedness, once called it *La Ville Complète* and despite its wounds it is still very versatile, very rich in talents and attractions. It is called by its doting *Syndicat d'Initiative Touristique* the Florence of the North and *La Ville Musée*. Epicures have long called it *La Capitale de la Gastronomie*, and Sisley Huddleston, who learned to know the French cuisine and all things French as have few Anglo-Saxons, affirmed that it carried the art of cooking to a "new high."

As a cathedral city, too, Rouen is supreme, despite the scars of war. No one of its churches equals, all things considered, the cathedrals of Chartres, Reims or Amiens, but it has no less than three, two great ones and a small one, which are of the very first rank in interest. Bit by bit we shall try to catch the colors of them, but first we may peer behind the curtain of the city's past, always exciting, sometimes seamy, and then view some of its present amenities.

It seems that practically everything has happened in Rouen. It is almost another Paris. Dismissing the story of Chilperic, of Charlemagne and of Louis le Débonnaire, let us get on to Rollo, or Rolf, who established at Rouen the Duchy of Normandy. It was in connection with this that Charles the Simple was so humiliated, an incident invariably played up by school textbooks. The monarch required that Rollo, in payment for the dukedom which he had won by force of arms, should go through the customary feudal ceremony of kissing the king's foot. Rollo refused to do this, but upon the king's insistence signaled to one of his attendants to perform the ceremony. The attendant jerked up the king's foot so sharply that the Simple Charles tumbled to the ground. Whereupon the Normans roared with laughter and the king, badly frightened, laughed with them, pretending to consider it a delightful bit of friendly horseplay.

The anecdote, only a trifle more threadbare for its retelling here, is, after all, significant. The Northmen were a proud, enterprising, stalwart people, quick to resort to violence but marvelously quick also to adapt themselves to new surroundings. The one important act of Charles the Simple was his cowardly overlooking of a gross insult. Had he been a strong king instead of a weakling, France might have been drenched in blood and might finally have exterminated one of the most vital elements which has ever come into the formation of the French nation. As it was, the Normans, with incredible speed, became more French than the French themselves and largely developed all French institutions, spreading their language and their art wherever they went. We shall examine the Norman character at our leisure through the lens of present-day Normandy, as appealing a region as one can find in the whole of France; but let us not forget that Rouen is its capital, though lying near its eastern boundary. Here in 1911 the city staged a great celebration called *Le Millénaire de Normandie*, recalling the ceremony of 911 so humiliating to a French king, so immeasurably important to the French nation.

Fourteen other dukes succeeded Rollo, including William the Conqueror, Richard the Lion-Hearted and John Lackland, whom the French call Jean-sans-Terre. This John, who was king of England and the only English king of that name, was the last duke of Normandy. By his oppressions and abominations, notably the murder of his nephew Arthur at Rouen, he gave Philippe Auguste the excuse to rob the English crown (obtained, of course, for the Norman line by William the Conqueror) of the dukedom of Normandy. Never again did the English possess Rouen or Normandy except for the thirty years from 1419, during which unhappy interval Joan was tried there and burned at the stake.

In general the city has prospered since the forced departure of the English in the middle fourteen-hundreds. It has developed its varied riches, commercial, artistic, literary, and has held its place as the best-loved provincial city of France. My feeling, as I write about Rouen, is strangely reminiscent of the attitude of the miserly small boy who hesitates to unwrap his Christmas present, preferring rather to prolong the thrills of anticipation. Perhaps it is pardonable to be leisurely at least in picking out one's hotel, and in eating one's first Norman meal.

On a prewar visit to the city I was charmed with the advertising of the then conspicuous Hôtel Lisieux, which proclaimed itself an "*ancien manoir du XVe siècle, ou l'évêque Cauchon, instigateur du procès Jeanne d'Arc, habita et mourut subitement en 1442, à la chambre no 6, au-dessus de la fontaine.*" What, I asked myself, was supposed to be my reaction and that of visitors generally, whether French or American? Were we expected to leap at the chance to sleep in the hotel, in the very room, "number 6 above the fountain," where Bishop Cauchon suddenly died? I, at any rate, did not so leap but selected a cheerier-sounding hotel near the Jeanne d'Arc sector of the city. The Maid *is* cheery, for she left this life in a blaze of never-to-die glory, whereas Cauchon ended as common carrion on a town dump.

I walked from my hotel to the Vieux Marché and viewed the exact spot where the Maid was burned. A swarthy little beggar girl appointed herself my guide, sensing a chance to earn a *pourboire*. I had oriented myself carefully by study of a map, so the little cicerone was quite unnecessary in my life, but she was so pathetic and pinched-looking that I made a great business of asking her all about Jeanne d'Arc as though I had just heard the name for the first time and was eager to receive all the information she could supply.

She showed me a gold mosaic marker in the pavement proclaiming it the exact place where the faggots were kindled, but actually a cobblestone cross in the middle of the adjacent street which separates the two portions of the market "marks the spot." Near by, attached to the market wall, a moving statue of Joan in the flames bore these words cut into the stone:

*J'ai fait cette oeuvre avec amour à la gloire de la sainte de la patrie.*

M. Real del Sarte 1928

The sculptor's love and skill produced, it seemed to me, a worthy work to embellish this very sacred spot. The statue survived all the bombardments of the war but by an odd chance the inscription was destroyed and is no longer to be seen.

My first Norman meal issued its earnest and savory invitation in this very square, the Vieux Marché. Here were, and luckily still are—slightly shaken by the war but not destroyed —two of France's most celebrated restaurants, where patrons partake of *sole normande* and *caneton à la rouennaise*, washed down with *cidre de Normandie*. With some difficulty I rejected the invitation of both of these places (on later occasions I have accepted with relish) in favor of a tiny hole-in-the-wall which I discovered on the quaint rue St. Romain directly opposite the *Portail des Librairies* (Portal of the Book-stalls) of Notre-Dame. At a table in one of the south windows of this restaurant (and it, too, has come through the war) I sat down to enjoy a long and delicious Norman meal, feasting my eyes at the same time on the strange conglomerate glories of Rouen's greatest church, its true cathedral.

The towers and the soaring spire were all visible from my coign of vantage. What an array they are. First, the Tower of St. Romain on whose street I was. At the base this tower is primitive Roman, in its middle stages transitional in style but still severely square, and in its upper stage utterly Flamboyant, like a woman who has first begun to use cosmetics at the ripe age of seventy and, liking the effect, daubs them on a little too lavishly. This tower contains the queen of bells "Jeanne d'Arc" (do not expect to escape the Maid in any part of Rouen), which tips the scales at an even twenty-three tons.

This tower of St. Romain is the north one of the west façade.

It suffered from bomb hits and fire in the Liberation and all but succumbed, but it was fortunately shored up in time and saved from collapse. To balance it on the south side is the world-famous Butter Tower, built, like so many other ecclesiastical beauties of France, from money paid by the faithful for indulgence to eat butter during Lent. This Butter Tower is pure Flamboyant from base to lofty crown, all graceful frills and furbelows. The effect is not, however, in the least like that of the Tour St. Romain, for this south tower is all youth and eagerness. It wears its elaborate party dress with utmost naturalness and has no need to rouge its fresh young cheeks or paint its lips. I must be pardoned for this flight of fancy. The Butter Tower's beauty "got me" as I gazed at it from my restaurant window. And then, too, the *cidre de Normandie* was rather potent.

The central spire of the cathedral, a nineteenth-century production of iron and bronze, is unmercifully damned by most critics, who are especially discouraged because it is so strongly built that they feel lightning can never destroy it as it has its many predecessors. I do not think we need worry overmuch about this spire's lofty ugliness. Notre-Dame-de-Rouen is full of architectural faults and is easily great enough to stand one more. The amazing west façade itself is the target of unending abuse. It is florid, surcharged, blatantly ornate, decadent—all these adjectives I cull from a single critic's comment—yet James Fergusson, stingy of compliments, called it a "romance in stone," and John Taylor Arms, securing a special permit from the police, spent four uncomfortable days in the island of safety in the middle of Place Notre-Dame, jostled continually by the crowds entering and leaving trolley-cars, choked by the whirling dust, in order to make his wonderful drawing of this façade. He must have thought it worth while. The trolley-cars have disappeared and likewise most of the dust, for the square has long since been repaved, but Mr. Arms's drawing remains to enthrall all beholders of it.

The war damage to the cathedral, especially to the lower south portion (and the St. Romain Tower) was so considerable that the whole edifice was closed to the public for some four years but it is being reopened. The interior fairly glows with romance. It contains, for example, in one of its chapels, the tomb of Rollo himself, and in the south ambulatory the lion heart of Richard the Lion-Hearted. As if that were not enough in the way of relics and tombs, it contains also the tomb of Louis de Brézé, grand seneschal of Normandy, who was the husband of Diana of Poitiers. This lady—who *may* not have been the mistress of Francis I during her husband's life, though she certainly was the mistress of Henry II after her husband's death—kneels devoutly at the head of the dear departed, while the Virgin stands at his feet. We will meet Diana again, queen in all but name, at Blois. I note in my journal this sole comment about Diana, the Correct Widow of Rouen: "Her nose is too long."

The most famous tomb in this cathedral, by all odds, is that of the Cardinals Georges d'Amboise, uncle and nephew. Its finest portions are the work of the master sculptor Jean Goujon. Both cardinals kneel in an attitude of prayer. It was the elder D'Amboise who gave the money for the beautiful stone crown which surmounts the Butter Tower and who gave also the sumptuous and much debated screen which connects this tower with the Tour St. Romain. He was a great cardinal and the first state minister of Louis XII. He ought to have been Pope and would have been if jealousies had not barred his path.

Christian humility, however, was not a passion with him, as one may assume from a perusal of the inscription which adorns the tomb. "I was the pastor of the clergy, the father of the people. The golden lily, the oak itself were subject to me."

This inscription is not in French but in medieval Latin. I had seen a translation of it and was eager to see what I could do thus fortified, with the original, but alas this tomb is in the Lady Chapel, which is shut off by an iron grille. One may see it only under the direction of an impatient sacristan who tows around large parties. In the particular party on the occasion to which I refer were some twenty young girls, evidently from a *pensionnat de jeunes demoiselles*, and—myself. After a few hasty moments given over to general admiration of this great work of art, I started busily deciphering the inscription, especially the charming portion about the lily and the oak. I had got as far as *Lilia Subdebant Quercus et Michi*—the last *was* that way, whatever the Latin textbook says—when I noticed that I was alone. The *jeunes demoiselles* had lightly departed from the Lady Chapel, and the sacristan, his expression distinctly sour, was waiting for me to leave too, so that he could lock the iron gate. I wish I could learn to like French sacristans as a race. They are really as good as the rest of us. What would my attitude be, I wonder, if I had to show the tomb of the Cardinals d'Amboise forty times a day.

One other thing of many in the interior of this rich cathedral must be mentioned, the Gothic stone staircase in the north transept, leading to the canons' library. One would say nothing short of alabaster could lend itself to a treatment so delicate and graceful.

Inside the library one is shown, among other reliquaries, the *fierte de St. Romain,* recalling the most gorgeous and interesting medieval spectacle which Rouen was privileged to witness, namely the *Levée de la Fierte*, which took place annually on Ascension Day. Briefly, this was the "Raising of the Reliquary" by a condemned criminal who had been selected by the cathedral chapter, and who was thus pardoned and absolved. The lucky man was then made much of by the clergy and by the populace, to whom he symbolized the Penitent Thief. He was crowned with white flowers as he walked in the procession. The cathedral was packed for a sumptuous mass, and to conclude all, the criminal was tendered a magnificent banquet and allowed to go free.

From all over Normandy and even from England came crowds for this "Privilege of St. Romain." One recognizes the same psychology that in our own land today makes the tabloids and those to whom they cater yearn over a criminal, be he ever so rotten a human hulk, who is "making a gallant fight for his life" in the courts. There were no movies in the fifteenth century but there were vaudeville shows of a primitive kind, taking their cue from a jolly Norman who first popularized light entertainment in the valleys of the Vire near Caen (les Vaux-de-Vire, hence vaudeville). Perhaps some of these freed criminals made a good thing out of it by showing themselves to gaping crowds. Or perhaps after a bit they slipped back into their old congenial "calling."

In the centuries before the great holocaust of 1940-1945 the cathedral of Rouen suffered much from the usual agencies of destruction, war, lightning, vandalism, eighteenth-century restorers and mad Revolutionists, but more especially it suffered, at least in its sensibilities, at the hands of Calvinist fanatics. Protestants of today are naturally much more prone to dwell on the iniquity of the St. Bartholomew Massacre and the Revocation of the Edict of Nantes than to think of the other side of the picture. The Huguenots of Rouen entered Notre-Dame one day in 1562, ten years before St. Bartholomew, and perpetrated the maddest acts of sacrilege. Mass was being celebrated when these fanatics burst into the church and rushed up and down the nave and into the choir, hacking confessionals and pulpit, smashing and overturning holy statues, wrecking whatever they could reach. They put the Sacred Host (to Catholics the very body of the Lord) in the mouths of little stone beasties, and yelling derisively marched about church holding these animals aloft. To cap it all they built a great bonfire in the square and fed it with hundreds of crosses, missals and sacred objects of all sorts.

On every visit to this cathedral I have found it most difficult to tear myself away. Always something caught my eye just as I thought I was decisively leaving. There are, for instance, the ambulatory windows (removed and hidden during the war, but due to find their way back), one of which inspired a story of Gustave Flaubert, a native Rouennais, another of which is marked in Latin: "Clement of Chartres Made Me." This latter window, which tells the story of Joseph and his brethren, is a sort of Rosetta Stone to students of thirteenth-century glasswork. It is the only one now existing which is definitely signed with the artist's name, and it serves to establish the family relationship of Rouen and Chartres glass, which could otherwise only be guessed at.

The two other churches of Rouen that insist on attention are St. Ouen, which largely escaped war damage, and St. Maclou, which was very badly hurt and is not yet reopened to the public. The former is often called the most beautiful Gothic church in France. One should learn to be chary of that phrase "the most beautiful," but I suppose no one ever will—myself least of all. Even Baedeker, who invariably had himself well in hand, used to call it "one of the most beautiful Gothic churches in existence," and those familiar with the Baedeker patois could read between the lines. He had nothing stronger in his vocabulary. He did *not* use this ace of trumps in writing of Chartres, Reims, Beauvais, or Amiens, but saved it for St. Ouen of Rouen. I am sure I will do well to leave my own description of St. Ouen unwritten. The central tower alone calls for a word. It is at least in its upper stage the *ne plus ultra* of pinnacled Gothic. This upper stage is the oft-sung *Couronne de Normandie,* a superb eight-sided open-work lantern. The *suisse* (sacristan) who sold me a taper to light my tortuous way up to the "Crown of Normandy" told me that the tower had been awarded by an association of architects the first prize as *the* most beautiful Gothic tower ever built. Its architect, he added, like the soldier beneath the Paris Arch of Triumph, remains *inconnu.*

I was amazed at the number of ancient churches I saw as I looked down upon Rouen from this sky crown. No one of them has been completely blotted out by war, though several have been reduced to partial ruin. Their names I checked up from my map, St. Vivien, for example, and St. Nicaise (both masculine saints). And of course there is that near neighbor St. Maclou, which is not so venerable, in fact not venerable at all, as French churches go, for it was built in the fifteenth and sixteenth centuries. It is the third of our trio of great churches in Rouen, though in size very much smaller than the other two.

The identity of this saint eluded Elizabeth Robins Pennell, who writes of it in a tone of mild concern, curious evidently, as anyone would be, to know what manner of saint should lend his name to such a strange, brilliant, inexplicable edifice. It eluded me also, in spite of a painstaking search, until—at last—I found it in an obscure reference work. Maclou appears to be the same as Malo, the Welsh priest who left his name to one of the most charming seaports of Brittany. His Rouen church is absolutely unique in having a pentagonal main porch which looks almost like a rounded apse. Some of the rich carving of the doors is attributed to Jean Goujon whose work enriches the Lady Chapel of the cathedral. The church of St. Maclou as a whole is one of the supreme achievements of the late period of florid flamboyance, which could so easily— and generally did—sink to vulgarity.

On one of my prewar visits to the Norman capital I did what every visitor sooner or later must do. I took the steamer trip to La Bouille, some twelve miles down the twisting Seine, and back. It was an eye-opener to me for I had somehow felt unconvinced by Rouen's claim to be the first port of France. For half the twelve miles, it seemed to me, there was an unending succession of anchored freighters, docked freighters, moving freighters of all nations. There were vast *basins*, sheds, warehouses and *parcs de stockage*. But eventually the signs of commerce grew thinner, the boat stopped at Croisset, the summer home of Flaubert, and chugged slowly on to the village of La Bouille (which means either The Fisherman's Pole or The Grape-Basket).

It was dark when the little craft, creeping back upstream to Rouen, nosed in to its wharf between the Pont Boïeldieu and Pont Corneille. Both the musician and the dramatist, in whose honor these bridges were named, were natives of Rouen. Pierre Corneille's statue stood at the center of "his" bridge on the western tip of the Ile Lacroix. This man, very great in the estimation of his contemporaries and still great in posterity's acclaim, helped to make Rouen a sort of intellectual shrine. Molière, Blaise Pascal, Madame de Sévigné and many others who were not natives of the city loved to come here for its literary atmosphere.

A view of Rouen's river is at present no less an eye-opener than it was before the war, but in a sadly different sense. It shows what even a pre-atomic war could do. To call that section a mess is as mild an understatement as is the standard British phrase "knocked about" to describe a ruined town. It all looks like the day after hell, and the day must run into years before France can restore to the river front even the semblance of order. This physical story of war is as legible to anyone with eyes as the stone Bibles of sculpture were legible to untutored medieval beholders. But one may lift one's gaze to the skyline of the city in the background. It is still *La Ville Orgueilleuse* extolled by Jean des Vignes-Rouges. It is still Rouen the Proud.

We have swung around the pivot of Paris, the Ambulatory of our imaginary Cathedral, from Chartres to Rouen. Let us not quite lose sight of this structure until and unless it becomes a burden. We shall turn our eyes westward, viewing the Chapels of our North Aisle, the stern, strong, sincere Norman churches that Henry Adams loved so well. Let us see if their round arches appear to us as they did to him "like old cognac compared with the champagne of the pointed and fretted spire."

## CHAPTER XI

# Westward through Normandy: Evreux—Lisieux—Caen

As WE work our way into the core of Normandy—architecturally speaking, for once—we must try to age rapidly; for otherwise, if Henry Adams is right, we are unlikely to enjoy its cathedrals. Norman architecture is older, firmer, less exciting. "Young people," he says, "rarely enjoy it."

By our plan, essentially a geographical one, we must turn back the pages of time by a century or more as we wander deep into Normandy. Rouen, though the capital and heart of that province, is scarcely within the architectural frontier. Only the cathedral's Tour St. Romain would qualify in any significant way as Norman.

You will object very justly, having crossed the frontier, to being introduced first of all to Evreux, which, as a cathedral town, is very un-Norman, but Notre-Dame-d'Evreux is so curious that it can scarcely be passed by altogether. It is the ultimate in Mixed Art. No two portions of it resemble one another; for it was ravaged times without number by fire, and after each conflagration some part of it was rebuilt in accordance with the taste of the time. The nave is partly of very early date, therefore more or less true Norman; the choir is early Gothic; the north portal rich and very beautiful Flamboyant; the west façade as dowdy Renaissance as you would care to find. Its two towers are especially recommended for their masterful ugliness. One questions whether architectural ineptness can exceed that displayed by "Big Peter," the north tower; but then one's eyes wander to the jumble of the south tower and force one to admit that Big Peter was a mere beginner in uncouthness. The *Guide Bleu* finds this church interesting *malgré son peu d'unité*. I should be inclined rather to call it interesting *because* of its "little of unity," though such a statement does injustice to the opulent north portal, the handsome central flèche and the fine glass of this church.

One must pause here, and disagreeably often in a few ensuing chapters, to give the grisly facts of war. Evreux, Lisieux and Caen all suffered horribly. Evreux caught it in the German invasion of 1940, while Lisieux and Caen had their turn in the Liberation battles of 1944, but the net result to all these unfortunate towns was much the same. Their business quarters are wiped out and with them something also of the glory of old France. But of the churches which chiefly concern us in this part of Normandy only the cathedral of Evreux was pitiably hurt. A part of its south tower, the uglier one, was chopped clean off and the tip of Big Peter was likewise smashed. The dowdy west façade was made dowdier by bombs and shells. But the church was not knocked out. It is open now, and its glass, saved and stored like that of Cathedral France everywhere, is finding its way back.

Evreux has furnished church annals with an unusual number of colorful bishops, notably that Jean de la Balue who is reputed to have had all the vices except hypocrisy. He was depraved, greedy, treacherous, a born intriguer, which enabled him to become the confidant of the King of Intrigue, Louis XI. He won the cardinal's hat for distinguished service in inducing France, despite her sworn word, to ride roughshod over the so-called Pragmatic Sanction and join the other Wolves of Europe in attacking Maria Theresa, the young queen of Austria. Finally his love of intrigue was his undoing, for he was caught plotting against his own patron, King Louis, and rewarded this time by eleven years imprisonment, much of it in one of those horrible open cages, devised, it is said, by La Balue himself, in which the unfortunate prisoner could not lie down at full length nor even sit up straight. The detestable cardinal is pictured rather intimately in *Quentin Durward;* but one does not, in Scott's picture, see the full blackness of his character, nor does one learn of the honors heaped upon him by the papacy when finally he was released from his eleven years' confinement.

Marie-Josèphe-Rose Tascher de la Pagerie Bonaparte, Napoleon's discarded Joséphine, was a celebrated resident of Evreux during a part of 1810—it was an interval between her two stays at Malmaison—and she still retained the empty title of Empress of the French. I have found no record of any visit paid her by her former lord while she was at Evreux; but of course he frequently "consulted" her while she was at Malmaison. How odd must those meetings have been.

We know that Joséphine went over with Napoleon his list of prospective brides and urged him to decide upon Marie Louise. Historians, or rather gossips, are divided in regard to Joséphine's private life while at Evreux and Malmaison. Generally it is called a dignified retirement, but a curious letter, written at this time in the emperor's own hand, gives a different picture. It came to light in 1865 and was sold for a large sum at public auction. The letter closes, after promising an early visit (to Malmaison), with these words: "I will give you warning so that there shall be no lovers with you that night. I should be sorry to disturb them."

Cardinal de la Balue and poor Joséphine were anything but Norman characters and I should have hesitated to introduce them here had the cathedral of Evreux not sounded such a jangling note.

A scant fifty miles west of Evreux lies Lisieux in a totally different atmosphere, both architectural and social. The blatant potpourri of Notre-Dame-d'Evreux gives place to the imposing early Gothic of Lisieux's St. Peter. The cardinal and Joséphine give place to Sainte-Thérèse-à-l'Enfant-Jésus, a young Norman girl who died at Lisieux and became a saint as recently as 1925.

Thérèse pervades Lisieux even more than Jeanne d'Arc pervades Orléans. Indeed her prodigious new basilica, set high on a hill opposite the railway station, very far overshadows the grand gray cathedral. Pilgrims in hundreds or thousands crowd into the basilica every day of the year, while only an occasional visitor finds his way to St. Peter's. The basilica, with a more or less Byzantine cast of architecture, seems to have taken its cue from the Sacré Coeur church of Montmartre in Paris and it looks even more colossal, a domed mountain flung against the sky. On the floor of the crypt, no less vast than the nave above it, are these words set into the floor: *Si Quelqu'un Est Tout Petit Qu'il Vienne à Moi* (If anyone is very small let him come to me). These are sweet and modest words but the basilica is anything but modest. Like Oslo's Vigeland Fountain it has outgrown itself and become a "layout." It has a view terrace (viewing the station and the railway yards) that can accommodate ten thousand people. Behind the edifice the layout climbs the hill in huge, fancy stairways, monuments and the fourteen Stations of the Cross, with an enormous crucifix at the top. There, too, is a statue of Sainte-Thérèse scattering stone roses at her feet.

In the lower town the little saint is literally *everywhere*. There is a building housing a Panorama of Miracles performed by her (and adjacent to it a handy establishment named *Brasserie Café Bar Restaurant du Panorama des Miracles*). There is a Diorama too—*Le Plus Beau du Monde*—where the events of her life are set forth in wax figures, in the manner of Madame Tussaud's. The saint's body, or a few bits of it as I was told by a priest, lies in a magnificent tomb in the Carmelite church, which is visited by throngs daily. Buses roll into town every few minutes and a motley of pious pilgrims, unblushingly exploited by commerce, saturates every street and eating place and shop. Pilgrim and visitor alike are beset at every step by postcard and curio hawkers. Scenes from the girl's life are garishly depicted on myriads of cheap colored postcards and the dripping sentiment and sanctity blazoned forth on some of these cards is, to most tourists at least, depressing. One card which I remember very well, shows the little girl at the age of six walking in a garden with her father. She is pointing to the sky, in which the letter T plainly appears, written in stars. *"Regarde, papa!"* she exclaims. *"Mon nom est écrit dans le ciel."*

Since we cannot escape Sainte-Thérèse we may as well take a moment to learn who she was. Born at Alençon in the edge of Normandy in 1875, she early moved with her parents to Lisieux and there entered at a very tender age a Carmelite nunnery. She was the youngest of nine children. Four of these had died in infancy. The rest, all girls, had, without exception, taken the veil; so piety evidently "ran in the family." Thérèse was extremely beautiful—one must accept the universal testimony on this point—and as good as she was fair. She devoted her short life to good works and died at the age of twenty-four. She lay in death on an open bier for all to see, as the Carmelite custom was, and possibly her beauty had something to do with the sudden conviction which came to the mourners that there was a peculiar sanctity in the body of the dead girl. Cures occurred and the story of them spread throughout France. During the first World War French soldiers turned to her for help almost as much as to Joan, and five years after Joan's canonization the "Little Flower of Lisieux" was also canonized.

Enough of Sainte-Thérèse, who is undoubtedly a very sweet and lovable saint but who tends to impede progress on the Norman road. Lisieux is still interesting despite its tawdry pilgrim aspect and the sad destruction of nearly all of its Old World streets, which were among the quaintest in France until 1944. On one of those old streets, it is said, a merchant named M. Creton developed the manufacture of a printed cotton cloth which soon came to be called cretonne the world over. The strong, dignified cathedral is not much damaged except for some shell and bullet scars. It faces a large square and a much larger area "opened" by war, permitting, at present, a superb view of it, especially when the afternoon sun illumines its mellow gray façade and interesting towers.

One enters the cathedral—it is no longer one in the strict sense—and finds St. Peter there in dignified bronze in the north aisle, his great toe shiny from devoted kisses as in so many similar statues in European churches, for example in those of Beauvais and Poitiers and in St. Peter's in Rome. On the pedestal are the words: *Tu Es Petrus; Portae Inferi Non Praevalebunt,* and indeed the gates of hell did not prevail when they swung wildly open in the summer of 1944.

The Lady Chapel has a considerable celebrity because of its historical character. It was built by Pierre Cauchon, in expiation of his horrible crime in condemning Joan—it *was* horrible, though Bernard Shaw, in his famous play, works up something of a case for the bishop. Cauchon, driven out of Beauvais, forgotten by the English, who had promised him the archbishopric of Rouen, had secured, by much effort, this little see of Lisieux. Here he spent his miserable declining years and built this expiatory chapel. When he died in Rouen his body was brought here and interred, only to be exhumed some years later, as we have seen, and cast upon the town dump. One of the utterances of Ste. Thérèse carved on a block of stone in the wall now adds a touch of sanctity to Cauchon's chapel. Its piety is of that almost sensual type which would repel us if we entertained any doubt of the genuine ardor and holiness of this strange young saint: *Mon ciel il est caché dans la petite hostie ou Jésus, mon époux, se voile par amour.* She spoke of Jesus boldly as her spouse, a conception by no means new in religious thought, but rather startling in the case of this flower-like girl of Normandy.

If one finds the air of Lisieux too holy or too tinseled with commercial sanctity one may quickly push on to the noble city of Caen, second only to Rouen in artistic interest. It is unquestionably one of those cities which inspire affection. Everybody loves Caen, and now perhaps more than ever since the historic Battle of Caen (1944) which, (with the St. Lô breakthrough) broke German resistance but in the process literally erased two-thirds of the city, "rubbing out" some nine thousand buildings. The cultural loss was great, the museum being razed, the beautiful church of St. Pierre emerging as a mere skeleton of itself and other fine old structures too numerous to list suffering damage or annihilation; *but* the cultural loss was by no means two-thirds of Caen's total wealth in that field. By sheer luck—in this case one can only call it that—the two celebrated abbeys built by William the Conqueror and his wife Matilda came through almost unharmed.

The luck consisted in their respective locations to the west and east of the town. The battle, one of the bitterest, longest and bloodiest of the whole war, was fought *in* Caen and over it and down upon it. It is impossible to believe that any structure, even a Norman church, caught in that cyclone of steel, fire and high explosives, could have survived in recognizable form. As a matter of fact William's church received but thirteen shell hits, a mere nothing in a battle of such titanic forces. Matilda's church suffered more but was not severely battered. It is still, or again, open to the public, a cool calm refuge from the choking desolation which crept so close to it and left so evil a trail.

When we turn from war to look at the city's more distant past we find that the one thing about it that really matters is William the Conqueror, but to omit mention of Charlotte

Corday while on our way back, in time, to William, would seem an unpardonable discourtesy to this strange heroine of the French.

It is fascinating to think of this Norman girl, raised in a convent, but as different as possible in her outlook from Thérèse of Lisieux, poring over Plutarch and the work of Rousseau and Voltaire, brooding incessantly over the crimes perpetrated by Marat against France, and especially against the Girondins who were her neighbors. There was nothing of the woman about her, says a French writer, except her agreeable face and her voice, which remained always childish. She was not much given to reading the Bible but evidently liked the apocryphal book of Judith for she underlined in it passages that excited her, especially the part which tells of Judith's departure from Bethulia for the tent of Holofernes. The climax of Judith's bold venture came when she approached Holofernes as he lay upon his bed and with his own falchion "smote twice upon his neck with all her might." The climax of Charlotte's equally bold venture came when she stood over the hideous Marat as he sat in his bath, and, watching her chance, plunged a dinner knife into his chest with such force that it pierced the lung, the aorta and the heart. Judgment of Charlotte must always be mixed. Lamartine called her *"l'ange de l'assassinat,"* the Angel of Murder. She was guillotined four days after that murder but in the course of time her remains received a signal honor, for she now lies buried in a special tomb just outside the Expiatory Chapel in Paris which Louis XVIII built to the memory of Louis XVI and Marie Antoinette. Charlotte's "neighbor," in a similar tomb on the other side of the chapel, is Philippe Egalité, Duke of Orléans, father of Louis-Philippe.

At the end of the street where Charlotte lived looms the castle of the Conqueror, long a ruin and now still more so, since 1944. This structure is of small interest except for its associations. One is not primarily concerned here with William as a Conqueror. It is not until long after his death that he was first given that sounding title in place of the inelegant one he carried through life—William the Bastard. One is not even concerned here with his parentage, though Falaise is near by where Robert the Devil, his father, became enamored of Arlotta, the tanner's daughter. It is with William as a marrying man that Caen's fortunes are involved.

He selected as his bride Matilda, the daughter of Baldwin V of Flanders, who was descended both from Charlemagne and Alfred the Great. Matilda's beauty and accomplishments matched her pedigree and William determined to have her. To be sure, she was married already—Augustus Hare mentions this, though no one else seems to. Then, too, she was a second cousin to William and therefore ineligible because of consanguinity. Furthermore—a point which was more disconcerting than any other—she scorned the bastard duke. Now if there was one thing more than all else that made William foam with rage it was to be twitted about his illegitimate birth. When he heard that Matilda was spurning him for this reason, he rode, hot with wrath, to her father's castle, rushed into Matilda's presence, and seizing her by her long hair, dragged her back and forth as he strode about the room. Finally he flung her down and rode off as hastily as he had come. Needless to say, this gentle wooing was successful. William married Matilda in 1053, and that in defiance of the papal prohibition. Some six years later William wrung from the Holy Father the necessary dispensation and then, having had his way, he "repented," and he and Matilda, to show how sorry

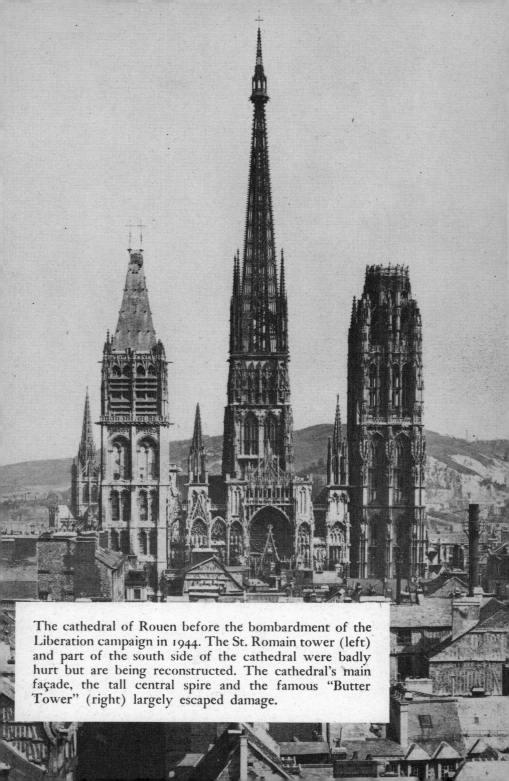

The cathedral of Rouen before the bombardment of the Liberation campaign in 1944. The St. Romain tower (left) and part of the south side of the cathedral were badly hurt but are being reconstructed. The cathedral's main façade, the tall central spire and the famous "Butter Tower" (right) largely escaped damage.

The dim towers are those of the Abbaye aux Hommes in Caen, built by William the Conqueror. The Battle of Caen (1944) passed by the outlying abbey but wiped out a square mile of the city's center. *Commissariat Général au Tourisme, Photo by Touring Club de France.*

they were, built each a beautiful abbey church at Caen. These are the structures, pre-eminently, which give Caen its Romanesque flavor.

Matilda's church, the Abbaye aux Dames, was begun first and completed in four short years. In it lies Matilda's body and also that of her daughter Cecilia, who became the second abbess of the institution. Sir Francis Palgrave paid William's queen a fine tribute in these words: "As for Matilda, a true woman, her goodness, her virtues, may be frequently traced in history—her interference, never. Her patience under trouble and tribulation constitutes the main feature of her biography." She bore William eleven children (some say only nine or ten) and her lord was apparently faithful to her in an age when scarcely anyone would have criticized him for unfaithfulness.

William's church, the Abbaye aux Hommes, called also St. Stephen's, is typical of the massive character of its founder. There was certainly nothing trivial or weak about the Conqueror, nor is there, unless in some of the later additions, about his church. William's body was interred in the choir and on his magnificent tomb of marble and gold and precious stones an inscription, prepared by the Archbishop of York, recorded his great achievements, but *not one word* was said about his little affair with England in 1066.

This tomb was destroyed by the Huguenots and its contents rifled, except for one of William's thigh-bones, which was rescued and later reinterred in another sumptuous tomb. The Revolutionists, not to be outdone in sacrilege by the Huguenots, destroyed this tomb also and carried off the lone thigh-bone. Where is it now? Where is even the dust of it? It would be more potent in the view of many than the whole body of most saints. "He was mild to good men who loved God," said a Saxon chronicler, "and stark beyond all bounds to those who withsaid his will." We have seen how "stark" he was to Matilda when she withsaid him, but when he secured her and became her husband he was a good husband.

One is likely to meet William and Matilda in almost any Norman town, but the intimate sense of companionship is somewhat lacking elsewhere; for Caen is theirs and they are Caen's.

## CHAPTER XII

# Across the D-Day Cotentin:
# Bayeux—St. Lô—Coutances

MOST of that Norman peninsula which juts out so far into the
English Channel opposite the Isle of Wight and which was
the very core of battle in the heroic operations following
D-Day (June 6, 1944) is within the ancient district called *Le
Cotentin*. The name is a lineal descendant of Constantinus, the
Constantine Land, and is said to refer to the Roman emperor
Constantius the Pale, who was the father of Constantine. It
is today, despite its ghastly ordeal in the Liberation campaign,
one of the most fertile districts of a fertile country and the
natives will tell you that if you have a few minutes to spare
you can watch the grass grow before your eyes.

Bayeux, which experienced an almost miraculous escape
from war damage, is on the edge of this old division of *basse
Normandie;* St. Lô, of terrible and hallowed memory, is well
within it; Coutances, though on its western edge, is its ancient

capital. Bayeux is the only one of the three which has always enjoyed, or endured, tourist popularity, but since the war St. Lô has been the nucleus of battlefield France for American trippers, whether they come in reverent or merely curious mood. Its name is a headline of history and will remain so, though battles of almost equal intensity flowed and ebbed over this entire peninsula from the Seine estuary to the coastline opposite Mont-Saint-Michel, on the border of Brittany.

Bayeux's enduring fame has been based chiefly on the Tapestry of Queen Matilda, which is not a tapestry and which Matilda did not make. I would not disparage so significant a work of art and so priceless a record of history, but one does tire of the endless reiteration of the story of the good queen and the ladies of her court, working so patiently and lovingly to produce this immensely long pictorial record of William's conquest of England. The tapestry is really an embroidery, worked in worsteds of eight colors on a band of white linen seventy meters long (about two hundred and thirty-five feet). It was wrought by Anglo-Saxon workmen and given, perhaps by Matilda, to Odo, the Conqueror's half-brother who was the youthful Bishop of Bayeux. Because it is more picturesque to think of the virtuous queen and her ladies doing this work, one is told the story glibly by reputable guide-books and by less reputable human guides. Despite this hoax, or calmly oblivious of it, the tapestry—it has earned that name through long possession of it—has a big story to tell, and the story is substantially true even if colored to extol the Conqueror.

It commences with a scene in which Edward the Confessor decides that William shall be his successor as king of England, and ends with the Battle of Hastings. One follows William's fortunes by wandering around and around a small room in the *ancien évêché,* in which the work is displayed in long glass cases hermetically sealed. At almost all seasons crowds of tourists are in this room and three-fourths of them, in normal times, speak English. Signs throughout the room give the warning in English, "Do not talk too loud," but there is no law to fix the maximum vocal content of talking, and when I have been there the room has usually seemed like one in which sixteen ladies have just assembled for bridge. I find it disconcerting, while puzzling out something in connection with Harold's death, to hear a woman across the way reading in stentorian tones: "Here Duke William and his army arrived at Mont-Saint-Michel. And here crossed the river Couesnon. Here Harold rescued them from the quicksands and they arrived at Dol."

The tapestry has had, as one might expect, an exciting career. It was formerly called *La Toilette du duc Guillaume* and was displayed in the cathedral on festival days, being exactly the right length to stretch completely around the nave. In 1792 it was appropriated by the local Revolutionary soldiers for a wagon covering but was fortunately bought from them by an art-loving *citoyen* and replaced by a substitute canvas. Perhaps the buyer, in order to allay suspicions as to his loyalty to the new regime, explained to the soldiers that the tapestry was just what he needed for blanketing his horses. How very illuminating are acts of vandalism such as that contemplated by the soldiery of Bayeux. They indicate not only inherent lawlessness but a deep social bitterness come to the boiling point. The priceless old tapestry of Bayeux and the thigh-bone of William the Conqueror were equally detestable objects to the fanatical and unthinking *Emancipés.*

The view from the windows of the tapestry room is almost as priceless as the tapestry itself. One gazes across a green little

park to the cathedral, which seems gay beside the stern structures of Caen. It is most often characterized by the veteran
adjectives, "noble" and "glorious," and both of them fit. When
I first saw it from the windows of the *ancien évêché* a heavy
mist was playing about the spires, half concealing them at
times, and there was an effect of mystery about them as though
they could, if they liked, continue upward forever. The style
of the church as a whole is Norman Gothic, but the west
towers, which excite the warmest ardors in all who write of
them, are of the Romanesque era. A notable characteristic of
the Normans as distinguished from the "French" is this: What
they began they completed. "Not one of the great French
churches," says Adams, "has two stone spires complete, of the
same age, while each of the little towns of Coutances, Bayeux,
and Caen contains its twin towers and flèches of stone, as solid
and perfect now as they were seven hundred years ago." (St.
Gatien of Tours, Ste. Croix of Orléans and other less-than-
great French cathedrals do have stone spires that are quite or
nearly twins.)

Of the many interesting persons connected with Notre-
Dame-de-Bayeux three stand out: Odo, the boy bishop; Agatha, the conqueror's unhappy daughter; and a *femme inconnue*
whose epitaph is carved on the side of the south tower. Odo
was the *legitimate* son of that Arlotta, or Arlette, who bore
William illegitimately to Robert the Devil. At the tender age
of thirteen he acquired this rich see from his half-brother for
no better reason than that he wanted the money in it. He
became a warrior, a man of energy, even a man of religion
when it suited his purpose. He built a predecessor of the present cathedral, which was consecrated in the presence of William and Matilda. An ancient crypt still existing under the

sanctuary is supposed to have been built by him. He does not lie in it, however, but very far away in Palermo, where he died while on his way to the Crusades.

Another of our characters, namely Agatha, does lie in the crypt built by Odo. She was as unhappy a girl as ever lived. Forced to travel to Spain for a political marriage with a prince whom she hated, the girl wore her knees almost to the bone with incessant praying for help. Finally help came in the form of death before she reached her dreaded goal. This crypt of Odo "appears to invite one," say Théophile Gautier, "to recline on a stone and await the Last Trump." I sensed the invitation but curtly declined it, for I was in no mood for gloom or mystery. The sun, I suspected, would be breaking through its morning shroud of mist and I was eager to emerge to the invigorating Norman out-of-doors.

The Latin epitaph to which I have referred on the south tower was unable to depress my spirits, for the passing of the old crone, whoever she was, seems to have been a blessing to Bayeux. The last four lines of this epitaph give to the deceased this quaint and vigorous shove into eternity:

> You can show to the dead your wrinkled old face,
> Aged Dame who caused us to lose a whole day.
> We regret truly more that whole day of joy
> Than a hundred old women of your alloy.

She is believed by some to have been a certain Isabella of Dover, sister of the Bishop of Bayeux and mistress of Robert of Gloucester, but I puzzled out the name *Léticie*, which was the only name on this south tower. There is no indication as to whether or not it belonged to the wrinkled old dame.

The square in front of the cathedral is inadequate as a vantage point. It seems to be mostly taken up with the Hôtel du Lion d'Or, which advertises "Comfortable Rooms. Flurished Terrass" (whatever that is), and with a post-card shop which fills one show window with assorted pieties and the other with kissing cards depicting amorous couples under a violent moon. To the north of the cathedral, however, there exists a very charming enclosure, completely dominated by an enormous plane tree, which, if the leaves are not too advanced, furnishes an unsurpassed grille through which one may gaze at the superb twin towers. This is the choicest viewpoint of Bayeux.

Saint Lô, outstanding victim and heroine of the Allied invasion of Normandy, is situated on and high above the River Vire. The contrast between Bayeux, which came through the war almost without a scratch, and this unlucky town, which was crushed to dusty powder, is as dramatic as anything in France today. On June 6, 7, 8 and 9, 1944, St. Lô suffered preliminary but terrific bombardments by Allied air forces, and on July 25 three thousand American bombing planes made history by attacking an area of but ten square miles in this neighborhood to soften it up in preparation for an all-out attempt of ground troops to break into Fortress Europa. The area was "softened"—no doubt of that—and the breakthrough was achieved. The cost to St. Lô, as a city of homes and business, was complete annihilation.

Of the church some substantial fragments remain, particularly the walls of the apse, but these fragments form only a part of a shell of its old self. The west façade is gone. The north tower, with its spire, was blown to bits. The spire of the south tower succumbed to the artillery bombardment of

the Americans and then of the Germans, who had the doubt-
ful honor of finishing it off. Those who knew and loved the
old church now see barely enough of it to serve for identifica-
tion purposes.

After the Liberation a plan was entertained to leave St. Lô
in its state of spectacular ruin as a sort of war monument, but
this did not work out. The call of home was too strong and
the dispersed inhabitants came back, to live in cellars and then
rebuild. The racket of reconstruction noises now rivals, in a
small way, that of Amiens.

St. Lô is a hill town, in all of its older portion, and what
is left of the church of Notre-Dame perches up aloft like an
ecclesiastical scarecrow, or rather like a drawing of a hill in
hell imagined by Gustav Doré. One may mount to it from the
west and south by rue du Maréchal Joffre or from the east
by rue du Maréchal Foch, but the heroes whom these streets
honor seem figures from a primitive era of warfare, so greatly
did the horrors of fighting multiply, especially for St. Lô, in
a quarter-century interval.

Immediately to the west of what was the church's west
front is the pathetically named Place des Beaux Regards, whose
outlook was one of the finest in Normandy. Notre-Dame-de-
Saint-Lô brooded over the lower town and spread the vision
of its own ripe Gothic beauty far and wide over the fertile
countryside. Few churches in France commanded so wide a
view or presented so glamorous an appearance to those who
approached it, by whatever means of transport. It was not one
of the region's somber and severe churches but rather of the
champagne type, pointed and fretted. It even veered to the
Flamboyant, but one Norman characteristic it did possess. Its
two spires were nearly alike. A special curiosity of the church

was—and happily still is—its outside pulpit of sculptured stone, a celebrated "bit" for artists and photographers. Protruding from the north wall near the apse, it managed, by almost incredible luck, to escape destruction. I have never seen anything at all similar except in the tiny Roman church of St. Quirin in Luxembourg City.

One need not be totally pessimistic in thinking of Notre-Dame-de-Saint-Lô. It is rather more than a mere memory. One begins to believe that since the town is resurrecting, the lovely old church, for centuries the cynosure of all resident and visiting eyes, will finally do likewise.

Coutances, capital of the Cotentin, sits upon a hill almost as abrupt as the hill of St. Lô and it looks out not solely upon verdant countryside but upon the Atlantic, more ocean here than channel. The cathedral spires serve as a compass for mariners and can be seen for many miles.

Six or seven hundred buildings and homes in the center of the town were burned to the ground in 1944 in an incendiary bombing raid by American fliers which some of the inhabitants claim was needless, being based on faulty intelligence work. Whatever the degree of justice in that assertion, the tragedy is undeniable. A great area along the main stem of the town, north and south of the cathedral, was burned out and the cathedral itself was damaged, though not very severely. It is being restored as fast as possible.

Coutances is the very marrow of Normandy and its church is more Norman than any other of importance. The spires are simple and severe and the façade, though cousin to the great gray front of Chartres, is extremely earnest in its outlook upon life. This does not mean that the cathedral of Coutances is Romanesque like the abbey churches of Caen, for it was built two centuries later. It does mean, and it serves to prove, that strength, simplicity and grave majesty can be or could once be implanted in even the graceful soaring Gothic style.

The central tower of the lantern—or *plomb*, as the natives call it, meaning plummet—is the outstanding glory of this cathedral and the most ultra-Norman of all its features. It is the greatest of its kind and indeed Viollet-le-Duc calls it the only one, ignoring, for example, the feeble and unsatisfying lantern of Laon, which is of a later period. Apparently France was never able to work out the problem of a large central lantern over the *croisée* of a cathedral, topped by a soaring spire. Even Coutances has no spire surmounting its *plomb*. Perhaps the central spire of Beauvais was the one grand achievement of this kind; but that, as we know, was doomed to quick collapse.

A story is told by everyone—and I repeat it, for it is good and probably true—that Marshal Vauban, the master engineer of Louis XIV, was so struck with the massive yet gracious loveliness of the Coutances lantern that he had a carpet placed directly under it and lay there on his back for nearly half a day admiring its beauty. I found no carpet at hand nor any lackey to spread it for me, so I tipped back my head and stared upward until my neck threatened to crack. It took much less than half a day for this threat to manifest itself.

Behind the cathedral is a beautiful garden, that of the former bishop's palace. It commands a grand view eastward and a still grander view *upward* to the cathedral towers and turrets. From this point the central lantern completely dominates the church, while the western spires, though sixty feet loftier, seem incidental. Within the old palace of the bishops a butter market was in progress on the occasion of a prewar visit which

I made to this garden. Big red-faced men were hurrying in and out, and I felt that if the cathedral towers were cousins of those at Bayeux, if the façade was cousin to that at Chartres, then surely these busy traders were Norman cousins to the butter and egg men I had so often seen in the Faneuil Hall section of Boston.

Coutances is a good place in which to introduce oneself, if one has not done it long before, to that excellent institution of all French provincial towns, the *jardin publique*. Nearly always the gardens are fine and well kept, but this one of Coutances is exceptional. It lies on a steep slope at the western edge of the town and adds a notable view to its other attractions. The mild influence of the ocean, warmed by the Gulf Stream, accounts for palms and other semi-tropical trees in this Norman garden. I remember also an impressive Chinese gingko tree and a still more impressive cedar of Lebanon. The whole garden, as a tablet states, is a *legs* (legacy) from Jean-Jacques Quesnel-Morinière, a leading benefactor of Coutances. It was once his private garden. A circular hedge-bordered labyrinth, called locally *le Colimaçon*, is its showiest feature, and if I were ever to "pray my way to Jerusalem" I should certainly elect to do so in this maze rather than on the hard stone floor of some old church.

Beautiful as is the public garden, attractive as are several other features of the city of Constantius, one is inclined to consider every moment wasted which is not spent in or near the cathedral. This is generally conceded to be the purest of the pure Norman churches, dating from the best period. By much looking at it one comes in a sense to know Normandy.

## CHAPTER XIII

# A Path into Brittany:
## Mont-Saint-Michel—Dol—St. Malo

BRITTANY'S contribution to what we are calling the French Cathedral is comparatively slight yet we can scarcely ignore it altogether, for the old country of the corsairs is full of color and its churches sometimes reflect this color in charming and unexpected ways. Unless one is determined to see practically all of the cathedrals in France, one is unlikely to visit those of Rennes or Vannes. Unless one has much time, one is unlikely to push so far westward as Quimper, though this trip would be highly rewarding. Dol and St. Malo, however, are interesting cathedral towns easily accessible from Normandy; and Mont-Saint-Michel, that far-famed curiosity made half by nature and half by man, lies directly on the path from Coutances.

Every traveler who comes to this part of France visits the celebrated Mount—who would dare to pass through Pontor-

son without taking the six-mile northward run?—and though
it lies quite outside the plan of this book I cannot forego an incidental word about it. In spite of the dreadful plague of way-
side shopkeepers and omelette sellers (this is the native habitat
of the Mère Poulard omelette, and during the war an acquisi-
tive patron named Hermann Goering made off with the reg-
ister of the establishment, for its autographs), the Mount im-
presses me as one of the genuine wonders of Europe.

I have climbed to the abbey and wandered with a large party
(as one must) through all its varied halls and cloisters, I have
gazed from the upper terrace at the retreating sea, and when
the tide was literally out of sight in the distance I have walked
completely around the rock on the wet sand. Never, it seems,
did man, through many generations, embellish nature to better
effect. It has been left to the present generation to try, without success, to destroy the militant charm of this unique place.
The church and the Archangel Michael, who surmounts its
spire, stand high above the world, including the tawdry flim-
flam of commerce in the Mount's only street; and, ignoring
petty affairs below, seem "to threaten heaven itself."

There are recurrent campaigns to reclaim for grazing
ground the flats surrounding the Mount, which are covered
by the sea only at high tide. Artists, architects, lovers of the
picturesque, all who in the slightest degree value sentiment
and tradition always rise up in wrath. They point with horror
to the neighboring Rock of Dol which was once an island
but now emerges from a checker-board of market gardens. As
long ago as 1884 Victor Hugo made the following eloquent
plea for the saving of the Mount, which was even then threatened:

"Mont-Saint-Michel is for France what the great Pyramid is for Egypt.

"It must be kept from mutilation.

"It must remain an island.

"At any cost this double work of Nature and Art ought to be preserved."

But the profit motive is hard to combat and Mont-Saint-Michel is today far less the Mount in Peril of the Sea, as it was once called, than the Mount in Peril of the Land.

The tiny River Couesnon which flows into the bay exactly at the point where the Mount rises is the boundary line between Normandy and Brittany. A few miles to the westward lies Dol-en-Bretagne. It is a small archaic little town with many twelfth-century houses, the most famous of which, called *La Maison des Plaids* (where, of old, Scotch plaids were examined), is now occupied by a shop which sells *"Cycles—Motos—Machines-à-Coudre,"* one of the few concessions to modernity noted in this old Breton community.

The cathedral (still called by this title even in guide books, though it lost the technical right to it in 1790) is dedicated not to the Virgin but to Saint-Samson, an early bishop of Dol. I had previously made the acquaintance of this bishop on the island of Guernsey where a granite quarrying town and a quaint church bear his name (spelled Saint Sampson). He is the patron of the island and both there and on the mainland still enjoys unusual saintly popularity, for during his lifetime and afterwards he was an indefatigable worker of miracles. His church at Dol is noteworthy for its evidences of English influence. It has, for example, a square apse of the type seen at Laon, the only further examples being at St. Malo and Poitiers.

In every case this oddity is directly traceable to English influence. An English bishop named Thoman James lies within the church of St. Samson in a sumptuous tomb of Renaissance style designed and sculptured by three Florentine brothers named Juste. It is odd that an artist family from the city of the Medici should have come to this distant Breton town to make a mausoleum for an English bishop. These brothers and a son of the oldest of them, Juste de Juste by name, later achieved celebrity by their work in the city of Tours, where they became darlings of the Valois. Not only the fact of their presence in France but also the very French sound of their name aroused in me so much curiosity that I "ran them to earth" and learned that their original Florentine name was Betti.

When I first presented myself at the church of St. Samson I found the doors locked. I wandered idly around the church until, on the secluded north side, I came upon a wobbly black lamb all alone. He bleated piteously at sight of me and I bleated back in a tone that seemed to assure him of my friendliness. We were both excluded from the sanctuary and for a few moments we discussed the hardness of our lot and the severity of Mother Church. Then I invited my little companion to come around and take a look at the two beautiful porches on the south side, which he did and was thereby much diverted, for he had never happened to notice them before. These porches, called the great and the little, are like exquisite lace pockets on a somber gray coat. One is ornamented with thirty-eight bas-reliefs and the other with delicate sculptures.

The town of Dol is situated at the southern edge of a great marsh, reclaimed from the sea by means of a system of dikes. All this district was once a forest, later inundated and destroyed by the sea. It still contains thousands of tree trunks that have been buried in briny mud for many centuries. It is said that the wood of these *arbres engloutis* takes on an extraordinary hardness when exposed to the air and furnishes for cabinet work some of the best material to be found in France. In the heart of this marsh rises the lofty granite rock mentioned above, a dreary picture of what Mont-Saint-Michel may become if protective measures are not firmly maintained.

Some fifteen miles northwest of Dol lies St. Malo on its small island of gray rock. It is a phantom city, bombed by the Allies and then burned to the ground in a wanton fit of anger by the retreating Germans in 1944. Hardly any life was left within it after the Liberation. Even two years later residents of neighboring communities considered it unlikely to be rebuilt, but like St. Lô it *is* being rebuilt, or at any rate a beginning is being made. Home, it seems, cannot be bombed out of human hearts, nor burned out.

St. Malo is the historic city of rovers and corsairs and deepsea fishermen. It was once almost independent, giving open defiance to the Duke of Brittany. It was a cathedral city as well as a great stronghold. But alas times grew soft and pitifully civilized. No longer were the stout-hearted Malouins prone to hear mass and then start out to seize a rich merchant ship or attack some distant city of fabulous wealth. "Of the episcopal city," moaned a French writer, "the Revolution has made a curacy, of the privileged city, which was half autonomous, a sub-prefecture. Of the military stronghold peace has created an insignificant spot, a summer resort much frequented by the English; and the corsairs' harbor is become a dock for the exportation of fowls, butter, vegetables and fruit."

It is quite true that in our day as in his, Percy and Cicely and little Violet with their sand pails infest the beautiful sandy

beaches where once good pirate oaths, Breton oaths with a
Welsh tang to them, whipped their rude way through the flying spume, but one may easily recapture the far past by walking
on the city's high and massive ramparts, designed by the same
Vauban who liked to lie on his back beneath the lantern of
Coutances. A circuit of St. Malo on Vauban's ramparts leaves
on the memory an ineffaceable impression. On the inner side
the relics of the gray houses of the city huddle behind their
walls in the manner of Dutch polder villages. They have need
to, for the tide surges at the equinoxes to the tremendous height
of *fifty* feet above low water and, if high winds drive the waves
on, they can occasionally hurl themselves over the ramparts.
On the outer side, except in one small section, lies the surging
sea or the quiet corsairs' harbor. On one of the islets, Grand-
Bé, which one can reach dry shod at low tide, François René,
Vicomte de Chateaubriand, lies buried. His tomb was located
here by his express wish and was marked by a simple stone
cross without inscription, but the Nazi forces, when in occupation, built a blockhouse over and around it and the tomb is now
entombed.

Chateaubriand was not given to personal modesty. The lack
of inscription on his tomb was egotism veiled in a pretense of
modesty. He had an extremely brilliant but declamatory genius.
Much of his work appears like an elaborate tissue of pretense
when viewed in the revealing light of his posthumously published memoirs. He was either a man of marvelous luck or an
opportunist of special talent. He had posed in youth as a free-
thinker but on the eve of Napoleon's reinstatement of the
Christian religion appeared the Breton's dramatically timed
apology for Christianity, *Génie du Christianisme*. It made him
the hero of the hour and Napoleon well rewarded him. On the

eve of the Corsican's fall, March 31, 1814 (it was on March 31, too, that the Allies entered Paris) appeared his pamphlet *De Bonaparte, des Bourbons, et de la Nécessité de se Rallier à Nos princes Légitimes*. Naturally he became at once the darling of Louis XVIII, who said this pamphlet had been worth a hundred thousand men to him.

In St. Malo one feels rather "pervaded" by this man. Near the main city gate is a bronze statue of him. The chief square is named for him. Many tourists stay in the Hôtel de France (one of few structures not destroyed) where he was born, and prior to the war nearly all visitors made their way to the grave on Grand-Bé where he is buried. In other parts of France, however, one hears or sees the name Chateaubriand almost exclusively as the label of a superior steak.

Facing on one side the crashing surf and on the other the square named for Brittany's literary prodigy is the grim castle completed by Duchess Anne of Brittany. One of its enormous towers, erected as an especial affront and humiliation to the Malouins, is called to this day Quiquengrogne, meaning roughly "Whoevergrumblesaboutit." It is a reminder of Anne's determination to curb the proud spirit of this city.

In the very center of St. Malo rises the much damaged cathedral, now only the parish church, of St. Vincent. To reach it from Place Chateaubriand one used to wind through narrow twisting streets which proved very confusing unless one was armed with a good map. When I first made my way to it I perceived three English women standing before its ugly façade in the rue de la Paroisse. They were of the cheerful, uninhibited ultra-Cockney species always numerous in that era in French and Belgian ports reached by cross-channel steamers. Confusedly they were leafing through their guide books when one of them burst out with exactly these words, "Wy, this is the sime church, you silly ass, that we was just in." With resounding laughter they hastened away in search of another church—*any* other.

St. Vincent is a terribly wounded war veteran and barred to visitors at present, but when it is open to the public one descends seven steps to enter, through its portal, a cathedral interior as weird as any to be found in France. The Roman nave and transepts are extremely dark and heavy. They seem also to be somehow corpulent—in other words, fat—but not at all jolly, like human beings who are built that way. I cannot describe them except to say that the ensemble reminds me of the fat man of the circus who has dressed up of an evening in his best black suit and has fallen asleep with his arms and head slumped down on a table. But on the other side of the room his daughter, lithe and slender and gaily dressed, stands on tiptoe chatting with the canary. The daughter, in our runaway figure of speech, is the amazing Gothic choir, "*juste orgueil des Malouins,*" built by Bishop Rousselot de Limoilan in the fourteenth century. It is as chic and elegant as the nave is gross and gloomy. I have never seen a sharper effect of contrast in a cathedral interior.

The signs I read on the church bulletin board on a prewar occasion betrayed—as if one could ever forget it here!—the close ties between this Brittany seaport and the perennial British tripper. A poster for a forthcoming show (net proceeds to be given to the St. Vincent parish) announced leading turns by *Les Dazzling Dancers* and *Le Petit Lord*. Another poster, of equal but no greater prominence, urged upon visitors from *outre-mer* the merits of the Catholic religion. It read in English:

"The religion taught in this church is exactly the same as that taught in every church in the land before the 'Reformation.' Its communicants number 360 million—etc., etc.," Some militant Protestant, possibly the Petit Lord or even one of the Dazzling Dancers, had carefully penciled out the quotation marks from the word Reformation.

At the entrance to the Gothic choir a mosaic inscription on the floor shows the exact spot where that intrepid Malouin, Jacques Cartier, knelt to receive the episcopal benediction on Pentecost Sunday, 1535, the day before he set sail with a small company of mariners on the voyage that was to take him far up the St. Lawrence River in the New World. He left St. Malo on May 16 and reached the mouth of the great river after eighty-six days. It was the tenth of August, the day sacred to St. Lawrence, and Cartier, feeling himself to be under this saint's protection, gave his name to the river. A statue of the mariner is one of the most interesting sights of the St. Malo ramparts. With his left hand he holds a rudder. With his right he strokes a thoughtful beard.

The many stirring events which the old cathedral witnessed up to the present century are dramatically set forth in a booklet by a local historian, M. Herpin. He pictures the triumphal mass that celebrated the return of a native son, Duguay-Trouin, after the capture of the Brazilian capital, Rio de Janeiro. He pictures, in opposite vein, the anguish of the Malouins when English cannon balls in 1693 smashed part of their beloved choir. The worshipers, heroic in adversity, marched slowly through the gloomy nave, chanting one line of their litany:

*A Furore Anglorum Libera Nos, Domine*
(From the fury of the English Deliver us, O Lord)

In 1944 the descendants of those worshipers had far more cause to pray for deliverance from *Furore Teutonico,* for German incendiarism brought far more ruin to St. Vincent than any number of seventeenth-century cannon balls could have done.

The apse of St. Malo's cathedral is quadrilateral (though not quite square), which I take to be less an evidence of English architectural influence than an evidence of the Malouins' desire to secure every possible inch of space for their structure. This curiously shaped apse crowded up to and almost into the (late) rue Porcon de la Barbinais, which was on a much lower level. It now crowds up to empty space.

If our imagination is good we can see the original owner of that street's long name bidding a last tearful farewell to friends and home as he sails off for Algiers and certain death. The story is a moving one. Porcon had been a prisoner of the Bey of Algiers and had been dispatched to France on an almost hopeless political mission. He had failed through no fault of his own. The Bey had sworn that if Porcon did not succeed, or if, having failed, he did not honorably return and pay with his life the penalty of failure, six hundred captive Frenchmen would be killed in his stead. Porcon returned. On a day in 1667 his aged parents and a great crowd of his friends, convulsed with weeping, saw him depart forever from St. Malo. He seems not to be much mentioned in the ecclesiastical records of the city. I judge that he rarely darkened the doors of the cathedral. No doubt he was a corsair, though he is euphemistically called a "merchant-service officer." If there is a special compartment of heaven reserved for those who are brave, regardless of the ethics of their profession, then Porcon of St. Malo must surely be "among those present."

Farewells seem to be of the very essence of this Breton port. Even now each year the *Terre-Neuviers*, Newfoundland fishermen, assembling as many sailing vessels as they can, receive a farewell blessing from cardinal or bishop and start out on their perilous journey to the Grand Banks, to fish for cod. Their oversea base is Saint-Pierre and Miquelon, those two tiny islands groups which are the very last remnants of the once vast French colonies in North America. It is said that on the average in normal times, six *Terre-Neuviers* are lost each season, but those boats that return, loaded with cod, are greeted by the Malouins with emotional enthusiasm. The hardy fishermen are given a welcome as rousing as that accorded to the successful corsairs of old.

St. Malo's habits do not die, nor does the city, nor the ancient hearth of its religion. One of the surest things about Brittany is its continuance through all wars and weathers.

## CHAPTER XIV

# Towers on the Loire: Tours

THE name Tours seems to suggest a rather definite need for us, who are trying to avoid confusion in our survey of the French Cathedral. We need to climb to some lofty eminence and look about us. Where, exactly, is this city on the Loire in relation to our imaginary structure? We find that though a fine pivotal point, it is outside the line of any true cruciform church oriented in the usual way and using Paris as the *croisée*, though no more outside than is, for example, the chapel of St. Radulphe in relation to its cathedral of St. Nazaire at Carcassonne. Since we shall scarcely wish to avail ourselves of the small boy's defense that we are "no worse" than Carcassonne, let us be quit of this imaginary church forthwith and consider the remainder of ecclesiastical France, especially the widespreading Midi, as the rambling palace of our bishop, or better still, of our archbishop. The *archévêché* shall easily blanket all irregularities.

Henry James is for many travelers on the Loire the one indispensable cicerone. His *Little Tour in France* was copyrighted by him in 1884, but it still has a good sale, whereas scores of books on the same subject published since then have long ago perished. One never thinks him out of date when he climbs into a carriage for a long afternoon's drive to some goal which you and I can reach by motor in an hour, for he had a deft touch and a sure gay humor which make him attractive company in any age.

Tours was for him a city "sweet and bright." Its province was "a region of easy abundance . . . the land of Rabelais, of Descartes, of Balzac, of good books and good company as well as good dinners and good houses." All these good things the novelist seems to have vastly enjoyed and his pleasure has communicated itself to generations of tourists in this château district.

Now I suppose I have betrayed my cause. It is of châteaux, I admit, rather than of cathedrals that one first thinks when the Valley of the Loire is mentioned, yet Tours itself unquestionably strikes the ecclesiastical note, though serving as a rallying point for the annual scramble of château tourists. Saint-Gatien-de-Tours, the city's cathedral, is one of the major cathedrals of France.

By luck of location, as in the case of the abbeys of Caen, St. Gatien virtually escaped damage in the Ruin of 1944 which liberated France. The tornado of battle cut an irregular path up the center of Tours from the Loire for a quarter of a mile, destroying everything that lay in the way—about a fifth of the city. It swirled within two blocks of the cathedral in two places but did not touch it except with a few whiffs of violence. In cutting its path the storm did, unhappily, demolish the house

where Honoré de Balzac was born, at 39 rue Nationale. I recall that in prewar times a curious bust of Balzac used to look
down from the wall of this house and a tablet proclaimed that
he was born *le Ier Prairial, An VII*, which is, being interpreted
from the Revolutionary calendar, May 20, 1799.

Rabelais and Descartes, whose statues at the approach to
Pont Wilson have been reconstituted to center two lovely circular flower gardens, are claimed as Tourangeaux, or "Tou-
rainians," though neither the lusty novelist nor the founder of
modern philosophy was strictly a native of Tours. Balzac, un-
deniably a native, was considered by Henry James to be the
link between those two so-different celebrities. His "strenuous,
laborious" moods recall Descartes; his jovial, full-feeding
moods recall Rabelais.

More intimately bound up with the fortunes of this city than
any writer or philosopher was a great monarch, the Spider
King, as he is called by a modern writer. His ruined spider's
nest, Plessis-les-Tours, is now within about half a mile of the
widening city. I refer, of course, to Louis XI. To me this king
is the most interesting of all the eighteen Louis of France, not
forgetting the ninth, who was the Saint, or the fourteenth,
who called himself the Sun. The Spider King was a wonderfully *intricate* human being. One loathes him for his hateful
cruelties and treacheries. One despises him for his small-caliber
bargaining with the saints, whose effigies he stuck all around
his ugly hat. One certainly does not admire him for his associates—for Oliver le Daim (meaning Fallow-Deer), who was
his barber and confidant; for Tristan the Hermit, his infamous
hangman; for Cardinal la Balue, whose character we glimpsed
at Evreux. But, for all this Louis the Eleventh, "the terrible
king," conceived in his brilliant, twisted brain—modern

France. He was—we hate to use the phrase—"the father of his country." And for Tours he was almost life itself, for he founded and fostered the silk trade there, which was long the city's main support.

It is high time for us to make the acquaintance of the cathedral in which, no doubt, the king offered some of his most artful prayers. Its fantastic western towers, completed after Louis', time, loom high over the city and seem to be its very sign and symbol. They are queer, clever towers, almost twins. The word "exquisite" seems to apply to them, and in much the same sense as it applied to Beau Brummell in his great days. They seem to wear their bizarre and showy clothes with utmost coolness, quite aware that other towers, if similarly dressed, would look ridiculous. Where else in France or in all Europe do Gothic towers, even dressy Flamboyant ones like these, dare to wear rounded Renaissance helmets and succeed in doing so without becoming a laughing-stock? The towers of St. Gatien are never laughed at, but are rather admired, as clever people are admired. I doubt if they are *loved* by anyone, as the towers of Chartres are loved, or respected (perhaps they would not want to be) as the sincere old Norman towers are respected.

This cathedral was called by Walter Scott the most magnificent church in France, but to most of us such a statement seems absurd. Had the author of *Quentin Durward* never seen or heard of Reims, Amiens, Bourges? St. Gatien is not even grandiose, for its proportions would scarcely warrant this adjective. It is, however, *suave*, and its history is very great.

Before entering the cathedral every visitor gives himself over to enjoyment of its Flamboyant west façade, whose bril-

liant frivolities are agreeably toned down by "a charming
mouse-colored complexion." One oddity will strike the beholder at the first glance. Its great rose window, supported by
eight lancets, is not a true rose but a sort of square with slightly
curving sides, stood upon one of its angles. It is sometimes
called a lozenge window but this is obviously incorrect, for
all its angles are equal. The whole scheme of the glass in this
central portion of the façade is called locally *le grand housteau,*
which term is borrowed, along with the idea, from Bourges.
The builder of this façade was a nephew of the great architect
of Saint-Etienne-de-Bourges, and this idea is thus a legacy from
one of the celebrated cathedral builders of the late Gothic
period, Guy de Dammartin, whom we shall meet in a later
chapter.

The term *grand housteau* is as interesting as the effect it
makes. It is not to be found in any French dictionary, but a
certain Abbé Villepelet in a monograph on the Bourges cathedral explains *housteau* as an ancient Berry word for *ouest,* so
each of these huge and oddly conceived windows at Bourges
and Tours forms for its own cathedral the Great West.

St. Gatien and its predecessors have an immense past. The
name-giver, a missionary who came to Tours about the year
250 and converted the city, is almost lost in the shadows of the
Dark Ages, but as one marches on, a century at a stride, one
encounters many a great name. The third bishop was Martin
of Tours, the saint who first won fame by dividing his cloak
with a beggar at Amiens. He is an exceedingly popular saint
for, in addition to having performed two hundred and six
authenticated miracles since his death, he has become the patron
of drinkers and of convivial parties. Once upon a time I en-

tered the sacred portals of the Vintners' Corporation in London and there, sure enough, was a life-size statue of St. Martin of Tours dividing his coat with the beggar.

Striding on two or three paces through the annals of St. Gatien, we meet first Gregory of Tours, bishop, historian, saint; and then the scholar Alcuin, who was Charlemagne's teacher. There are more celebrities, many more, worth meeting; but let us take a long forward leap to Anne of Brittany, that vigorous duchess whom we saw at St. Malo erecting the tower Quiquengrogne. She married three times and all of her husbands were kings. The first, to whom she was married by proxy only, was the oft-wedded Maximilian of Austria, called "King of the Romans." Somehow this marriage never "took." Ignoring it, Anne presently married Charles VIII of France and, when he died, Louis XII, who thus clinched for France the rich duchy of Brittany. Her marriage with Charles was blessed with four children, but one by one all of the children, three boys and a girl, died in infancy.

This brings our thought directly back to the cathedral, for the richest treasure of St. Gatien is the white marble tomb of the children of Anne by Charles VIII. It is conspicuous in the right transept, a thing of exquisite taste and beauty often attributed to the brothers Juste, who went from Florence to Dol to make the tomb for Bishop James, but almost certainly not executed or designed by them. No one knows surely who did the work, but investigation seems to support those who point to Michel Colombe of Tours, the patron of the brothers Juste.

Extraordinary confusion seems to exist as to whose bones lie in this wondrous tomb. It is quite safe—and lazy—to say, as ever so many books do, "the children of Charles and Anne," but one is eager to know the facts more definitely. Henry

James speaks of "the little boy and girl," who "lie side by side on a slab of black marble." This is a rather painful error as the sculptured robes of the infants, decorated with symbolical dolphins, proclaim to every visitor that the royal children were both *dauphins* of France and therefore boys. (The word *dauphin* means dolphin. It happened to be a proper name, Delphinus in Latin, attaching to an old noble family and passed on to French royalty as the title of the King's eldest living son, the heir to the throne.) A familiar guide, generally meticulous in marshaling its facts, mentions this tomb as that of "the four infants" of Charles and Anne. As a matter of fact the correct story is carved on black marble tablets placed at either end of the tomb. The older child was Charles Orlana, the first-born. He died at the age of three. The second, named simply Charles, was born a few months after his brother's death and lived but twenty-five days. I have never seen infants in marble more natural and sweet. Charles Orlana wears his crown and Charles (whom Henry James thought a girl) wears a baby hood. The noses of both children are chipped off but their sweet slumber is undisturbed by this little misfortune. Every visitor is tempted to linger in the presence of these charming children. They are worth forty archbishops.

On one early visit to Tours, in a lush year of tourism, an American theatrical troop arrived and swarmed like a herd of ants directly into my hotel. The corridors resounded with such comment as "Ain't this a swell dump, Stella?" To which Stella, chomping steadily, replied, "You said it." I recalled a billboard notice I had seen on the old stone bridge of Tours, a garish advertisement of "Chicago's Follies," the forthcoming theatrical attraction. The girls of the chorus were pictured therein with pigs' tails emerging from their ballet costumes, a charming bit of twentieth-century symbolism, I thought, and here were the little dears rooting about in my hotel.

In spite of occasional exotic follies, there are many things of noble dignity and many things of romantic appeal about this old city on the Loire, but one must select only a fragment from so rich a repository as Tours. I propose to salt down in my memory for permanent preservation one thing above all else, that which a local guide-book, printed in laborious English, calls "The Thumb of Ch. VIII's Children."

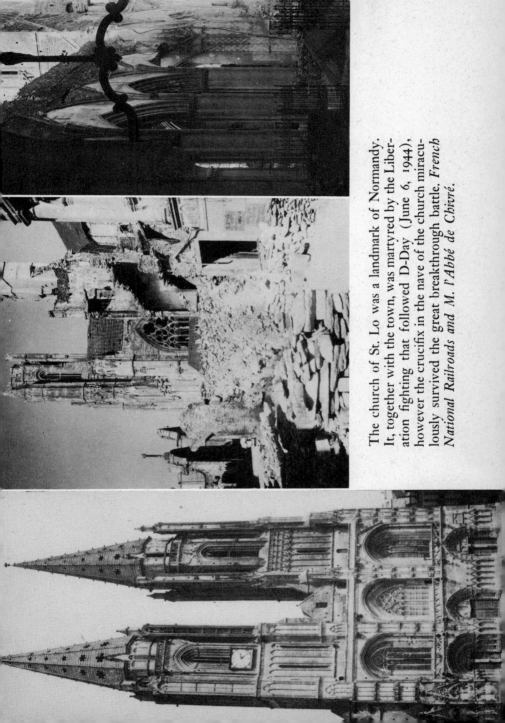

The church of St. Lo was a landmark of Normandy. It, together with the town, was martyred by the Liberation fighting that followed D-Day (June 6, 1944), however the crucifix in the nave of the church miraculously survived the great breakthrough battle. *French National Railroads and M. l'Abbé de Chivré.*

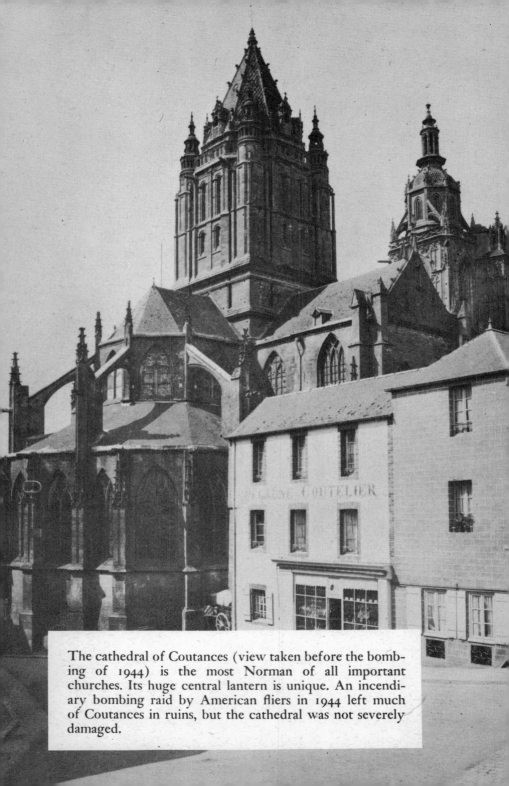

The cathedral of Coutances (view taken before the bombing of 1944) is the most Norman of all important churches. Its huge central lantern is unique. An incendiary bombing raid by American fliers in 1944 left much of Coutances in ruins, but the cathedral was not severely damaged.

## CHAPTER XV

# *Le Mans and Black Angers*

LE MANS, the capital of ancient Maine, is one of a half-dozen cathedral towns easily seen in one-day trips from Tours, which shall be for the plan of this book a small Paris. Tours still has such a special "personality," indefinable perhaps but sensed by all, that it makes an agreeable hub of travel, a good place to come back to several times; and as a practical note one may report that the hotels were not caught in the wave of war that engulfed the city.

The meaning of Le Mans, if one chooses to be a literalist, is rather shocking. It is Meal-Worm or Grub or White Maggot or, especially, Larva of the Cockchafer. And the Cockchafer is a May-bug or a June-bug, according to what part of the world you live in. A knowledge of this curious archaic meaning is not, however, vastly important to the Anglo-Saxon visitor. What is of some importance or convenience is a facility in juggling with the French definite article. Many who have visited France a dozen times have difficulty in acquiring glibness with it. If speaking French we should, of course, go *au* Mans, and return *du* Mans, yet how guilelessly, in practice, do we leave the original *le* untouched in this and all other place names similarly formed.

Le Mans has one thing in common with most towns the world over. It presents its ugliest front to the traveler who approaches by train, but the city itself has always been cheerful. I recall an incident in one of the decrepit prewar streetcars (now replaced by trolley buses). They were all "manned" by women, stocky wind-blown *Manceauses* who wore black tabliers and tri-color scarves. Each trip became a sort of party, especially for those who stood on the front platform. *Prière de ne pas Parler au Conducteur* read a conspicuous sign but the *ne pas* had been penciled out and the resulting affirmative command was obeyed by everyone, to the obvious pleasure of the lady motorman who joined heartily in the repartee and enjoyed the broad jokes of the *commis-voyageurs*. At one of the stops on my first trip a pathetic old blind cripple boarded the car. The motorwoman descended to help him on, then pulled his bushy whiskers jocosely, cracked a joke and returned to her duty. The cripple received her pleasantries with as much of a smile as his poor blind face was capable of and spent the rest of the trip poking the lady with his cane, or trying to. She would dodge from one side to the other but when the old man scored a hit all the "guests" on the front platform roared with laughter. The whole scene was to me a gorgeous page torn out of that humorous, tender, coarse, fascinating book called Life. And—the little red trolley car never left the rails.

The cathedral, Saint-Julien-du-Mans, is one of the very great churches of France. E. A. Freeman, whose architectural judgment is held in high esteem, rated it unblushingly ahead of Chartres. Few would agree with him, yet the overawing effect of the chapel-circled choir towering above the Place des Jacobins is one of those things which the most hurried tourist never forgets.

I acquainted myself with the exterior of this church—its eastern end at least—in the manner I most enjoy, from a café table in the square. To be sure, the immediate foreground was then dominated by a horrible monstrosity which pumped *Essence Tourisme* into thirsty gasoline tanks; but this, after all, was an appropriate note in the Le Mans ensemble for gasoline scored in this town one of its great triumphs. Wilbur Wright was the scorer, but more of him anon. We are in the Place des Jacobins and St. Julien demands all our attention.

How grand, how utterly improbable this cathedral is. I was a little reminded of Beauvais. St. Julien possesses a nave but one has almost to hunt for it. It is a small Romanesque structure quite lost beneath the protecting shadow of the giant transepts. Its effect is nearly as incongruous as that of the cathedral in St. Malo. The whole church covers, architecturally, four or five centuries in two daring leaps. Nave to choir was the first leap and nothing could possibly be bolder. The old Roman wall had to be removed by special permission of the king of France to make this choir and its ring of chapels possible. The transepts, built two centuries after, were the second leap. They are so huge in their proportions that with the cathedral's only tower on the south end they give visitors the impression of being the nave, with the choir running off inexplicably at right angles.

Stained glass, returning now as everywhere, is the greatest glory of a glorious cathedral. The nave awaits return of the very oldest colored window in existence except possibly one in a monastery in Bavaria. Its lower half, which alone is the original, is of an extraordinary rich red hue seldom matched in even the great thirteenth-century days. The choir, which is of the latter period, has many of those wonderful guild windows which one sees at Chartres. The bakers, the drapers, the furriers, even the *cabaretiers*, which means *publicans*, are here, each group shown in characteristic attitude at the bottom of the window it gave. If in the mood, any tourist could be happy here for hours, not precisely studying the glass but letting its color soak into his system.

A king and a queen of England are intimately associated with St. Julien. Henry II was baptized here and Queen Berengaria lies buried here. To many well-informed persons Berengaria is hardly more than the name of an old ocean liner, but to Richard the Lion-Hearted she was a good wife. She was the daughter of Sancho VI, King of Navarre and to wed her Richard repudiated his betrothal, made during his infancy, to Alice of France. The royal wedding took place at Limasol on the romantic "Copper Isle," Cyprus, which was birthplace and home of Aphrodite. Berengaria's beauty and accomplishments became a legend throughout the world, but alas she did not stay with Richard until death did them part. For some obscure reason she became estranged from him late in life and while she now lies in this cathedral of Le Mans, her husband, or at any rate his heart, his *coeur de lion*, lies, as we have seen, in the cathedral of Rouen.

The chief historical figure in one's picture of Le Mans is not, however, Richard's queen; but rather a bicycle repair-shop mechanic from Dayton, Ohio, U. S. A., who invented an amazing machine that would fly through the air. Here in Le Mans he demonstrated his invention and awoke the tremendous interest of the Old World. The New World, so alert and progressive, had looked on during this man's experiments, but had refused to risk a nickel of its good money on a fad so obviously impractical as this invention. It was Léon Bollée of Le Mans who really introduced Wilbur Wright and his invention to mankind.

The American aviator stands—in stone—at a corner of the Place des Jacobins and it is well for the cathedral that it happens to be so majestic, as a common church here would certainly have to play second fiddle to Wilbur Wright's first. The statue is quite unlike most statues and commands attention even from those who constitutionally hate such things. The aviator, heroic in size, is in the act of climbing from a shaft of stone up to the sky. He is nude, which at first thought seems scarcely the correct presentation of a gentleman from Dayton, Ohio, but the French think of Wilbur Wright as deathless and timeless like Icarus, *son précurseur*, who is pictured at the base of the statue adjusting the wings to his sandals. A synopsis of his life is set down from the 1900 *Expériences de Vol Plane aux Dunes de Kittyhawk* to his world-shaking successes at Le Mans.

Rue Wilbur Wright (or Whright on one sign for years) descends very sharply from the Place des Jacobins to the banks of the River Sarthe. It is almost a tunnel, but emerges on as quaint an old quay as one could find in France. The Sarthe is not much of a river, but it is navigable from this point for small boats, thus making Le Mans a port. One should really never *descend* a street named rue Wilbur Wright; so I, having done so, will hasten to undo the mischief and mount again to Place des Jacobins to be a little nearer to the sky and gaze again at St. Julien, which fairly bumps the blue dome.

The story of Le Mans is full of amazing characters, such as a false Joan of Arc who hypnotized the local bishop and made a mighty fool of him. The burlesque poet Scarron is another. This gentleman, besides being a poet and a canon of the cathedral, was a first-class libertine. He numbered among his amorous conquests two of France's most famous beauties, Marion Delorme and Ninon de Lenclos, and married a third. Therein lies the climax of his adventures. He had become a horrible paralytic. The story, constantly told and occasionally denied, is that Scarron and two young comrades once covered their bodies with honey, rolled in feathers, and then raced wildly through the streets of Le Mans. The Manceaux, young and old, human and canine, delighted or scandalized by such madness, raced after them. The joke took on an aspect of real danger to the perpetrators until finally the three were forced to leap into the Sarthe. The poet's two comrades were drowned and he, though rescued, was crippled for life by paralysis.

His physical ugliness grew to ghastly proportions. He was a burden to himself, a horror to others, yet somehow his cheerful wit stayed with him. He wooed and won a young girl named Françoise d'Aubigné. "I would rather marry a *cul-de-jatte*," she said, "than the convent." The hyphenated word is an unlovely one meaning a legless cripple who sits in a bowl. Scarron sold his ecclesiastical *bénéfice*. The wedding took place and Françoise became in effect the devoted nurse of a monster who was, at the same time, one of the most brilliant wits in France. This strangely assorted pair, established in Paris, succeeded in making their home the center of the capital's literary life.

Scarron mercifully died. Françoise became royal governess,

then royal mistress, then queen of France. She is known in history as Madame de Maintenon and her second husband was, of course, Louis XIV. Quite an upward jump, that, for the widow of an ex-canon of Saint-Julien-du-Mans.

The cathedral to which Paul Scarron rendered his dubious service is virtually unknown to the genus tourist. One cannot account for this, since Le Mans is easy to reach from Tours and not difficult from Paris. It can bide its time, however. Anything so superb will surely come into its own. It will be some day "discovered."

Angers is as far west of Tours as Le Mans is north. Henry James had a bad time with this town and called it a sell but having said that he spent the rest of his chapter unsaying it. The old capital of Anjou seemed to him too dressed up with new and uninteresting boulevards. Also he found "an effect of perversity in a town lying near a great river but not on it. The Loire is a few miles off, but Angers contents itself with a meagre affluent of that stream."

These querulous objections the author would undoubtedly have forgone had he had the good fortune to fortify himself while in the town, with a *Cointreau*. This liqueur is made in Angers and has carried the town's name to the four corners of France. It is based on orange flavor and is, in my unexpert opinion, the very finest of all French liqueurs. I feel myself to be lacking in enterprise to have set down this glowing testimonial without having first made some "arrangement" with the *société anonyme* which manufactures the fiery cordial; but if it entices a few persons to the Angevin capital who would have been deterred by Henry James I shall feel repaid.

There is an enormous old castle in Angers, the château of

the counts of Anjou. Nowhere in France have I seen any castle more grim and dour. Seventeen towers, all short and very stout, surround its outer wall, and being striped zebra-fashion, they give something of the impression of the awkward squad of a prison chain-gang. This castle was built and dwelt in by Saint Louis but one must think back still farther in history to perceive the true significance of the spot. Here roughly was the court of the hereditary counts of Anjou, most of whom were named Fulk. They were a bold and multi-colored lot like the various Baldwins of Flanders—Fulk the Red, Fulk the Good, Fulk Nerra (the Black) who was very wicked and built an abbey or made a pilgrimage to expiate each major crime, Fulk the Young, who achieved many important things, of which the greatest was the begetting of Geoffrey Plantagenet.

Geoffrey was, of course, the founder of that dynasty of English kings which lasted longer than any other dynasty since the Conquest. His nickname, *Plante Genêt,* or Broom Plant (a sprig of which he always wore in his hat) was not, except in one or two cases, taken over by his descendants and historians object to the term "Plantagenet Dynasty," but it is picturesque, convenient and popular so historians will object in vain. To me the accomplishments of Geoffrey's favorite plant were a revelation when I looked them up. The broom will not only sweep your floors but will cure you of dropsy. Its seeds also form a passable substitute for coffee, and one species, close cousin to Geoffrey's own *genêt,* will yield a good yellow dye.

In later but still medieval times "the good King René" was the dominating figure of Anjou. He stands now benign and handsome on the boulevard that parallels the castle wall. King of what, you ask, unless you are far better posted on general information than I was. He was king of Naples, though he never succeeded in ruling or scarcely even in entering his turbulent kingdom. There was enough else to occupy his attention. He was Duke of Anjou and of Lorraine, Count of Provence, Prince of Sicily, ruler also of Jerusalem. But he disliked all this arduous ruling and finally took refuge in literature and the fine arts which he loved.

Yes, there is a cathedral in Angers and a double-starred one. Saint-Maurice-d'Angers is, to be specific, a Gothic cathedral of Angevin type, which refers especially to the curious domical vaulting of the interior, a sort of freakish Byzantine effect which is a peculiarity of the region. I like the *Guide Bleu's* phrase for this odd effect, *voutes bombées comme des coupoles*, rather better than I like the effect itself. The aisleless nave of this cathedral is another oddity which has both partisans and opponents. It is like a large rectangular room with a high *bombé* ceiling. When I first saw it, the room was filled, every square centimeter of it, with a vast crowd doing honor to Jeanne d'Arc. The Maid's banners, emblazoned with the names *Jhésus Maria*, were hung all around the nave. In the choir was a most colorful array of clergy, with the Bishop of Angers at their head. The choral mass was rich and stirring, especially when the treble of the boys' choir, supported by organ, rang through the great open stretches of the domed nave.

St. Maurice is magnificently placed on the highest ground of Angers. From the square before its Gothic west front, which is the cathedral's showiest and least interesting portion, one fairly tumbles, by the Montée St. Maurice, down to the quays of the

River Maine. As I prepared to do so a violent shower came on, for no apparent reason. I hesitated between dashing for shelter around the corner in the shop called *Au Talon Louis XV* or tobogganing down the *Montée* as numerous long-skirted priests were doing. I chose the latter course and found an apology for shelter on the quay, whence I could gaze at the rain-beaten waters of the world's *shortest* river. The Maine has a total length of about seven miles. Just above Angers the Sarthe, the Mayenne and the Loir unite and merge their identity in the River Maine, which no sooner acquires an identity than it throws it away in the wide yellow waters of the Loire.

Do not be confused by the rivers Loir and Loire. They differ as sharply as Smith and Smythe, or, for the matter of that, Clark and Clarke. I understand that the French tongue and palate are capable of differentiating between their two names and the French ear is capable of catching the distinction, but such hair-splitting differences are beyond me. When I come to a river in France whose name is *Lwar* I always say, "Pardon me. Do you spell your name with or without an 'e'?" The name means, quaintly, dormouse and like a happy pair, male and female, the two rivers make their way westward side by side for a hundred miles or more. As sometimes happens, the lady is built on a very generous scale while her mate is thin and worried looking.

From the towers of St. Maurice-d'Angers, to which I climbed, I could see in the distance the two dormice or at least the valleys through which they traveled. And Black Angers lay sprawling at my feet. The town is far less black than it used to be, but the slate, which was formerly much used in construction work and gave the town a somber appearance, is still ex-

tensively quarried. It is the chief source of Angevin wealth—
unless, as I half suspect, the much advertised Cointreau, which
looks like water and tastes of orange fire, has clambered into
first place. However this may be, the union of gray-black slate
and orange fire have made, so far as I am concerned, a good
modern setting for the home town of Geoffrey Plantagenet.

## CHAPTER XVI

# The Maid and the Salamander:
## Orléans—Blois

THE cathedrals of the Loire valley, excepting perhaps that of Tours, are not in any sense great, but they are exceedingly interesting as showing the utter collapse of good taste. If this book were based on architectural chronology rather than geographical convenience, the picture of Orléans and Blois would have to bring it to a dreary close. I rejoice that it is not so designed, for that taste which produced the great Gothic cathedrals was a thing of such divine quality that one would have said it could never die. How is it possible that men who must have seen Chartres, Reims and Notre-Dame-de-Paris could have perpetrated the cathedral of Blois?

Sainte-Croix of Orléans is much more understandable. It is a large Gothic cathedral erected by competent and hardworking men of the seventeenth and eighteenth centuries who had not one spark of the original fire that had burned in men's hearts in the twelve hundreds. It is even noteworthy as the only important Gothic cathedral which has been achieved in France since the Middle Ages, but one rather hopes that no more will be attempted. Modern architects and stonemasons cannot conceivably recapture that intense zeal, born of the feeling that the Mother of God stood at their elbows counseling, directing, urging them on, to make for her a worthy abode. Of what value is advanced science in construction when set against a primitive zeal like that of old?

On a prewar trip I went direct from Chartres to Orléans. The difference between what one may fairly call the original Gothic and the warmed-over Gothic was startling, shocking. The towers of Chartres are very dissimilar while the towers of Orléans are exact twins. All sorts of things, I suppose, are wrong with Chartres and nothing much is wrong with Orléans, but "oh the difference to me!" It was quite as great, I assert, as the difference between Lucy living and Lucy dead and stuffed by a taxidermist could have been to William Wordsworth. Chartres is a Dante among churches, a Da Vinci, an Abraham Lincoln. Orléans seemed a man about town faultlessly dressed for dinner.

It is perhaps unkind to speak thus of Orléans cathedral, for both it and the surrounding city suffered very severely in the Liberation. The church has been a *chantier* ever since, resounding with the noises of reconstruction work. Its twin towers and its west façade were badly battered and its glass—very garish eighteenth-century work—was destroyed. The center of the city, around Place du Martroi, is a pathetic desert of stone and dust but large new business constructions are under way. This courageous rebuilding program provides a focus for the thought of the community, which seemed, in prewar times, to concentrate on its famous Maid of Orléans.

This strange saint has a hold on all France, even atheistic France, such as no historical character has over any other country. She is absolutely inescapable from Normandy to Marseille, from the Champs Elysées to Montmartre. Statues of her are *everywhere*. Streets and squares by the hundred bear her name. Learned academicians write new and learned tomes about her. Music halls represent her and not irreverently. Politicians make great capital of her. To the church she is, of course, patron saint.

One might by rule expect the Maid to be without honor in her own city, the city which she delivered, but Orléans fairly outdoes itself to extol her. I have postcards of more than a dozen statues of her, all of which are in Orléans. She is represented all the way from a peasant girl in simple attitudes of prayer to a ridiculous plumed Zenobia, sword in hand, whose vast hips and opulent breasts test the quality of the meshed steel which encases them. Commerce has, of course, appropriated Joan. Whether you wish jelly or perfumery or a good "T.S.F." (radio) you are likely to find the Maid's likeness imprinted thereon.

One of Orléans' war tragedies was the gutting of the ancient house containing the Jeanne d'Arc Museum. It is now a ghost, bearing only its empty title carved in stone above the door. In it, before the war, I saw three of Joan's signatures, or rather exact replicas of three signatures. They had little in common except the obvious difficulty with which they had been penned. Even the spelling was not quite consistent. In two cases it was Jehanne and in the third case Johanne.

The nave of the cathedral was filled at the time of my first visit with gay banners left over from the *Fête de Jeanne d'Arc* which had occurred only two days before. On each banner appeared the names of one or more of Joan's captains and supporters. One bore the names of her brothers, Pierre and Jean d'Arc, who were small fry and disgraced themselves nine years after their sister's death by supporting the claim of a false Joan and actually conducting her to Orléans. Another banner boldly bore the name *Bâtard d'Orléans*. This was the celebrated Dunois, greatest of Joan's helpers, natural son of the Duke of Orléans. Every one spoke of him, even the Maid, I suppose, as the Bastard. He was a shrewd leader and a gallant warrior. Few opponents save that remarkable young Scot, Quentin Durward, ever succeeded in so much as denting his helmet. At Orléans the Maid and the Bastard were brilliant partners in a brilliant feat of arms, but I shall make no attempt to set down this long and familiar story here.

Forty miles down the Loire as one returns toward Tours, lies Blois, the Salamander's favorite home. All over France one finds, here and there, the emblem of the salamander but in Blois it seems to dominate the town. At the very station one is importuned to buy postcards with this emblem and explanations of it set forth. The local guide-book uses it as an appropriate cover design. The most conspicuous wing of the celebrated château in the center of the town is that constructed by the royal Salamander himself and his device is all over it both inside and outside.

Francis I was an extraordinary monarch. Few kings have been so universally popular during their lifetime and few have left a name more dazzling on the pages of history. Yet he was not by any means great except as a Lothario among women and a good fellow among men. In those fields he was surpreme for his charm and his genuine affability were noteworthy. Fortunately he added to these qualities a genuine and intelligent devotion to the arts and it is this quality in him that has made his name live. He was the sponsor and patron of the new art, the French Renaissance, which did great service in reviving national artistic enthusiasm and which committed a monstrous crime in causing the old Gothic to be despised.

The motto of the Salamander was *Nutrisco et Extinguo*— I subsist on it and I extinguish it. The *it* is, of course, *fire* in the case of the crawling four-footed salamander. The two-footed royal Salamander meant by "it" just what Elinor Glyn and Clara Bow meant, when, some four hundred years later, they succeeded in grafting the pronoun upon the "street language" of America. Francis lived on love, breathed it forth, and devastated the ladies who were about him in his nomadic court life, but unlike the mythical salamander he never extinguished the fire. He came much nearer to extinguishing, through the prodigality of his gifts to his mistresses, the solvency of France itself.

The château where Francis lived at Blois far outshadows the cathedral and although this book must not trespass on the great and glamorous field of the Loire châteaux in general it would be overconscientious in denying itself any glimpse of the great building which sounds the keynote of the town. Well I remember my introduction to this building. With a group of ladies, all English except one, I stood in the courtyard admiring the unsurpassed beauty of that spiral outer staircase called *L'Escalier d'Honneur* in the Francis I wing. We were waiting for the guide who was a little too deliberate, we thought, in giving us his attention. Presently he arrived suave, urbane, equipped with excellent English. One of the English women, ruffled by the long delay, prepared to bait him. I could feel it coming.

"Whom does that figure represent?" she asked severely, pointing to one of the female statues in a niche on the stairway.

"We do not know, madame," replied the guide with becoming dignity. "It is supposed to be an allegorical figure representing peace."

"Isn't it Diane de Poitiers?" The question boomed forth in a heavy and threatening contralto.

"No. It is not that, though sometimes it is called so."

"I beg your pardon, guide." The lady's tone was annihilating. "It is Diane. I recognize it. I have seen a postcard of it."

"I have been working in this château, madame, for some ten years. We do not think that it is Diane."

"Excuse me for contradicting you, but I am positive that it is." The militant lady was growing excited, but the guide, inclining his head gravely, said, "Shall we go in now, please?" My respect for French guidehood rose enormously as I witnessed this passage at arms.

The emblems, devices and varied monograms within the château were to me the most enticing thing about it. I came to look for them and to recognize them with delight as we made our rounds through countless rooms. Of course the salamander motif was most conspicuous but there were many other emblems.

Louis XII, the Salamander's predecessor, who was the second husband of the unfortunate Anne of Brittany, is recognizable as Le Porc Epic, the Spiny Pig, that is the Porcupine. His device stands over the main doorway of the Louis XII wing.

A pair of wings always represents Louise of Savoy, the

mother of the Salamander. The symbolism is a bit self-conscious here. The French word for wings—*ailes*—is pronounced exactly like the letter "L" which stands properly enough for Louise.

Francis' wife, Claude, is represented by a swan pierced with an arrow. The lady was *dépourvue d'agréments physiques* and even limped a little. Therefore she was never able to command anything more satisfying than respect from her sultan-like lord but she was loved by the people for her gentleness and purity. Her motto, a bit cold and cheerless perhaps, was *Candida Candidis* (white upon white).

Of the numerous crowded initials and monograms in the château none is so amazing as that of Henry II, son and successor of the Salamander. It was something like this:

The H is for Henry. The two uprights of the H are for II. The C is for Catherine de Medici, Henry's wife. The D is for Diane of Poitiers, his mistress.

The three sons of this cheerfully bigamous monarch all came to the throne in turn and the third of them, who was Henry III, perpetrated in the château of Blois one of the foulest murders that ever stained the castle's checkered annals. The victim was the Duke of Guise, *Le Balafré*, which means "Scarface," a nickname not unknown in America. The story is very familiar and can only be given here in skeleton form. Guise was a bitter opponent to Henry and a claimant to the throne of France. Henry invited him to Blois and laid a deliberate trap for him. He carried his plans to the uttermost length of compelling a group of nuns to *pray* for the success of his murder.

Very early on a winter's morning, two days before Christmas, Le Balafré responded to a summons to Council from the king. He had had countless warnings of danger but spurning them all went boldly to the château.

"He was eating some prunes, by the fireplace, when the Council was called to order. The king was not present.

"In a moment the king's secretary entered and said: 'Monsieur, the king asks for you; he is in the old cabinet.'

"The Duke threw his prunes on the table, asking: 'Who'll have some?' then he went to the king's cabinet. When he came to the tapestry which hung before the door, the assassins fell upon him. He fought furiously and the struggle lasted two or three minutes. The end was in the king's own chamber, at the foot of his bed, Henry crying 'Finish him!'

"When he was finished, Henry approached the body, and touching it with the end of his sword, said: 'Mon Dieu! how tall he is!' "

The quoted paragraphs from a popular guide are almost the very words of the suave gentleman who told the story to the English ladies and me. This murder, brilliantly fictionized by Dumas, was one of the great classics of crime. To the weak and vicious monarch who planned it to the minutest detail its success was convincing. Here, beyond question, was heaven's answer to prayer. The king's hired pleaders must have stated their case well when invoking the divine blessing.

But the story has a sequel. Just seven months later Henry himself was murdered—by a hard-praying monk named Clément.

This cheery subject seems to lead one's thoughts directly to the Cathedral of Blois which is a standing monument to the murder of architectural taste, though much of it was built by Louis XIV's famous architect, François Mansart, who gave his name to the mansard roof. How is one to account for a cathedral so bad lying within a stone's throw, so to speak, of Chartres, Le Mans and Bourges? The answer is that Saint-Louis-de-Blois was not born of the old faith but was laboriously erected, without enthusiasm, and chiefly for a political purpose—to aid in subduing and overawing the troublesome Huguenots.

Critics call the style of this church "bastard Flamboyant." True Gothic had come to be despised, yet the architects paid it the dubious tribute of superimposing upon a mongrel Flamboyant structure certain superficial Gothic trappings, "gaping gargoyles and stunted buttresses." They perpetrated all sorts of crimes, also, even on the Flamboyant. The curious fact has been pointed out that many of the thoroughly bad churches of France are dedicated to St. Louis. What a peculiar misfortune for one of the noblest men that ever lived! He became fashionable, alas, as a saint, at a period when architectural taste, at least in the matter of churches, was at a very low ebb. The royal saint who built the incomparable Sainte-Chapelle at Paris was thus doomed to lend his name and patronage to a group of ugly, uninspired churches throughout the land he ruled.

If the cathedral of Blois is in itself an unmitigated failure, its setting, high above the Loire, is nevertheless superb. The garden of the *Ancien Evêché* behind it is one of the most delectable places in all the Loire valley. It commands a magnificent view and its own attractions match those of the distant prospect. I well remember—and always shall—the ordered ranks of the horse-chestnut trees snowing their pink and white blossoms steadily upon myself and others who walked beneath them. And the flower patches were of bluest forget-me-not bordered now with white pansies and now with yellow.

Jeanne d'Arc is conspicuous in this park and effaces memories of sordid and philandering kings. This particular statue of her, an equestrian one, given by an American, was executed by a Massachusetts sculptor, Anna Vaughan Hyatt, whose other statues of the Maid, on Riverside Drive, New York, and in the Cathedral of St. John the Divine, have attracted wide interest.

The steeply sloping river-edged town of Blois is wonderfully attractive and *sympathique*. "Seated on the north bank of the Loire, it presents," says Henry James, "a bright, clean face to the sun and has that aspect of cheerful leisure which belongs to all white towns that reflect themselves in shining waters."

To me, as a Bostonian, Blois had a special appeal. It was a sort of message from home, for the name De Blois is a familiar and respected one in the capital of the Bay State. In Boston, to be sure, it rhymes with Joyce and Royce but none the less all those who bear it must have, I suppose, some blood in their veins inherited from dwellers in this town. They are wandering sheep from the fold of the royal Salamander.

## CHAPTER XVII

# Poitiers, Mighty in Battle

POITIERS seems almost like a light-flooded prize-ring; for three great fights, if not precisely "billed" here, did actually occur and each was essentially a no-quarter fight between two individuals. I shall appoint myself announcer and call the fights one by one. The megaphone is at my lips.

### Clovis the Frank versus Alaric the Visigoth
### Time, 507

Clovis had been a Catholic Christian for nearly eleven years and had found the new religion a very profitable venture. It was a powerful buttress to his ambitions and made him in the eyes of his people a holy leader. He turned his attention southward and beheld a distressing thing. "It grieves me," he said, "to see the misbelieving Visigoths [they adhered to the Arian branch of Christianity] in possession of the fairest province of Gaul." With his customary vigor he undertook to rectify this sad state of affairs. Energetically he marched his Frankish army southward and near Poitiers engaged Alaric and his Visigoths in battle. It was rather a world-shaking struggle, for upon its outcome hinged the leadership of Europe. Clovis won and to complete his triumph slew Alaric with his own hand. He was thus the lord of Gaul to the very Pyrenees and the Roman Catholic cause was in the ascendant.

I raise the megaphone again to my lips.

### Charles the Hammer versus Abdur Rahman the Arab
### Time, 732

Established Christianity hung again in the balance. This time, however, the aggression was from the other side, and not from mere heretical Visigoths either but from the terrible Arabs, who had a religion of their own. Their religion exalted and glorified battle instead of merely winking at it. There is no soft talk in the Koran about turning the other cheek. To kill Christians was the dearest desire in each Moslem breast for it not only satisfied a natural longing for bloodshed but it definitely helped the slayer to attain salvation.

Mohammed, the prophet of Allah, had died exactly one hundred years before and this was the year of years to push upward into Europe and capture for Islam the fair land of the Franks. Abdur Rahman was a frightful fanatic and his men were by reputation the hardest-riding fiercest-striking Arabs of all. He arrived at Poitiers in October and started on for Tours.

Charles Martel, the Christian champion, was King of the Franks in all but name. A harmless adolescent named Clotaire bore the title of king, but Charles Martel was Mayor of the

Palace which meant absolute ruler of the Franks. The name Martel was ancient French for Hammer, though it has been modified in modern French to *marteau*. This Frankish Hammer had struck repeated and successful blows against Neustrians and Aquitanians, but the fanatical Arabs were of the type who did the striking first.

Charles awaited them. Christendom was shaken as with a violent ague. Prayer was the order of the day; for surely the God of the Christians, if pleaded with earnestly enough, would take the trouble to save his own.

The Arab horsemen suddenly swept forward with yells that rent the canopy of heaven. They fell savagely upon the Franks, but to their amazement they found that the keen steel swords of Damascus glanced like willow wands from the strong iron helmets of the Franks. They found too, and had no time to be amazed, that heavy Frankish battle-axes did *not* glance from soft turbans. Both sides were brave and the carnage was horrible, but Charles the Hammer won. The repeated charges of Arab cavalry broke upon the massed Frankish warriors, who resembled, says a contemporary chronicler, "an immovable wall frozen by the cold."

School textbooks refer to this famous battle, whose date is actually remembered by three children out of four, as the "Battle of Tours." One knows not the occult reason for this curious title. The French call it the Battle of Poitiers and they ought to know. It occurred almost without question at Moussais, some five miles north of the city.

We are ready for the third bout.

*Edward the Black Prince versus John Goodfellow*
*Time, 1356*

This is the "Battle of Poitiers" of the English and American textbooks, an incident of the Hundred Years War, but really the third battle of that name. British hearts swell with pride at the mention of Poitiers, and with good reason; for Edward and six thousand men soundly whipped John of France and sixteen thousand. His strategy has been likened to Napoleon's at Arcola, for by means of sixty men-at-arms and one hundred archers Edward really turned the tide of battle. Consider the wonder of it! One hundred and sixty men would be no more than a decent meal today for one machine-gun nest, but this intrepid body of fighters was ordered to ride around the flank and attack the French from the rear. They did so and actually created on their enemies the impression of a trap—two armies fighting against one.

The French dauphin disgraced himself by fleeing with his eight hundred lancers; but the king, *Jehan le Bon*, which means really John Goodfellow (a nickname given him because of his convivial habits), fought like a lion with his youngest son, a boy of fourteen, beside him. The picture of this father and son has always been like a drop of balm to the French heart. The boy was a veritable prodigy. He fought brilliantly and is thought to have saved his father's life several times.

"Look out at your right, father," he would shout, or "Look out behind you, father." Finally the valiant pair were disarmed and captured. The Black Prince conducted them to London and treated them with utmost courtesy and even deference, for he had been thrilled by their bravery. At the entry into the English capital he rode beside them bare-headed and at a great banquet he waited upon them himself.

Battles and churches are the warp and woof of Poitiers.

There are not three but seven churches of genuine interest, a most remarkable family, for the Poitevins began building temples to the Christian God almost from the moment they heard of him and one of these, the Temple St. Jean, still exists. It is the oldest Christian church in France.

You are watching me narrowly to see if I am going to start with firstly and conclude with seventhly and, since I fear your beady eye, I will not, though I confess to being tempted. I can think of no other French city where the *variety* of church architecture is so extraordinary.

In Notre-Dame-la-Grande, the most interesting of the family, I had, long ago, an odd experience. I was certainly the tourist *par excellence*, for I carried in my hand not one but two guide-books, one of which was the telltale red-covered Bae-deker. I fumbled with a camera too and was looking over some postcards which were on exhibition just inside the door. At this point a well-dressed French lady approached me, held out a five franc bill, and asked for four francs. I could not understand her desire to enrich me by one franc so I counted out five brass francs in exchange for her bill. She thanked me, obviously not taking notice of what I gave her and then took a one-franc sacrificial candle from the sacristan's sales table and after lighting it fastened it upon a spike before a statue of the Virgin. Very gradually it dawned upon me that she had taken me for the *sacristan*, so I put a franc in the slot for the candle she had "bought." Always that wonderful old Ro-manesque-Byzantine church will be associated in my mind with the candle incident. I do not consider the prying tourist an especially lovely object in a French church but compared with the sacristan he is a delight to the eye. I could scarcely resist playing my rôle a little further, shambling up to the lady and muttering some nonsense about the dates of every object in the church.

The façade of Notre-Dame-la-Grande is its great glory, being both Romanesque and elaborate. The round arch is its dominant note but saints and apostles dress it up charmingly and give to it a resemblance to repoussé work, which means, if I may insult your intelligence for a moment, the appearance of having been beaten up into relief from the inner side as though a goldsmith and not a mason had done it. The gable with its striking medallion of *le Christ triumphant dans la nue* and the stumpy little conical towers *à la* fish scale complete what is perhaps the most appealing Romanesque façade in France. It is like dark wine of some amazing old vintage whose name is lost.

In the garishly renewed interior of the church is one treasure which the Poitevins prize highly, a miracle-working "Virgin of the Keys." She has a whole *"trousseau de clefs"* in her hands to recall her first miracle. In 1202 a traitor stole the keys to the city gates and was about to sell them to the English when this Virgin intervened and miraculously took them from him and saved the city. The only trouble whatever with this miracle is that England already *had* the city in 1202 and had been in possession of it for fifty years. But the faithful of Poitiers are little worried about what historians have to say. After all the Virgin is there in plain sight, the keys in her hands to prove that it is all true, and the sacristan for a few paltry francs will sell to any doubter a learned *opuscule* explaining everything.

The church of St. Hilary is one other architectural curiosity which flatly refuses to be ignored. Its interior is a scramble of round bays, gloomy arches and massive pillars which give the illusion of an ancient temple with endless colonnades. There are *six* aisles beside the nave, a high record among French churches. The vaulting is a system of queer octagons and the choir, on a level a dozen feet higher than the rest of the church, is surrounded by apses. There are really seven beginnings and as many endings to this queer church which grew hit-or-miss out of previous churches ravaged and half ruined by various invaders, especially Abdur Rahman the Arab.

Yes, there is a cathedral in Poitiers, but one is in danger of overlooking the fact. It is large and hopelessly uninspired, heavy and dull outside, uninteresting inside except for a trick of construction to make it look twice as long as it is. The architect narrowed the nave and aisles and lowered the arches toward the choir so that one looks as if through the wrong end of a pair of binoculars. The cathedral seems to go on and on almost to infinity.

The wooden choir stalls do whip lagging minds into attention, for they offer an excellent opportunity to study at close range a medieval church "zoo." Built in the heart of the Great Decades, they contain in the *écoinçons* every animal that the wood-carver had ever heard about from the quaint Bestiaries of the time. Do you, in this pale era, have a clear idea of the appearance of a griffin, a basilisk, a phoenix? If not, come to Saint-Pierre-de-Poitiers.

The griffin has the head and wings of an eagle, the body and tail of a lion. Of his four feet two are aquiline claws and two are leonine paws. He is a grim and efficient watch dog. *Cave Gryphum!*

The basilisk is half barnyard hen and half serpent with bat's or dragon's wings for good measure. Do not let the beast fix his eye upon you or you will die on the spot and the sacristan will be annoyed. I have tracked the basilisk through many works of reference in an attempt to reconcile this Poitiers monster with other basilisks in other churches. This labor was lightened for me by a famous dictionary which brought a smile to my wan cheek by asserting boldly that the basilisk was hatched by a serpent from a rooster's egg. I had heard of suckling fathers but never of egg-laying roosters. More power to them!

The phoenix is a bird too familiar to require much description. Insurance companies have exploited him everywhere. I say "him" advisedly, for there was never really but one of him. He lived for six hundred years in Arabia, and then, feeling old age creeping upon him, built a funeral pyre of gums and spices, fanned it into flame with his stiff old wings and burned his body only to emerge from the flames a fresh young phoenix. We see him in one of the north choir stalls of Poitiers actually achieving this miracle, which puts to shame the puny efforts of Steinach and Voronoff to renew youth.

Eleanor of Aquitaine and her English husband, Henry II, commenced this cathedral and it was somehow or other completed after two and a half centuries. This Eleanor was a most remarkable creature. Adams calls her without qualification the greatest of all French women. She was the dominating kind, much better as someone else's wife than as one's own. At the age of fifteen she married the French king Louis VII and brought him the immense dowry of Aquitaine which was perhaps a quarter of modern France. But Louis fell under the influence of St. Bernard and grew almost ascetic. Eleanor was disgusted. She went with him on a crusade but amused herself at Antioch, according to report, by love affairs with a handsome Saracen slave, with her uncle, Raymond of Poitiers, with Saladin himself.

Finally she wearied of her monkish husband and got him to declare that their marriage had been irregular. It was therefore annulled. She took herself and her vast lands to Henry of Anjou who presently became king of England. For Eleanor it was off with the old king and on with the new. She was queen or dowager of England for nearly fifty years and her jealousy became legendary. It is she who is supposed to have poisoned "Fair Rosamond," one of Henry's mistresses.

Eleanor cuts a tremendous figure in any story of Poitiers but the city is more closely associated, in name at least, with the Duchess of Valentinois who was the celebrated Diane de Poitiers. I have mentioned this lady in connection with Rouen, where she was a correct widow, and in connection with Blois, where she was an incorrect but very potent queen, the "left-hand queen" of Henry II, whose real wife and queen was Catherine de Medici. Diane was in her fortieth year when she became the mistress of Henry, who was nineteen. What an easy mark the boy king must have seemed. Diane, a ripe and vigorous woman, was reputed very beautiful, though her portraits do not fully bear this out. She knew, at any rate, how to dazzle a boy king. She had married the seneschal of Normandy four years before Henry was born and could have been a mother to him, but she chose rather to be his mistress. It is a tribute to her strength of will and cleverness that, although Catherine de Medici was twenty years her junior and was clever as well as youthful, Diane absolutely effaced her rival during the whole of Henry's life. We have seen that Henry's official monogram contained a linked C and D for Catherine and Diane but the legal union was practically all that the young queen could call her own. She was forced to remain discreetly in the background while a rapacious outsider won and retained all the king's devotion.

It is not difficult to imagine what Catherine must have thought of Diane, what sizzling epithets she must have secretly hurled at her, but she had sense enough to smile and bide her time. When Henry died Catherine finally asserted herself. Diane was then sixty and her most strenuous efforts to retain her youthful looks were insufficient. Catherine was in her prime and took pains to humiliate her old rival in every possible way. Her unabating spleen is easy to understand. For twenty years she had been repressing her rage and mortification. Now she hunted "the other woman" through a depressing old age to a dishonorable grave.

A more appealing figure than either of these selfish beauties or even than the great Queen Eleanor is that of a certain peasant girl. Did you perchance assume that you had *escaped* the Maid of Orléans? Indeed you have not, for a great episode of her career took place in the *Salle des Pas Perdus* of the Poitiers Palace of Justice. Hither she was sent by the puzzled King Charles to be questioned by the Doctors of the University who composed the French Court of Parliament. They were to determine whether she was a witch or a spy or perhaps a genuine ambassadress of heaven. The learned men put her through a severe cross-examination of four weeks duration and finally professed their belief in her genuineness. Jeanne hastened to Blois and then to her great task at Orléans.

The picture of this seventeen-year-old girl questioned so earnestly by the most learned men of France is strangely moving and also strangely reminiscent of a similar scene in the temple of Jerusalem when a certain Child of Nazareth was

Laon's cathedral rises from a lofty ridge. Unique in France, its towers commemorate the oxen which toiled up the slope dragging stones. Sixteen of the beasts peer out from the towers.

The immense brick fortress which is the cathedral of Albi is dedicated to Sainte Cécile, gentlest of the lady saints. Its west tower frankly forgot religion and became an impregnable stronghold.

The cathedral of St. Front in Périgueux is a curiosity. It is Byzantium-in-Aquitaine. Mother of all the domed churches in France, it attained its present appearance, a disturbing dream of the Orient, through restoration.

Notre-Dame-la-Grande of Poitiers, though an ancient Romanesque church, manages to present a west front that has been compared to the work of goldsmiths rather than masons.

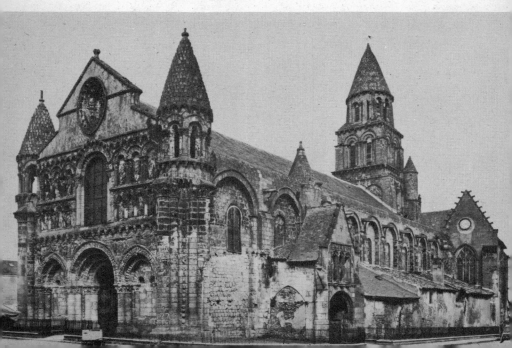

found arguing with the doctors. Jeanne d'Arc was the conspicuous outcropping, claims Adams, of a common type of medieval French maiden. She was no great shock to the men in the street, who fully expected her to do what she promised. "There were Jeannes in every village. Ridicule was powerless against them. Even Voltaire became what the French call frankly 'bête,' in trying it."

Poitiers is one of the towns one easily loves. Its situation on a high promontory between two rivers is full of charm and its streets are quaint and winding. Calvin and Coligny both took shelter here; but Protestantism, which tended to cause an architectural blight on such cities as it captured, never secured any great power in this stronghold of the old church. The cathedral, which was made a *Basilique Mineure* by Pius X in 1912, contains a large bronze Saint Peter (his great toe shiny, as usual, from the kisses of the faithful), and across the River Clain rises the colossal gold Virgin of the Dunes to guard the city and remind it and us that the Queen of Heaven is still a power to be reckoned with.

## CHAPTER XVIII

# Domes and Minarets in Aquitaine:
## Angoulême—Périgueux—Cahors

THERE is a marked touch of the Byzantine about many of the cathedrals of old Aquitaine. Scholars are at great pains to explain this and the explanations simmer down virtually to this: the influence is there because, as you see, it is there. There is vague talk about Levantine merchants and trade routes, but one of the chief Levantine colonies was in Limoges and the cathedral of this city is anything but Byzantine. It is most interesting, however, regardless of causes, to find in the heart of France such an extraordinary group of domes and minarets. Angoulême is a surprise, Périgueux a positive shock. By the time we reach Cahors we are hardened and behold without a blush what even a refined spinster has described in her book as "two heavy Byzantine domes like twin breasts" surmounting the cathedral.

My earliest memories of Angoulême are of *brass,* shaped into

musical instruments and blown with lusty lungs through tire-
less lips. Scarcely had I settled myself in a hotel and enjoyed
dinner than my ears were smitten by the brazen strains of the
Priests' March from *Athalia*. I emerged into the glorious June
twilight to find the town band drawn up in a circle in the
Place de la Commune and mightily at work. The band of
Angoulême was not wonderful but the acoustics were. I
walked almost completely around the ramparts from the Jardin
Publique on the west to rue Paul Abadie on the east (Paul was
the "great restorer" of the Second Empire and did some of his
worst work in Angoulême), but nowhere could I shake off that
band. The Prize Song, the Largo, the Marche Militaire were
successively murdered and I overheard the whole thing and
was powerless to stop it.

Angoulême, when in its more rational moods, is one of the
fine old French hill towns much too little known by Anglo-
Saxons. Even Henry James confesses to skipping it on his
"Little Tour in France." Like Poitiers it occupies a promontory between two rivers but the promontory is much higher
and sharper and the view magnificent. Until the late seventeen-
hundreds the town was living in all the unsavory squalor
characteristic of the Middle Ages. The refuse from the bishop's
stables was dumped regularly on the cobbles of the main square
and householders threw their garbage and rubbish into the
street before their doors. There was occasional talk about purchasing a town garbage cart but "each mayor," comments a
local historian dryly, "left to his successor the honor of realizing this progress." No attempt whatever was made to light
the town and nocturnal brawls and robberies were common.

In 1776, the date of an important event in Philadelphia, the
town of Angoulême voted to purchase three lanterns, but two

years later the town fathers were still debating as to whether they should be placed on the streets, and if so, where. Then quite suddenly Angoulême began to wake up and has become one of the most progressive hill towns of France.

The cathedral, dedicated to St. Peter, is an interesting conglomeration but is primarily Byzantine or at least domical. Its three inner domes, over the nave, are covered externally by the slanting roof but the central lantern is a huge "breast" which dominates the church and even the town. The north tower is a sort of Florentine campanile with six stages, and has the amazing distinction of having been torn down by Abadie and his wreckers and rebuilt by them in the same way from the same materials. The turrets of the west front are fish-scale cones in the manner of Notre-Dame-la-Grande and the pediment is of the Rhine Rhenish, that is, ornamented by many a round arch applied to the surface. The gable completes the architectural mélange, being purely Abadian, for the pet architect of Napoleon III had a free hand to do what he liked.

This man Paul Abadie must have been nearly half as active as Viollet-le-Duc himself. He restored a number of churches and built new ones almost by the dozen, including two at Angoulême. His crowning triumph came in 1874 when his design won the great contest for the erection of a church on the hill of Montmartre in Paris. Tremendous storms of abuse had raged around his head and yet the Congress of Architects, after ten years' consideration, voted for Abadie's plan and today his church floats like an astonishing Byzantine banner on the summit of the Wicked Hill. It is the first thing travelers see when they approach Paris from the north or east and it has unquestionably added its note and not a slight or unimportant one to the immense symphony that is Paris. The architect drew his inspiration straight from Aquitaine and particularly from St. Front of Périgueux which he had restored, so if you know whence came the Aquitanian urge toward the Byzantine you can trace the full pedigree of the Parisian basilica of Sacré-Coeur. Nobody likes this church but somehow everybody loves it, at least if it is sensible enough to "keep its distance." It seems scarcely to be meant for prayer but rather for being gazed at from afar.

"Spicy" is the adjective that characterizes Angoulême's history, both secular and ecclesiastical. Where the Hôtel de Ville now stands, built by the inevitable Abadie, there once stood the *château comtal*, and here Marguerite d'Angoulême, called also Marguerite de Valois, was born. This clever noblewoman, who was also a queen of Navarre, was characterized by a sweet disposition and unusual strength of mind and yet it is largely her own fault that she is known today to the literary bootlegger of America. She wrote devotional poems, charming letters and the Heptameron. This work, which critics praise for its charm and even for its fine feeling and delicate sentiment, is devoted to sensuality, like the Decameron of Boccaccio upon which it is modeled. Five gentlemen and five ladies are marooned by floods on their way home from the Pyrenees and beguile the tedious days by telling love stories. Each guest was to tell a story to the others for ten successive days; but Marguerite died when only seventy-two stories had been completed, so the work remains a Heptameron or Seven Days' Tales. Since there is evidence that Marguerite's court circle, which was one of the most brilliant in Europe, collaborated with her in the writing of the Heptameron, it would appear that brilliant gentlemen and ladies of the sixteenth century actually did talk to one another in the unabashed vein of the party pictured in the book.

Marguerite was born six months to a day before Columbus sighted the first island of the New World. She was the beloved sister of Francis I and became the maternal grandmother of Henry of Navarre. A charming, gay and yet spiritual woman, she should somehow be brought out of shabby obscurity and allowed to make her headquarters, say, in the Women's City Club of Boston, Massachusetts, though perhaps she would like to be consulted about this arrangement.

The cathedral of Angoulême has had a checkered story and here too there has been spice enough for any church. Cruelty, which has so often been the handmaid of religion, had its place when harassed Huguenots were compelled to stand, dressed only in their shirts, to hold the lighted candles for the Catholic masses which they abhorred. Revenge, which is properly Jehovah's, had its place when the Huguenots in 1569 flew at the hated cathedral and tore down its south tower, ruined its lantern and furiously smashed its grand sculpture.

Bishops of all stripes have raised the Sacred Host in Saint-Pierre-d'Angoulême but none more strange in character than Octavien de Saint-Gelais who was gently styled the Gentle Bishop. This youth, given to gaiety and amorous adventure, was a favorite of Charles VIII and suavely overrode the candidates of the Angoulême chapter for bishop when a vacancy occurred. With the king's backing he had himself installed as bishop. He had to prepare as an integral part of the installation ceremony a metrical paper on some religious subject. What he chose was the very rankest travesty, and its success shows the abject subservience of the chapter at that time. His paper, dedicated to Charles VIII, dealt with one of the most unsavory love affairs of Aeneas Sylvius Piccolomini, who became Pope Pius II. Of course there was sounding piety in the paper, which proclaimed itself "under the shield of the Holy Trinity," and its most voluptuous passages were handled deftly and with faultless taste. It was accepted as not without ecclesiastical merit and how the Gentle Bishop must have roared with laughter when he discreetly met his friends after the ceremony.

Octavien was not a phenomenon. There were many of his type in many a medieval church, tongue-in-the-cheek bishops who were in the game for what they could get out of it; but there were more, far more, who were sincere, devout, even wholeheartedly consecrated. It is silly to believe anything else, for great cathedrals do not rise at the behest of prelates like Octavien.

The cathedral of Angoulême is an appealing one today, despite its jumble of styles and despite the hard, eyepiercing coldness of the interior which is an unpleasing tribute to Paul Abadie's mathematical mind. It is in a perennial state of poverty and the faithful communicant as well as the visitor has to be continually prodded and urged to give. This pathetic lament is posted on the door:

"Some time ago our clock stopped after several ineffectual repairs and now we are obliged to stop the harmonious peal of bells, owing to the bad state of the belfry. Soon our beautiful organ will be out of use." The dirge goes on and on followed by a tearful appeal for money and the assurance: "God will reward you a hundredfold!"

In connection with this printed appeal I received my first intimation that I was approaching Spain for the whole thing was set into Spanish, commencing with the flattering saluta-

tion: *A los nobles visitantes de nuestra Catedral*—and concluding, *Díos se lo pagara con el centuplo!* I could not resist this
appeal, gave a sum of money (I have an impression that it was
at least a French dime) and transferred myself to Périgueux.

St. Front, the cathedral of Périgueux, is called the mother of
all the domed churches in France. It is one of the very great
curiosities of that country and it is even a great church in spite
of the ravages inflicted upon it by all its enemies. Time, fire,
the Huguenots and the Revolution all damaged it. They were
the ordinary enemies. But then, almost in our own day, came
Paul Abadie. I must pause to bring the ink in my pen to a boil,
for it is positively improper to write of Périgueux and Abadie
without raging.

No one seems to know who built the original St. Front or
why. It is Syria or Venice in Aquitaine and may have been
erected in the tenth or eleventh century. At that time and
until much later there were two Périgueux, an upper and a
lower. The upper, called the Puy St. Front, was centered
around the abbey and its amazing Byzantine church, the lower
or *cité* centered around the cathedral of St. Etienne, whose
bishop looked with undisguised jealousy at the powerful abbot
in the upper town. When the abbey, following the trend of
the centuries, inevitably declined and when Huguenots completely destroyed St. Etienne the bishop boldly "moved up
higher" and appropriated St. Front, which became the cathedral in 1669.

Until the commencement of the Abadie Crime (my pen
is almost at a boil now), this church was one of the supreme
treasures of architecture. It is considered not only as the
Mother of the French Dome but also the Mother of French
Gothic, by which is meant that here the round arch began to

grow obtusely pointed. But Abadie liked the round arch and used it exclusively. He liked stunning distant effects, he liked hard garish interiors. A few hundred thousand francs would have honestly restored St. Front under the guidance of an architect with intelligent affection for the past. Abadie was allowed to spend many millions for his personal glorification and for the utter effacement of the past. Listen to the mounting wail of a scholarly Périgourdin of the local Archaeological Society who witnessed the crime:

"We have watched these mighty piers torn down piecemeal—; we have seen walls and cupolas and the Gothic choir levelled to the dust—. Even the sculpture has been replaced, nearly all of which was in perfect preservation. Every scrap of this precious old work has been thrown away as rubbish and replaced by copies absolutely devoid of character and interest."

All this substantially true, but Abadie was not content. His fertile mind devised new uglinesses. The blatant crudeness of the oak fences enclosing the nave, the lighting posts placed at intervals, the incongruous walnut pulpit, the screaming garishness of the Stations of the Cross are all minor witnesses to his power.

I had read comparatively little of the Abadie Crime when I first entered the cathedral and was scarcely prepared—even by the Cathedral of Angoulême—for the chilling effect of the interior. It is a feeling hard to describe. An indefinite sense of unhappiness invades one's whole system. Certainly the Virgin of the thirteenth century would have refused to live in such a sanctuary. It would be suitable perhaps for Euclid's mother in some new mathematical religion. But the furnishings would have to be wiped out.

The plan of the cathedral is a Greek cross with a great central dome and four slightly smaller domes over the four arms. A special feature is the narthex or vestibule at the western end, this word being one which I am emboldened to use here because the Rockefeller church on Riverside Drive, New York, has made it familiar to many thousands, as it has also the word triforium. In the narthex there congregated in former times the catechumens, or candidates for confirmation. Today these catechumens gather in St. Front not in the narthex but in two curious choir chapels that look like bowling alleys and are called *confessions*. I saw and heard a large group of these children at work in one of the *confessions* and was considerably cheered thereby. They were good enough to be somewhat plausible as catechumens, bad enough to seem very much like real children and as pretty as only French children know how to be. The Abadie Crime worried them not the least bit in the world. From a distance, especially from the banks of the River Isle you look at St. Front and are in danger of forgiving or even acquitting Paul Abadie. The effect is magnificent, stunning. You cannot get enough of it. Is it all one church or is it perhaps the city of Stamboul? Can only seventeen thousand persons be accommodated in it or is the number one hundred and seventeen thousand? There are five domes and thirteen little minarets and the effect of the ensemble is like stepping stones from east to west, from the crowded old houses of Périgueux almost to heaven itself.

The Western tower is the brilliant climax of all this climbing. Placed on the highest point of the Puy it dominates the whole town. It is said to be the *only* Byzantine campanile in the world and it is also the only thing about the old church that Abadie did not damage. A heavy base, two graceful cubes, a rounded colonnade and a tiled conical dome. There you have the tower's inventory but its beauty can not be measured out in words. It is one thing that is remembered by those who have seen every cathedral in France.

Périgueux has ever so many things which those of tender conscience try to see, Roman ruins, the former cathedral, memorials to three great Périgourdins, Montaigne, Fénelon and General Daumesnil. But who cares about all that? The one thing worth doing in Périgueux is to gaze at St. Front and keep at a distance from it.

Cahors is an ecclesiastical anticlimax to Périgueux, but in every other way it is one of the most interesting towns of old Aquitaine. Its history reeks with picturesque wickedness, it has produced more than its share of famous men, including Pope John XXII and the fiery Léon Gambetta, and it is today one of those lost towns of southern France which are worth crossing an ocean or two to see. It lies within a perfect U formed by the River Lot and on three sides are steep wooded hills. The air is filled with the sound of hurrying waters and from the heart of a lofty rock emerges a limpid spring which formerly gave the town its name (Divona or Holy Fountain) and which now gives it an unfailing supply of purest drinking water, some two hundred gallons per second.

I first arrived in Cahors in the evening, a procedure I recommend to others. There is a wonderful mysterious charm about the place when night has fallen and all the 12,706 inhabitants have gone to bed. There seem to be no bright lights to attract human moths and the brooding stillness is so great that the river sends forth its cheerful little hum like an unending murmur of wind in trees. I walked through the main street of the town at nine-thirty, meeting scarcely a soul, and had come to the conclusion that I was almost a scandal, an outland brawler making the night hideous with my footfalls, when suddenly, entering the outer reaches of the enormous main square, I saw after all some bright lights and a milling crowd of at least fifty persons. Imagine my delight upon discovering that the night life of Cahors centered about a small portable stage on which a company of wandering actors was present-ing—*Hamlet.*

I joined the standing "mob" and gave myself up to the sheer delight of listening to the familiar classic lines rendered (and often ranted) by leather-lunged outdoor actors bent on killing off any competitive noise. Polonius was lecturing Laertes as I arrived and this is what I heard:

> *Le Prêteur perd son prêt et l'ami qu'il oblige*
> *L'Emprunt use le nerf qu'un bon ménage exige*
> *Mais surtout sois fidèle à toi-même: il s'ensuit*
> *Aussi certainement que le jour suit la nuit*
> *Que tu dois l'être à tous.*

How desperately feeble some of these lines sound when com-pared with the original. Survey the lumbering verbiage in the second French line above and then think of the bard's actual words, as crisp as an October day—

"Borrowing dulls the edge of husbandry."

And again consider the five most famous lines of this most famous masterpiece and compare the words of the French Melancholy Dane as they rolled over the heads of the awe-struck Cahorsins:

To be, or not to be, that is the question:
Whether 'tis nobler in the mind, to suffer
The slings and arrows of outrageous fortune,
Or take arms against a sea of troubles,
And, by opposing, end them?

*Etre ou n'être pas, telle est la question.*
*Vaut-il mieux endurer la persécution,*
*Les coups poignants du sort, ou bien prendre les armes*
*Contre cet océan de douleurs et d'alarmes*
*Et mettre à ses assauts un terme en résistant?*

I doubt not the translation is clever but it goes to show that Shakespeare cannot be really appropriated to another tongue. How downright laughable are the following attempts to achieve the impossible:

Ay, there's the rub. *Ah! voilà la problème.*
A little more than kin and less than kind.
*Un peu plus que mon oncle, un peu moins que mon père.*

But such quibbling complaints are after all unworthy of the scene. Rarely have I enjoyed an evening so much. Hamlet and Ophélie soliloquized or wept or went mad as the occasion demanded. Rozencrantz and Guildenstern did their duty. The grave diggers dug. And the stars shone and the river murmured.

The light of day revealed Cahors as little less charming than it had first appeared by starlight and lamplight. Lovely tree-shaded quays with interesting names, Champollion, Aguesseau, Cavaignac, bordered the river, and a fine wide boulevard, named for Gambetta, bisected the U of the town. This Boulevard Gambetta which in very early times formed the western boundary of the town is one of the outstanding provincial Main Streets of France. Besides being attractive, even, at times, fascinating in its own right, it is like the central theme in a colorful symphonic poem. It links on one strong thread patriots and base usurers, fighting heretics and hypocrites, generals and a poet or two.

First in interest though last in time there is Léon Gambetta himself. His father, who was a Genoese, kept a grocery shop close to the cathedral and a part of its sign, reading Bazard Génois, is still to be seen. For France it was an amazing stroke of fortune that the grocery business seemed to that man better in Cahors than in Genoa; he thus bequeathed a son destined to be a founder of modern France. By what is almost a fluke of chance, Italy had lost Nabulione Buonaparte to France a few decades earlier. Now, by another odd chance, she lost young Gambetta, whose genius burned with a purer flame than that of Napoleon and with almost as much power.

His life was too full and admirable to be packed into a nutshell here, but we cannot resist noting the romance and tragedy of it. At the age of thirty-three Léon met a lady, named oddly Léonie Léon. He could not have been much to look at, for he had accidentally lost an eye at the age of fifteen but she loved him and he loved her. This passion was the rudder of his life from then on, but how different was her fine influence from that of the various mistresses of the various kings of France. True, she never married him but this was solely because she feared to compromise his career. Oh yes, they sometimes lived together and those who will may condemn them for this irregularity. Léon consulted his Léonie frequently on the most vital matters of statesmanship and apparently her advice was intelligent and sound and utterly unselfish.

After eleven years of this liaison, she finally agreed to marry him; for he had never stopped asking her. The date was definitely fixed, but on a certain November day in 1882 when they were together in Léon's home at Ville d'Avray the great statesman, carelessly handling a revolver, shot himself in the hand. On the last day of that year he died from the resulting inflammation. Léon Gambetta, the pride of Cahors, the glory of France, was cut off in the midst of his usefulness and poor Léonie Léon lived on to become old and a bit garrulous. I hunted up Gambetta's birthplace in Cahors, a rather dreary gray plaster affair occupied by a cobbler, a painter, a tailor and an electrician. It is Number 9 on a street now named for another patriot who was thus honored all over Europe. It is rue du Président Wilson.

In its early days Cahors became notorious for a group of Lombard usurers who set up their shops in a little square just off the present Boulevard Gambetta. They must have been a hardboiled and detestable crew for they made the word Cahorsin synonymous with usurer and brought to the town an extremely malodorous reputation. Dante in the eleventh canto of the Inferno actually linked the city with Sodom. Hell, says the poet,

> "doth
> Seal with its signet Sodom and Cahors."
> ("*suggella
> del segno suo e Soddoma e Caorsa.*")

This frightful condemnation was called forth purely by the greed of the Cahorsin money-lenders, whom he characterized as "disdaining nature and her bounty." The tremendous spread of their operations is indicated by Matthew Paris who wrote in 1235 of "the horrible nuisance of the Caursines," which prevailed "to such a degree that there was hardly any one in all England, especially among the bishops, who was not caught in their net." The chronicler always did like to make a good story.

John XXII seems to guard the northern gate of Cahors, where the main *route* from northern France merges with the Boulevard Gambetta. His palace, though perhaps he never saw it, used to stand here and a crenellated square tower of it still exists. It is something of a distinction to be the twenty-second of anything that calls for Roman numerals. I do not think it has been done in this era except by the Johns of the Vatican, who reached XXIII. There have been sixteen Gregorys and fifteen Benedicts and of course eighteen Louis of France but only the Johns have exceeded a score, which is utterly unimportant except for one thing. The *last* of the Johns died in 1419. There have been fifty-five popes since then and not one of them has cared to call himself John. In part this is unquestionably due to the evil repute of John of Cahors who was XXII.

Greed and worldliness seem to be particularly unlovely in very old people and more especially in old popes. John of Cahors won the election at the age of seventy and, until death at last claimed him, he dragged the papacy, then in its period of captivity at Avignon, through a mire of controversy in which little except John's selfishness emerges clearly. He did a great

deal for his native Cahors but by the greater part of Europe
he was thoroughly and deservedly hated for his greedy extor-
tions. One of the most amazing things he did was to condemn
and even excommunicate the exalted Franciscans, allowing
four of them to be burned at the stake because they upheld the
literalness of Christ's teaching concerning the blessedness of
poverty. The kernel of the matter was that this teaching did
not harmonize with John's desire, for he was amassing a fortune estimated as high as twenty-five million florins. The Franciscans were a standing rebuke to him and he did not hesitate
to condemn them to perdition. The money rolled into the papal
coffers and Europe groaned under its burdens, waiting for the
wretched old man at Avignon to die, which he finally did at
the age of eighty-nine.

Like a refreshing breeze comes the thought of two beloved
generals of Napoleon, Bessières and Murat, who were born
near Cahors. The latter in particular serves to efface the sordid
memory of John XXII and bring high color to our picture. As
"the finest cavalry officer in the world," as the husband of
Napoleon's sister Caroline, as the picturesque King of Naples,
he is still the pride of the Cahorsins, second only to the lofty-
spirited Gambetta.

It seems almost an intended joke of this new-old town that
the street of a twentieth-century American war president leads
to the most perfect medieval bridge in France, the celebrated
Pont Valentré, which spans the Lot on the western edge of
Cahors. It is magnificent in its frowning yet somnolent beauty,
a bridge six hundred meters long, *à dos d'âne très accentué*, to
use a guide-book phrase meaning "very exaggerated donkey-
back." Three fine square towers and a barbican serve to guard
it and six Gothic arches support it. Only yesterday, in 1880

to be precise, was the last stone of this bridge laid, for the devil built it under agreement with an architect who exchanged his soul for the devil's skill, but since the soul was not to be given over until the last stone was laid the clever architect, a *Frater Barbatus* perhaps, compelled the devil to bring up *in a sieve* the water for the setting of the upper stone of the central tower. The devil was beaten by superior wit and a humdrum French Republican mason finally completed the job five or six centuries later. If you do not believe this story you have only to climb the tower, and look at the stone. It is new and so the story must be true.

The cathedral, dedicated to St. Stephen, has been awaiting our attention with phlegmatic patience. It is not great at all, but immensely queer. It has a touch of every style except perhaps the Abadian. The west front is by some chance heavily North German, the vast twin domes, greater in size than any built in France during the Middle Ages, are more or less Byzantine, the apse is Gothic. It is to the domes that one's attention is continually drawn. They really are what the lady writer called them and yet they are anything but voluptuous.

The interior of the cathedral is of a dazzling white-washed brilliance not unlike that of a well-kept hen-house but the cloister and the *maison des abbés* are full of ancient charm. I allowed a sacristan, loaded to the gills with dates, to escort me, and in spite of his dates I actually found the man interesting. He told me a great deal about Henry IV, who came from the gaieties of his court at Nérac in 1580 to capture and pillage Cahors. Being then a Protestant he took especial delight in sacking the cathedral and finally rode off with much of its treasure, including the *Sainte-Coiffe*, chief treasure of all, which is the very blood-stained shroud that swathed the

Savior in the tomb. Henry admired the *châsse* which contained the shroud but cared nothing for the sacred *coiffe* itself, which he threw to the ground. An old woman saw the blessed cloth, lovingly gathered it up—and sold it back to the town of Cahors for forty litres of wheat. This story may be true and so may the *coiffe* itself. The sacristan said it was made of "Cleopatra Cloth" twenty-five hundred years old, but did not explain why cloth already five centuries old was used for the wrapping of the Lord's body.

One point, one major doubt concerning this sacred *coiffe*, strikes the visitor instantly. If the Cahorsins of old believed firmly in the authenticity of this shroud and the blood stains which they saw upon it, why did they not build a cathedral worthy of it? There is no good answer to this, although one may say that it was, after all, only a relic of Jesus and not a relic of His Blessed Mother.

I am bothered by a suspicion that I have lingered too long in Cahors, but if I have been guilty it is because of my deep and lingering affection for the place. It is a Joseph's Coat among towns. All the colors, including black and white, are to be found here in plenty woven into that charming U-shaped nest which the hills and the river have built.

## CHAPTER XIX

# *Toulouse, the Languedoc Capital*

CATHEDRAL book writers as a race manifest an unreasonable skittishness in writing about the fair capital of Languedoc, simply because its cathedral happens to be very bad. But may one not argue that that is all the more reason for writing of it? Good cathedrals may be found in scores of towns, but where will one come across one so magnificently bad as St.Etienne-de-Toulouse? To me it is fascinating, like a blue-ribbon bulldog for ugliness, like Quasimodo for deformity.

St. Etienne had no single architectural parent nor is it even the result of labors by a dynasty of successive builders. It merely happened. It is a confessed accident. Somebody built the Romanesque nave in that dark century which followed "the end of the world," that is in the ten hundreds. It is wide and low and aisleless, an altogether squat and gloomy affair. Somebody else, driven by a dynamic bishop, started in the twelve-hundreds to build a lofty and impressive Gothic choir, intending eventually to destroy the ancient nave and build a new Gothic one. But three hundred years were frittered away on the choir and there was no money or enthusiasm left. The oddest thing resulted, for the choir and nave, while on parallel axes, are not on the same axis. To put it technically, the south aisle of the choir is a direct continuation of the central nave. One's vision must bend and cleverly avoid a massive central pillar in order to take in the whole interior of the church. And if this difficult feat is accomplished, one's mind reels before the shock of the gorgeous choir partnered with such a mean and sorry nave.

But this is not all. In the fourteen-hundreds somebody thought of giving the shabby old nave a new west front and this work was started but it seemed a pity to junk the fine rose window then two centuries old so the window was retained. It did not at all fit the new scheme, did not even come in the center, but was retained anyway. Its center is two or three feet off the line of the main portal and as a sort of apology for this defect another abortive portal crops up to the left of the main one. It seems to be a retention from the earlier scheme but has been blinded and blocked up and otherwise deformed. To crown this scrambled façade, there is a sharp *one-way* slant to the roof, north to south. It might be useful in the case of the rare Toulousan snowstorm but is otherwise completely ridiculous.

There is one tower only, which is a mercy. It stands in square brick ugliness at the north of the façade which I have been so pleasantly depicting. It has no style whatever, or rather a little of every style, with an unsightly white clock in its center like a navel.

At the present time great efforts are being made to erect a

worthy north portal in a style consonant with the Gothic choir, but this can hardly serve to mar the splendid ugliness of St. Etienne. Had the architects of Louis XIV only been entrusted with this job they would have created a Renaissance portal, which is the one incongruous touch now lacking.

This church has been called "not only artistically poor but mathematically insupportable," and yet mathematics of a very high order must have been summoned to make it hang together at all as a single edifice. The central pillar, for example, called the Pilier d'Orléans from the cardinal who built it, is an amazingly interesting and efficient liaison officer between the choir and the nave. It supports a complicated system of twisting arches and does what it can to promote harmony among the motley of styles. It is the most appealing thing about the church and at its base lies the body of one of the most appealing citizens of Languedoc, Baron Peter Paul Riquet de Bonrepos.

This immensely wealthy man devoted nearly his whole life to the successful attempt to link the Atlantic and the Mediterranean by a canal system, of which Toulouse is the center. He studied it for eighteen years, worked out a miniature of it on his estate, begged from Colbert, the minister of Louis XIV, permission to undertake the enterprise, and actually put the gigantic task through *entirely at his own personal expense*, variously estimated at five to twenty million dollars. By a tragic twist of fate he died on the very eve of the actual opening of the canal which has done so much for Toulouse, for Languedoc and for France. The baronial name of this high patriot seems peculiarly appropriate to those who gaze at his memorial before the *Pilier d'Orléans*. One can scarcely avoid murmuring it in reverent admiration. He earned his Good Rest by a lifetime of strenuous unselfishness.

Toulouse is the center of a romantic dying language, the language of *oc*. All southern France, with Catalonia as well, once spoke this tongue, while nothern France spoke the language of *oui*, by which is meant simply that in the south men said "yes" by the syllable "oc" and in the north by the syllable "oui." The north won in the long struggle and became modern French but at Toulouse the battle still goes on, waged picturesquely by a handful of savants who have a tendency to grow less earnest and more playful as the hopelessness and uselessness of it become more and more evident. The patois of the country people of Languedoc can scarcely be called any longer the language of *oc*. It is merely a bad French.

The society which cherishes this dying language is probably the most ancient literary society in Europe and certainly one of the most colorful. It is over six hundred years old and was called originally *Le Collège du Gay Sçavoir*. What infinite charm lies in that old name. What a clod must any educated Toulousan have been not to long for membership. Yet the name was changed after two or three centuries to *Académie des Jeux-Floraux* and as such it exists today. This change was due to one Clémence Isaure, a rich maiden lady of the fifteenth century who has become almost the patron saint of Toulouse. She revived this society, which was sadly languishing, and instituted the Floral Games, leaving a large legacy for their perpetuation.

I once hunted up the handsome medieval Hôtel d'Assézat, which is now the headquarters of the society, and after much ringing of a jangling bell secured the attendance of a wondrous ancient hag, the *gardienne*. She had but one tooth in her head and that a veritable tusk. I explained to her my desire to visit the headquarters of the learned academy but her face did not light up. Grimly she admitted that my wish could be realized. I asked her if Clémence Isaure was a real personage or only a myth as some assert. "That," she said, "is as you wish. One believes in her or not *selon gout*."

Wishing to win the favor of the dour *gardienne* I casually toyed with a young handful of pretty aluminum francs, whereupon a spark of real life glimmered upon the lady's leathery visage. The whole of her gigantic tusk was bared in what I honestly believe to have been a smile. She became positively chatty and took me through all the academy rooms and even up to the roof to see the view. Much floral lore I gathered from this *gardienne* and from hurried staring at the various exhibits. Nine flowers are distributed annually, on May 3, for the best poems and prose compositions in the pure *langue d'oc* which is spoken exclusively by members of the academy when in session. The highest prizes are the amaranth, eglantine and jasmine made of pure gold, the lesser prizes violet, marigold, primrose, lily and again eglantine in silver. The lowest or consolation prize is a silver carnation.

All this seems a bit silly to the cold-blooded Anglo-Saxon—like perfumed bonbons. One can hardly picture members of a British or American authors' club competing in passionate verse in a dead language in the hope of attaining a coveted gold amaranth, but it is after all merely one quaint manifestation of that local loyalty which crops up with varying intensity in every part of every land. The *langue d'oc* is the language of the old troubadours, the same in essence as the Filibrige of Mistral, and has a considerable surviving literature. For two or three centuries it was the most aristocratic language of Europe. For sheer glamour nothing seems to equal it, not even the dying Romansch of the upper Engadine. So it is not surprising that Toulousan poets and littérateurs have striven until very recently with ardor and occasionally with rancor for the revivification of the *oc* language. In the Place Wilson is a statue to Peire Goudouli, a Languedoc poet, with these words as an inscription, which I submit as a sample of the troubadours' tongue. The words translate themselves.

*Nourigate* (nourished) *de Toulouso me pläi de mainteni soun langatge bel.*

From the roof of the Hôtel d'Assézat unfolds a rather extraordinary panorama. Firstly the city of Toulouse, gift of the Garonne, is no mean city. It boasts about 250,000 inhabitants and possesses a very distinct individuality. One does not, somehow, confuse Toulouse with a dozen other provincial cities of France. The Dalbade, Daurade and Jacobin churches catch the eye and more than all mighty St. Sernin, the head of all the noble old family of Romanesque churches in France and the pattern for all churches which affect the "Toulouse style." On the horizon to the north is a monument of striking similarity to that of Bunker Hill. It marks the spot where Marshal Soult and Wellington fought in 1814 the last battle of the Peninsular War which crushed Napoleonic hopes. Sixty-five hundred men threw their lives away in a sacrifice which might have been to Moloch for all the good this futile battle did. Napoleon had abdicated a week before and was on his way to Elba.

The backdrop for the really immense panorama which unfolded itself for me as I stood atop the roof of Hôtel d'Assézat was nothing less than the glorious snow-crowned range of the Pyrenees. There is no mountain system in Europe quite comparable to that of the Pyrenees, which stretches like an immense and glittering curtain of frost between two sun-soaked countries. Toulouse is some fifty miles distant from this curtain but often enjoys a magnificent view of it and sometimes feels its cool influence.

Religious strife with all its ghoulish train of cruelties is the dominant note of Toulousan history. The Languedoc capital was almost a rival of Paris in importance and if any of its counts manifested a lenient or even decently Christian attitude toward heretics within their domain they gave offense or rather excuse to the greedy monarchs of France, who dreaded their ascendancy. The strife culminated in the humiliation of Raymond VII which we have witnessed in Notre-Dame-de-Paris, an affair in which the greatest feudal lord in Europe was exhibited in his shirt to a grinning populace while mass was sung and the Virgin praised. Thereafter the Inquisition was the bloody spiritual dictator in Toulouse.

For centuries religious rebellion and religious persecution alternated. In the middle of the sixteenth century four thousand Toulousan Protestants lost their lives and in the St. Bartholomew massacres three hundred more were murdered outright in one day. In 1619 Lucilio Vanini, a celebrated lecturer, was convicted of atheism. His tongue was torn out, his body burned and the ashes scattered before the wind. Even as late as 1762 occurred in Toulouse one of the most heinous religious murders in history. A certain Jean Calas, Calvinist, successful cloth merchant, was the victim.

This man, high-minded, placid, devoted to all the simple virtues, married a girl named Anne-Rose. Her last name, Cabibel, she was glad to exchange for Calas. They lived happily and produced six children, but religious storms began to play like forked lightning around their heads. Their children could not get jobs because they were despised heretics. One of them abjured the paternal faith, to the great grief of Jean and Anne-Rose. Another, Mark Anthony Calas, wanted to do so but lacked the courage either to risk damnation or to risk failure in this life. He became despondent and one day committed suicide by hanging himself in his father's shop. As if this were not tragedy enough for the anguished parents, a fanatic neighbor accused Jean of murdering his son to prevent his turning Catholic. Actually the court found him guilty though there were no proofs whatsoever. It was merely the old story of mob hatred stirred up by the priests. "Break him! Break the heretic!" snarled the crowd. The jurist Sudre defended him magnificently but the crowd "cried out the more."

Jean Calas was broken on the wheel nine days before his sixty-fourth birthday and his body thrown upon a bonfire. This sort of affair was meat and drink for the ever ready pen of Voltaire. With the same passionate enthusiasm he was to display a little later in defense of the name of the Chevalier de la Barre, victim of fury in Abbeville, he roused literally the entire nation of France. With indomitable energy he collected proofs of the innocence of Calas, wrote pamphlet after pamphlet in his defense, finally shamed the council of Toulouse into convening again and clearing, by unanimous vote, the memory of Jean Calas. This occurred exactly three years, to the day, after the condemnation.

There are three little sequels to this tale. Anne-Rose Calas was given a considerable sum of money by her chastened fellow-citizens and lived on for thirty years. David de Beaudrigue, chiefly responsible for her husband's legal murder, went mad and killed himself. And lastly, religious passion raised its ugly head again a full century later, almost in our own time, and made an effort to re-blacken the memory of

Protestant Calas. But the world had grown. This effort, vigorously fanned, awoke no spark of response. Its authors only succeeded in making themselves asinine.

I gazed long and earnestly one day not into but through the *vitrine* of the Maison Calas. The shopkeeper thought I was fascinated by his display of millinery, but I was in reality trying to determine whether the two *battants* of the entrance door were the same from which Mark Anthony Calas hanged himself. From this gruesome and profitless examination I presently strolled away to the cool and bosky stretches of the *Boulingrin*, presided over by a colossal golden figure of Clémence Isaure, "*Gloire de Toulouse*." The *Boulingrin*, as of course you know (if you are an eager collector of odd words), means Bowling-Green. The French are adepts at altering and refitting any word of any language to their own needs. For a people who can pronounce the name Rockefeller *Rock-Fellaire*, there is nothing startling about the word *Boulingrin*.

The churches of Toulouse, both major and minor, are exceptionally individual like those of Poitiers. Of the minor ones only the Daurade and the Dalbade need catch our eye. In these two words again we note the French facility for adaptation. The first means *deaurata* (made golden) and the second *dealbata* (made white). The golden church recalls an ancient Roman church on the same site, covered over with golden mosaics. In the modern church, under the altar, rest the bones—if any—of Clémence Isaure and here each third of May the gold and silver flowers of the Jeux Floraux are officially blessed.

The Dalbade, ancient worshiping place of the Knights of Malta, whose brick walls were once "made white" with chalk, was until recent times an impressive "Toulouse Gothic" church; but on April 11, 1926, at three in the morning the lofty north tower with its twenty-one bells fell and literally broke the church's back, cutting the nave clean in two. In the vestibule appears nowadays a printed lament describing the tragedy and concluding with these words in heavy capitals:

*"Sainte-Thérèse-de-l'Enfant-Jésus was prayed to for three days before the catastrophe. Plainly she saved the parishioners, the children, the priests. Will she inspire you to contribute to the rebuilding of the church?"*

My own answer, I have to say, and without intended offense to the faithful of that parish, is "no." Whatever little offering I gave was in spite of rather than because of that tinsel appeal, for I learned, though not from the official description of the tragedy, that a baker and his wife *were* killed by the falling tower. The sweet-spirited little saint of Lisieux should not, by all the laws of logic, be given credit for averting tragedy unless that unfortunate baker couple can be explained. Rather should the rising church or at least a chapel of it be dedicated to the two unfortunates who lost their lives. They were as good, I have no doubt, as the average. As matters stand this couple is hushed up as an unfortunate speck in the miraculous ointment.

Of all churches in this much-churched city the greatest, by far, is St. Sernin, dean of all French Romanesque churches. It is often called unblushingly the finest brick building in the world and certainly its splendid dignity makes the jumble of the official cathedral seem not so much charmingly ugly as feeble and absurd, like an old man trying to be funny by wearing his wife's hat.

The west front of St. Sernin is about as plain as any church façade could be. It has no pinnacles, no sculptured saints, no gorgeous rose window. It is not even completed, and yet its lines give a tone of nobility to the whole structure. The sole tower of this enormous edifice rises over the apse and, though almost an architectural dandy by comparison with the severely plain west front, does not in the least destroy the harmony of the church. It is the very essence of the Toulouse style, with five octagonal stages, diminishing in size as they mount upward.

I was once lucky enough to visit Toulouse at the time of *Pentecôte* when St. Sernin becomes even more than usual a Mecca for pious pilgrims. In the open spaces around the church a prodigious fair was raging even during the celebration of high mass. A French provincial fair in full blast must be *heard* to be appreciated. What an appalling bedlam of cheerful bickering and dickering it is! If there was any object short of a portable house and barn not for sale in the squares and streets surrounding St. Sernin that Whitsunday morning, I cannot now recall it. Many booths dealt in pious fripperies and many others in apparel and mundane household articles. I recall too a bookseller's booth at which one of the most prominently displayed books was a paper-covered abomination entitled *Le Véritable Moyen de Forcer l'Amour*.

Very few of the pilgrims seemed to be giving a second thought or even a first thought to this literature, so let us also pass it by and enter the gorgeous interior of St. Sernin. Gorgeous it was indeed that morning, for its very numerous holy relics were all "on parade" as they are every year on *Pentecôte* Sunday. I can scarcely convey any adequate picture of the profound sanctity of this church. A prayer before each one of its seven principal altars will win for the pilgrim exactly the same indulgences as are granted to those who pray before the seven principal altars of St. Peter's at Rome; and the number of saints and apostles whose bones (all or part) lie in reliquaries here pales all other French churches and perhaps all Italian churches. There are scores of them to say nothing of a piece of the true cross (authenticity established by a *Procés Verbal* in 1811), a thorn from the Crown of Thorns, a piece of the Holy Sepulcher and a piece of the Virgin's robe.

On Sunday the crowd jamming every portion of the huge church was too great to permit of any leisurely examination of the relics, so I squeezed myself into a niche close to the choir screen and watched at close range the celebration of high mass. The boys, the little red-robed acolytes, were of wonderful interest to me at this close range. I had wondered more than once what acolytes were really like. On this occasion I was so near that I could have reached through the iron grille and touched them. It was with a sense of real relief that I noted that acolytes are merely boys, just like other boys. These little red-garbed Toulousan cherubs, who were swinging censers, tinkling bells and opening great missals with such unconcern, were also fidgeting and snickering and playing practical jokes on one another and twisting their faces into uncouth grimaces.

I was more than surprised during this high mass to be singled out by a hawk-eyed priest in the ambulatory and almost *commanded* to visit the crypt—for a small fee, of course. I obeyed and found that nearly all the treasures of the crypt were being *exposé* in the nave, but of course my money was just as good in the priestly hand as if I had something for it. Perhaps I did have two bits' worth of pleasure at that, for, since nobody else was fool enough to visit the crypt when all

The cathedral of Toulouse, dedicated to St. Etienne, was built at various epochs and it turned out to be a strange conglomerate monster with nothing architecturally right about it. An impressive Gothic choir is concealed by a mean Romanesque nave, which is not on the same axis.

The west front of St. Gatien, the cathedral of Tours. The chief west window, square but with bulging sides, is called the *grand housteau* or "big west." Only one other important cathedral (Bourges) has the same curious feature. *French National Railroads.*

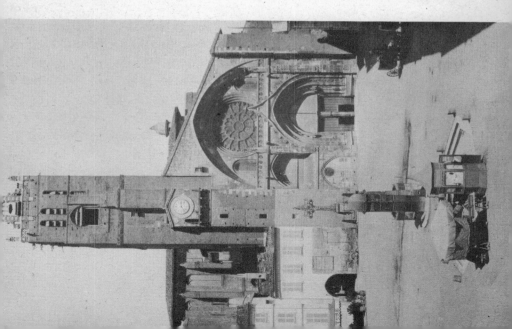

The enormous cathedral in Bourges France has five portals in the west front. It is great in every sense, and has stained glass that ranks second only to Chartres. *Commissariat Général au Tourisme, Photo by Touring Club de France.*

its treasures were gone, I had the place absolutely to myself and was able to study at my leisure the holy lore of St. Sernin.

This would make a life study and I could scarcely scratch the surface that morning or on several other visits which I made. A predecessor of this church was in high favor with Charlemagne and his son Louis le Débonnaire and *his* son Charles the Bald and all of these kings made vast contributions of sacred bones which have been retained in the present edifice. I find in my journal opposite the names of many saints, "Bones by Charlemagne" or "Skull by Ch. the Bald." Suppose we consider the roster a little more definitely. St. Sernin claims one or more bones from the following amazing array of apostles and missionaries:

| | |
|---|---|
| St. Peter | St. Philip |
| St. Paul | St. Simon |
| St. James Major | St. Jude |
| St. James Minor | St. Barnabas |

Of early or medieval church saints it boasts St. Thomas Aquinas, the great religious encyclopedist; St. Vincent de Paul, founder of the Lazarists; St. Gregory, the great Bishop of Rome; St. Catherine, the martyr; St. Agatha, the Virgin of Sicily, who spurned her lecherous ruler; and St. Edmund, King of England, who after eight hundred years in paradise was still sufficiently interested in this earth to save Toulouse from the pest in 1631.

Nearly all of these bones have their post mortem travels meticulously catalogued by the zealous clergy and authenticated, a bit ridiculously it may seem, by a *Procés Verbal*. Take

Jude, for instance, the *Patron des Causes Désespérés*. Scholarship knows nothing whatever about the apostle Jude except that he asked his Lord a question (John XIV, 22), but here in St. Sernin we find his bones and the whole story of them. They were taken from their first resting place in Mesopotamia to Persia and thence to Rome. Charlemagne came upon them, acquired them and sent them to Toulouse. For seven hundred years they were lost; then they were rediscovered amid salvos of rejoicing and "exalted" in the year 1511. Thus Jude, the zero of the twelve apostles. Barnabas, companion of Paul, has a comparatively simple story. He was found in Cyprus in 488 buried "with the Gospel of Matthew on his chest." So far as St. Sernin of Toulouse goes it is the now familiar story— Bones by Charlemagne.

I witnessed on the Monday after *Pentecôte* in this same church a ceremony of wonderful unconscious humor. The sacristan and two assistants were cleaning up after the great day. My own presence was due to my keen desire to see the head of St. Thomas Aquinas, one of the great heads of all time. I finally found it at the left of the nave wrapped tight in cloths and laid away in a sumptuous silver *châsse*. Presently I noticed that I was receiving dark looks from the sacristan. I was, in short, in his way, so I partly withdrew. At that moment he began calling the saintly roll in stentorian tones, and his assistants answered as they located the various saints.

"*St. Thomas-d'Aquin!*"
"*Ici.*"
"*Ste. Suzanne-de-Babylone!*"
"*Ici.*"

"*Ste. Jeanne-de-Toulouse!*"
"*Ici.*"
"*Ste. Scholastique!*"
"*Ici.*"

To me it was amazingly funny and I half expected to hear my name called as St. Touristicus, but then I suddenly recollected that I was no good as a tourist and rarely listened to the voice of conscience. It occurred to me that I had not visited a provincial museum since—Evreux. This really did shock me a trifle, so I made haste to leave St. Sernin and visit the Toulouse Museum, which rewarded me by catching and holding my attention. Its *grand cloître* and *petit cloître* are of particular charm.

Very numerous and noteworthy are the sights and historical celebrities of Toulouse, but it is the animation of the place that one remembers, and the Garonne and the distant white curtain of the Pyrenees. In the era of the *octroi*, those city customs controls that were a minor nuisance throughout France until their abolition in the present decade, I once used this city for a considerable period as travel headquarters. Upon each return the business of the *octroi*, silly survival of medieval feudalism, annoyed me. Unkempt officials glowered at my bag, wondering if it contained any jelly or squabs or country butter, but rarely asking. It was always a hot, slow business emerging from the station. But when finally I reached my room, overlooking the cool and shaded canal that Riquet built, I was "friends with everybody." The street was the Boulevard de Bonrepos, another tribute to the philanthropist and a restful invitation to the stranger who looks down upon it from his hotel window. I always offered a mental toast to Tolosa, ancient city of the Romans, Mecca of the medieval troubadours, modern metropolis of the Midi, bright capital of a dead language.

## CHAPTER XX

## *In the Shadow of the Pyrenees: Auch—Bayonne—Carcassonne*

IT IS pleasant to roam for scores of miles either west or east of Toulouse and be always under the protecting wings of the Pyrenees. Man has dared to look at their snowy peaks, their embattled glacial *cirques,* and then proceed to erect his own puny monuments within sight of them. We may admire such courage and in several cases the artistic intelligence that went hand in hand with courage. One such case is Ste. Marie of Auch, the "swan-song of French Gothic."

The name of this town, which was the old Gascon capital, excites our interest at once. It looks somehow Scotch. It looks *also* German. It seems even to be a suitable exclamation for one who has jammed his finger in a door. But it is actually the ancient capital of the Iberian tribe called Ausci and rhymes more or less with Boche. It has also a delightful old Iberian or Basque name which you may use if you prefer, Elimberris.

Whatever you call it you will like Auch, for it sits upon a striking hill above the Gers and is crowned by a massive yellow-gray cathedral which has the high distinction of being a worthy church erected in an unworthy architectural age. Almost I never went to Auch at all, for it has always promised tedious hours on a French *omnibus*, but I went all the same and rejoice that I did. It is, all things considered, one of the Unforgettables.

Many minutes before my train lumbered into the station, which is in the suburb of Goose Foot (Patte d'Oie), I saw the towering cathedral and was instantly reminded of distant Laon and St. Lô and Coutances. I always revel in the climb *à pied* to the summit of these hill towns and will do so as long as lungs and legs permit. A mere three hundred steps compose the *Escalier Monumental* which leads from the turbid River Gers to the lofty Place Salinis, a sort of Hanging Garden which commands a marvelous view. Here the sense of antiquity, of strolling centuries, captures the imagination and one can believe that this now somber and somnolent town on the hillside and across the river is historically a five-ply capital, of the Iberian Ausci, of the Roman province Novempopulania, of medieval Armagnac, of later Gascony, of the present-day *département* of Gers.

Ste. Marie is the whole sum and substance of the Auch of today, so far as we are concerned. One might chatter about the amazingly gloomy little Romanesque church of St. Orens or the bumpkin life of the main street (rue Gambetta) where small boys flatten their noses against the bookseller's windowpane wishing they had sous enough to buy his lurid offering called "Battling Malone"; but such trifling talk would be out of place in a town so overawed by one great church. This cathedral was actually begun about the year 1500, centuries after the Great Decades, and finished under Louis XIV, yet it is a noble and dignified Gothic church, incongruous to be sure in its jumble of styles but great enough to live this down and impress every beholder with its majesty. Its size is enormous for such a little town and what would be glaring, unforgivable defects in a smaller church are mere peccadillos in this vast and severe cathedral. The façade, of classical design, is wholly out of keeping with the Gothic style of the main structure and some of the interior decorations are fearfully and wonderfully garish, but few people seem much concerned over this. If you dress a seven-foot Gothic giant in a Roman toga and then make him wear a Neapolitan sash and a pink carnation, I imagine he would still contrive to look majestic.

One's interest in the interior of the cathedral is divided between the wonderful glass, finest of all Renaissance achievement in this line, and the still more wonderful carved oak choir stalls unsurpassed in France unless by those of Amiens. The glass was *painted*, mostly by one Arnaud de Moles, and offers a good opportunity for comparison of this sixteenth-century method at its best with the thirteenth-century method, the true *stained* glass which is to be seen in its perfection at Chartres or Bourges. De Moles and his contemporary artists did not hold to the old glass-makers creed, "My window shall hang as a rug on the wall." There is a very sharp distinction, too seldom understood by the tourist, between the early and the later methods. Clement of Chartres, one of the greatest of the early artists and almost the only one whose name we know, gave his glass its color *in the crucible*. Like his contemporaries he cared nothing for painting large scenes on cold glass and burning the pictures in. He obtained his effects rather by a marvelous blending of little bits of colored glass arranged in lead frames to form a design. The sun *filtered* through Clement's windows in a subdued and reverent manner. Arnaud de Moles, a fine artist, painted his designs outright upon the glass as if upon canvas and burned his pictures in. The sun lit up these pictures, very beautifully at times, but the effect was uncertain and not always pleasing. The lesser artists of the sixteenth-century school were roughly handled by the piercing light rays, and painted windows presently became so grotesque and absurd that the entire art of making colored glass died and fell into utter oblivion for two or three centuries.

We know nothing at all about this sixteenth-century painter of glass. He saved his very name from extinction by recording in quaint Gascon upon a window in one of the south chapels that he, Arnaud de Moles, had made *las presens berines* (these present windows) *en aunour de diou et de nost d.* (in honor of God and Our Lady) on the *XXV de Juhn mil V cens XIII*, a date which one may rather easily puzzle out. The other windows of the choir chapels are of such similar workmanship that it has been assumed that Arnaud made them all.

The subjects of these windows form almost as interesting a study as their method of manufacture; for along with prophets and evangelists the sibyls play a very important part in them. How amazing it seems that these pagan seeresses were able to crowd their way into the great company of Jewish and Christian notables and win prominent places in the windows of Arnaud de Moles. This was not, however, outside the bounds of precedent; for many of the church fathers, including St. Augustine himself, had proclaimed their belief that the sibyls were divinely inspired. So the prophetess of Cumae, she who sold her sibylline books to Tarquin the Proud, is here in Auch beside Saint John the Baptist and the Lamb of God.

One window, which I well remember, pictures the sibyl Europa, the drawn sword of Herod in her hand, standing between Joshua on her right and Amos on her left. Europa's bosom is as bare as that of any Follies girl and as generous in its contours as that of any Rubens model, but the son of Nun and the herdsman of Tekoah are quite impervious to the sibyl's flaunting charms. Another window represents the Apocryphal scribe Esdras in the act of assembling and editing the sacred books of scripture. "Abacuc," whom we call Habakkuk, is beside him, taking dinner to Daniel, who is in the Lion's Den in the *next chapel*. There seems no accounting for the glass painter's whim in placing Habakkuk in the wrong chapel. The prophet's attitude toward Esdras is extremely amusing. He appears to be surveying him with some astonishment and well he may, for Esdras wears upon his nose a modish sixteenth-century *pince-nez*.

I have an old book both learned and lively called *Une Visite à Sainte-Marie d'Auch*, written and published in 1852 by a certain Abbé Canéto, who styles himself Honorary Canon of Auch and of Ajaccio. This alone is odd, for one sees no plausible reason for linking of this Gascon town with the far-distant birthplace of the Corsican, but the contents of the book are still more entertaining. The good canon has a deft and even gay touch in dealing with the subject of each window. Many are the quaint details he gives concerning the interplay of prophets and martyrs and pagan sibyls and apocryphal saints.

The oaken choir stalls are no less remarkable than the glass for their subject matter, and in perfection of carving they attain the very loftiest level of art. There are one hundred and thirteen of them forming an ensemble of rich dark loveliness rubbed by countless canonical elbows into a lustrous polish almost like ebony.

Nearly any familiar Biblical story can be found and read in these dark carvings. On the south side, for example, beginning at stall 36, one finds:

a) King David with harp, crown and scepter.
b) Bathsheba, his extremely ill-gotten wife, with her bath prepared. She is called charmingly Betsabée in French.
c) Saul accepting David's offer of military aid.
d) David as a warrior but still with his shepherd's crook.
e) Goliath with his giant's pike-staff.
f) David slaying Goliath with smooth stones from the brook.
g) A Philistine soldier removing the debris of Goliath.

So it goes on, always quaint, always exquisite, and presumably capable of giving a certain spiritual nourishment to the uncritical and generally devoted souls of countless servants of the church. Ste. Marie of Auch may well give the most light-minded beholder of today a certain emotional thrill, call it spiritual, esthetic or what you will. At least it achieves the fine eminence of being almost the only great Gothic cathedral built in a decadent age.

Bayonne, in the very hem of the Pyrenees curtain and within sight of Spain, has the misfortune to be thought of, if at all, as a sort of accessory to Biarritz and yet it is in itself ten times as interesting as that fashionable watering place. It is a very real and very lovable little city quite able to stand erect and be somebody for twelve months in every year. I like it immensely. The Rivers Adour and Nive charmingly trisect it; Vauban's citadel, which never surrendered, frowningly guards it; the old château, dwelt in by a host of notables, gives it that historical glamour without which, say what you will, no town is really interesting; and the twin-spired cathedral, if not absolutely great, is remarkably satisfying.

I like Bayonne for its mystery as well as for its undeniable charm. It is a sort of *de facto* capital of French Basqueland and its true native sons, the Basques, are an ethnological mystery which has lured anthropologists to years of almost fruitless labor. Fifty-seven Basque skulls were once dug up from an old graveyard at St.-Jean-de-Luz and carefully measured to find their mean index, which proved to be 80.25 and which proved further that these particular Basques were midway between the brachycephalic people to the north of the Pyrenees and the dolichocephalic people to the south. Beyond that it proved nothing, nor have all other researches, including the long-protracted efforts of Louis Lucien Bonaparte proved anything of importance. Are these people primitive Iberians? Are they Berbers? Are they Atlantides, survivors of a lost continent? Were they perhaps even begotten and cradled right here in the Pyrenees by whatever evolutionary processes produced the human race? Let us leave the problem to others. They are an attractive people to look at and that is enough. The women are for the most part genuine beauties and rivet the gaze of many a male tourist. The men—well, one of them, Jean Borotra the "Bounding Basque," captivated the ladies of two continents so that for years a major tennis tournament could scarcely be a box-office success without him.

The language of the 600,000 Basques who are scattered over

both sides of the Pyrenees is as profound a mystery as their origin. It is a veritable island in a sea of Aryan speech, absolutely unrelated to any other known tongue. It is extremely complicated, with an amazing "post-positional" system a little like the Hungarian. First you plant your noun firmly and then attach to it definite article, preposition and adjective. The verbs draw to themselves like magnets the subject pronoun and the direct and indirect complements, so that each transitive form has no less than *twenty-four* combinations and permutations. Try to imagine it. And as if that were not enough, you must tack on various suffixes according to the age, sex and status of the person you are addressing. Suppose someone asks you in Basque if you know the Basque language. You do not, and wish to say so politely. First survey your questioner and then reply as follows:

    To a man—Eztakiat
    To a woman—Eztakinat
    To a child—Eztakichut
    To a priest—Eztakizut.

Add to these delightful complexities a system of nasal vowels and "wet" consonants; add a numeral system which is vigesimal (for example 54 = twice twenty ten and four, *berrogoi ta hammalaur*, a slight affinity to the cumbersome French *quatre-vingt*); add for good measure eight major dialects and you have a bird's-eye view of Basque. Why not pick it up while in Bayonne? It will be so interesting to talk freely with the natives in their own vernacular.

A further acquaintance with all things Basque may be most

pleasantly made in the Basque Museum, which has a unique personality. The most confirmed museum hater could not fail to respond to its appeal.

### Hemen Satrzen Dena Bete Erchean Da

This is the motto which welcomes you and it means "Whoever Enters Here Is at Home." Everything within is unexpected. One wanders through a stable, a beautiful underground chapel (with graveyard), a cider mill, a sandal-maker's shop, a charming inner court. One learns all a museum can tell of Basque games and dances and music. There is but one foreign note in this all-Basque museum. The place of honor in the main hallway is occupied by a bust of Thomas Garrigue Masaryk!

The *gardienne* told me that she spoke only the smallest smattering of French and that everybody in Bayonne spoke Basque. Why, she asked, did I not pick it up, as I have asked you. Ah, but there is a difference between the *gardienne* and me. She had a two-hundred-page Basque grammar to sell for about a dollar. *My* suggestion is prompted by sheer altruism.

Across the town from the museum rises the square stone bulk of the Château Vieux. Alfonso, El Batallador, King of Aragon, built it in 1130 and those who have for short or long periods dwelt in it are a kaleidoscopic succession. There is Edward the Black Prince and his great Breton opponent, Bernard Duguesclin. There is Pedro the Cruel of Castile, followed by four kings of France, Louis XI, Francis I, Charles IX and Louis XIV. The ninth Charles brought his mother with him (he could scarcely sneeze or say his prayers without her sanction); and she, known to history as Catherine de Medici, is alleged to have plotted here with the infamous Alva the Massacre of St. Bartholomew. Even Napoleon at his zenith once stayed in this château and here compelled the wretched Charles IV of Spain to abdicate in favor of Brother Joseph.

The above is only a partial list of the guests (generally self-invited) of this grim old pile of masonry. The others must do without our publicity, for we are eager to see the cathedral whose spires, admirable if recent, have long been nodding to us over the housetops and up every little street.

Notre-Dame-de-Bayonne is pure Gothic, started in the Great Era and completed, except for the spires, three centuries later. During more than two of these centuries the town was in English hands, which accounts for the Plantagenet arms in the first *travée*, three leopards on a red shield, which the sacristan points out with sibilant whispers to all Anglo-Saxon tourists. The Bayonne sacristan has other tricks in his bag, notably a wonderful open cloister whose charm he does his best to destroy by a running patter of comment in thick French interlarded constantly with the English words "sirteense century" whistled through ailing teeth. When one has finally shaken this man off, one may really enjoy the cathedral's splendid glass, its fine traceried triforium and best of all its Gothic sanity. One tends to grow a little weary of the endless oddities of cathedral architecture in southern France, the jumbled eccentricities and erratic experimentation. Notre-Dame-de-Bayonne is above all restful. You feel that you have got back at least near to the Great Decades.

A sign on the outside of this cathedral reads *Défense de Jouer à Pélote* but all the same a small boy was playing it, batting a hard rubber ball against the façade, when I emerged. I suppose a Basque boy must play pelota as surely as he must learn his catechism. It is played by professionals in Bayonne in a huge hall called *le Trinquet*, similar to the frontón of Spanish and Latin-American cities. Travelers see almost the same game, under the name *jai alai*, in Havana, and under the name pelota in Rio, but in those cities each player wears a long wicker cestus attached to the right hand. Here in Bayonne they play barehanded without even a glove for protection. Their speed and agility in keeping the little white ball in play are dazzling. I was fairly exhausted with following a fifty-point match.

One must not leave this fair, surf-smitten, mountain-shadowed Basqueland without a brief visit to Saint-Jean-de-Luz. Here is to be seen a true Basque church in all its curious glory. The church of St. Jean is like an ancient wooden hangar with an arched roof. On three sides of the aisleless nave rise three-tiered wooden *tribunes* like a town hall council chamber and at the other end an ultragorgeous altar-piece, all gilded and Spanish looking. In this church were married Louis XIV and Maria Theresa, Infanta of Spain (not to be confused with the great Maria Theresa). A special door, traces of which are clearly seen, was knocked out for this ceremony in the south wall of the nave and sealed up again immediately after the wedding.

The names both of persons and towns throughout the Basque district are a continuous source of entertainment. Perhaps we react only mildly to such names as Ttikia and Latxagu, but if we have a spark of the kid left in us what are we to do about Bigorre and Baigorry?

I once entrenched myself in this Basqueland and lingered here for nearly three weeks. It was June, the most gorgeous month of the year, but since the society calendar absolutely forbids any one of the least smartness to be caught in Biarritz or vicinity until August, I had the entire countryside and coastline to myself. Many a plunge I took in the silvery surf of the Silver Coast, on the beaches of Biarritz and Bayonne, using the open sands as bath house. Especially I enjoyed a certain beach called La Chambre d'Amour where I expected at any moment to see Cytherea rise from the foam. She never rose, which was fortunate; for I needed every atom of my attention to battle against the terrific cross-currents and undertow. Along the beach were always a dozen or more grizzled fishermen waiting, with that wonderful patience which only the French fisherman has attained in its perfection, for bites which never seemed to come. With poles planted in the sand and the leaded line far out in the breakers they talked and smoked—and watched me. One of them finally became so worried that he implored me to discontinue bathing here alone. Ever so many people had been drowned here. The strongest swimmer was helpless when an ugly current set in. I was forced to take his advice. To whisper the truth, I had been a little frightened all along. Bayonne and life in general were fair to look upon and I quitted the beach of the Chamber of Love with some alacrity.

I will record here and now two items about Bayonne which I find myself in danger of forgetting, for they ceased to interest me after some twenty hearings and readings. The name is Basque for "harbor"; and the bayonet, invented by a local citizen, takes its name from Bayonne. The first recorded jabs are said to have been made at Ypres in 1647, with which gory comment I must conclude my remarks about one of the most attractive cathedral towns of France. *Au revoir Bayonne et pays des Basques!*

Carcassonne is two hundred miles east of Bayonne, far the other side of Toulouse, our presumable base of operations; but it is still in the shadow of the same Pyrenees. I approach the subject of Carcassonne with some trepidation, for the glamor of this town has been played up by generations of romantic and excited scribes, capitalized by every tourist agency that knows its business, popularized even by the motion picture producers. In spite of all, and I do hope not because of it, I can never seem to develop any passionate interest in this wondrous walled city. It is a great curiosity, its outline against a sunset sky is unforgettable, its historic interest is great, but it is forced to live the year round in a depressing welter of tourist adulation.

My mother brought me up on Carcassonne. I imbibed it during the oatmeal and spinach era if not in actual babyhood. Gustav Nadaud's famous lines were a commonplace of the nursery and I poured out my childish sympathy on the poor peasant who lived only five "grand leagues" from Carcassonne and longed all his life to see it but was never able to finance the trip. It all seemed grossly cruel in view of the manner in which the peasant's family cavorted here and there.

> Ma femme, avec mon fils Aignan,
> A voyagé jusqu' à Narbonne
> Mon filleul a vu Perpignan
> Et je n'ai pas vu Carcassonne!

He finally undertook the trip but died on the way. *"Il n'a jamais vu Carcassonne!"* Along with Poor Disappointed Georgie who could not go to the circus and Suppenkaspar who died rather than eat his soup, this aged Languedoc peasant was one of the three sweet sorrows of my youth. Is it to be wondered at that I expected much of Carcassonne and was vaguely let down when I saw it?

Prosper Mérimée by his urgent pleas saved this walled city when its immense walls were in process of being torn down for materials with which to construct the Ville Basse. Then came Viollet-le-Duc and had the time of his life restoring the whole thing on a grand scale. I have long been threatening to say a word or two about this man Viollet-le-Duc and here in the presence of his greatest effort it really must be said.

Eugène Emmanuel Viollet-le-Duc must have had something of that prodigious mental industry characteristic of so many of his fellow-countrymen, Vincent de Beauvais, for example, and Voltaire. He wrote indefatigably, including two encyclopedias, which have become standard works, the seven-volume architectural dictionary and the encyclopedia of French furniture. Perhaps you consider this enough for one man, but for Viollet-le-Duc it was scarcely more than an appetizer for more work. As an active and supervising architect his industry well-nigh passes comprehension. I have wondered whether it would be easier to list the cathedrals and public buildings which this man restored or those which he did not restore. I will compromise by citing the names of eight of his more conspicuous efforts which bear directly on the contents of this book.

1. Paris—Notre Dame and the Sainte Chapelle
2. Sens—Cathedral
3. Châlons-sur-Marne—Cathedral
4. Laon—Cathedral
5. Amiens—Cathedral
6. Toulouse—St. Sernin and Capitole
7. Carcassonne—Fortifications and Cathedral
8. Clermont-Ferrand—Cathedral

His efforts for the most part were genuinely successful, though many think that he went too far. There can be no doubt of his love and respect for the Gothic of the Great Decades.

For me, since I am on the subject, there is one dark blot on the Viollet-le-Duc escutcheon. He built a church of his own in St. Denis outside of Paris close to the famous abbey church (which also he restored). I have gazed many times at his church, which was his own creation, and have even been inside it. I am willing, then, to say, regardless of what happens to me, that I consider it the ugliest church in France. It looks exactly like the old car barn of a small New England town, with a few ecclesiastical embellishments.

I think there is very little net gain in the practice of walking around the walls of Carcassonne, as nearly every visitor does under the leadership of a French guide. It is a hot and interminable business and, unless one is a professional architect, one knows no more after the trip than before. A more inviting and profitable occupation is to sit in a wicker chair in the superb terrace garden of the Hôtel de la Cité and sip a long cool drink. I saw an American gentleman doing just that while the rest of his party—and I was a trailer with them—trudged around on the path of duty. We came to a point on the wall directly opposite him. A *Saturday Evening Post* was on his knees, a glass was in his hand, a grin was on his face. The grin said plainer than words, "I'm having a good time and you are not." Of course he was a frightful barbarian but I had a sneaking respect for him at that. I think he took back a happier memory of Carcassonne than did his earnest wife who tried very hard not to miss a thing the guide said.

There are two cathedrals in Carcassonne, an old one in the

Cité dedicated to St. Nazaire and a present-day one in the bustling Ville Basse dedicated to St. Michael. This latter is an utterly dreary affair, not worth mentioning, but St. Nazaire is a delight, half Romanesque, half Gothic and wholly unconventional. When I first entered it, a funeral was in progress and I took my stand beside a pillar of the stern old Roman nave and watched the ceremony. The sacristan's versatility was amazing. He had scarcely finished making the preparations than he became suddenly a priest and began chanting the service antiphonally with a higher priest. The somber service over and the mourners gone, he put things to rights with lightning touch and addressed himself to me. He was suddenly all guide. Under his brisk tutelage I prospered greatly and perhaps appreciated the Gothic charms of choir and transept as much as I would have without him. The glass is wonderful here, full of those rich basic blues which the old glass-makers loved.

The chapel of St. Radulphe is the outstanding curiosity of the cathedral. It is completely outside the line of the church and on a much lower level. For four centuries it was sealed up with earth and masonry and for that reason is still called erroneously (and because tourists like it) the Lepers' Chapel. The sacristan pointed out to me a bas-relief in this chapel depicting a funeral procession. "Notice," he said gaily, "that the two acolytes *in front* are looking very sad. The others are laughing. It was so in this funeral just now."

Behind St. Nazaire is a large outdoor theater which draws capacity crowds in prosperous seasons for every performance, though it can accommodate five thousand persons. *Hamlet*, played by players of the Comédie Française, is said to be wonderfully effective here. The ghost appears on the old walls, the cathedral clock does the midnight chiming. A full moon often lights the stage. I confess I am eager to see this and compare such a sophisticated performance with the lusty efforts of the wandering troupe I saw at Cahors.

Carcassonne is really mystifying. If there is one Carcassonne today, why are there not a hundred? The situation of the old Cité is no more impregnable than many another. The stronghold's enemies were certainly no more soft of heart. One of its besiegers, indeed, was Simon de Montfort, arch persecutor of heretics. His body was buried for a time near the high altar of St. Nazaire. Whatever the reason this unique town of romance does exist and in spite of my own confession of weakness, due to too much early feeding upon the subject, I am glad to join in the chorus of gratitude to Prosper Mérimée, who awakened France and saved this treasure.

## CHAPTER XXI

# *Albi and Its* Cathédrale Troublante

THE phrase which I have appropriated to the title of this chapter is that of Louis Courajod, a French art critic. I think the adjective is the one perfect word for Sainte-Cécile-d'Albi. It means disturbing, disconcerting, but also much more than that. A majestic bit of mountain scenery, the Matterhorn wearing its sunset blush, the Cirque de Gavarnie when its thirteen waterfalls are roaring nicely, these are *troublant*. The terrific surf on the Portuguese coast is *troublant*. Even the smile of Mona Lisa is *troublant*, and the song of the Alderney skylarks disappearing in the blue. Whatever elates the spirit is *troublant*, especially if there is a touch of fear or mystery about it.

The cathedral of Albi is a grim brick fort of overpowering dimensions and yet it is also a church, Romanesque in plan, Midi Gothic in style, ornamented with an unsurpassed richness of detail and dedicated to the very gentlest of lady saints, Cecilia, who is the patron of church music. In this there is something to think about.

Physically this church seems impossible. It can't be true, we say over and over again as our train or car rolls into the outskirts of the town. Its massive corrugated red walls, with slits for windows, shoot upward like a row of planted rockets to be terminated by a severe military parapet behind which an army could take shelter. The west façade is not a façade at all, having not even a door, but is taken up with one prodigious dungeon tower eighty meters high, a plain fort in its three lower stages with some ecclesiastical concessions in its three upper stages. This tower fort is planted directly on the Rock of Albi at its western tip and a few yards from it the huddled town tumbles down to the swift red River Tarn.

The search for the reason for such amazing architecture takes us directly to one of the most terrible pages of church history, of the long story of religious oppression and cruelty. Ste.Cécile is an echo of the bloody and successful attempt of the Christian church to stamp out one of the most picturesque heresies that ever cropped up in France, the Albigensian heresy which took its name from this very town of Albi. Basically the Albigenses were anti-sacerdotal and of course that alone was enough to damn them in the eyes of the church. Their leaders inveighed constantly against the vice and corruption of the clergy, and since this corruption was only too obvious there were many listeners.

It is true that some of the doctrines of the Albigenses, though now very difficult to determine precisely, were peculiar and gave their enemies capital. They taught dualism, belief in a personal God of Good and an equally personal God of Evil. The former was exemplified in the New Testament, the latter in the Old Testament. Jehovah was plainly evil, for he encouraged evil things, including marriage. He delighted in sowing enmity among the people he had created, he cursed freely, and finally he admitted that he was evil for he was always "repenting."

The Albigenses appear to have had their own Pope and below him were the *Cathari* or *Perfecti*, who were called also *Bons Chrétiens*, but then there was a truly startling gap in the organization. The Perfect Ones lived most austerely, eschewing marriage, disdaining money, eating no animal food nor even milk or eggs, since these are tarnished by their connection with the idea of sex. But the *Credentes* (Believers) and especially the *Audientes* (Hearers) appear to have made little attempt to approximate in their lives the teachings of the Perfect Ones. They were free to live as they liked and believe as much as they chose provided only that they pledged themselves to be "hereticized" before death. Needless to say this extraordinary freedom won many converts and led to outrageous excesses on the part of some, which gave the whole body of Albigenses a bad name, though the *Perfecti* and very many of the *Credentes* continued to be above reproach.

Like a wave whipped incessantly by the bitter (and *just*) denunciations by the *Perfecti* of ecclesiastical corruption, the Christian Church shook itself angrily and prepared to wipe these heretics from the face of the earth. In the heart of the Great Decades (1209) Pope Innocent III preached a crusade against the Albigenses. The same indulgences and heavenly rewards were offered for this crusade as for former crusades against the Saracens; and like the clever salesman that he was Innocent explained to the faithful that "the labor was but small, the distance short, and yet the recompense was eternal."

Almost immediately 20,000 horsemen and 200,000 footsoldiers rallied to the battle-cry and for twenty years the south of France was convulsed with the struggle. Never was fighting more mad and merciless. In one siege where Catholics and heretics were inextricably entangled the papal legate was appealed to by a body of soldiers who feared for their own souls if they should chance to kill true Catholics. "What ought we to do?" they inquired. "Slay them all," roared the legate. "God will recognize his own." Finally the brilliant old Languedoc civilization was destroyed, but still heresy was not quite stamped out. For a century after the active fighting ceased the Holy Inquisition, developing from these Albigensian wars, hunted down stray heretics with a relentless zeal that has rarely been equaled in any line of human endeavor.

The Inquisition, as it grew up in Albi, makes us fairly hate ourselves for being members of the human race which could produce such a system of injustice and rank sadism and dare to call it a religious office. But the world *is* growing better and therein is comfort. What nation or church today would tolerate such regulations as were a commonplace of the Inquisition and openly supported by nearly every government in Europe? In heresy cases the human mind seemed to take leave of its wits and the human heart of its last trace of compassion. Consider a few of the regulations.

1.) Women, children and slaves could witness for the prosecution but not for the defense.

2.) A hostile witness proven also false could be punished for his perjury but his false testimony *was retained* and considered valid.

3.) Refusal to testify was tantamount to confession of heresy.

4.) Accusation by a heretic of relatives and friends resulted in freedom for the despicable tale-bearer.

5.) Torture of the defendant to secure confessions was definitely ordained by Pope Innocent IV and confirmed by Urban IV, Vicars of Christ, but,

6.) Confessions extracted by torture being obviously invalid, the defendant was required to repeat his confession "freely"—a quibble to make the Blind Goddess wince.

7.) Witnesses as well as the defendant were put to the torture unless their testimony was satisfactory.

8.) Any lawyer attempting to defend the suspect was deemed to be himself guilty of heresy.

9.) "There was never any case of an acquittal pure and simple" (H. C. Lea, an authority on the subject).

In the end the "obstinate" heretic, after enduring the most frightful tortures, was burned at the stake. Two hundred *Perfecti* so perished in a single day.

But death was not the end. Posthumous trials were frequent. The entire estate of the heretic defendant, if it had not already been confiscated as "fines," was taken at his death. The legitimate heirs were disinherited and even made ineligible for any civil office for two generations. Could greed and spleen be carried further? Church and state divided the spoils of many a saintly man whose only offense was to be suspected of some slight irregularity in his personal beliefs. The Holy Inquisitors themselves profited directly in proportion to the amount of money they brought in. The whole pack, with a few exceptions, were fastidious ghouls trying to hoodwink themselves and God.

A certain Bishop Bernard de Castenet was Holy Inquisitor of Albi toward the end of the twelve-hundreds and he it was who conceived the idea of this fortress-church. He was a very successful raiser of money and scores of wealthy heretics lay chained in the narrow episcopal cells with no light and with scarcely air to breathe, awaiting year after year their trials. Their goods and fortunes had been briskly sequestered by the bishop to swell his already immense revenues. Some of the heretics who were obnoxious the bishop walled up alive in their cells and others he tortured and burned, but for the most part he let them slowly die or go mad. Such a bitter storm of hatred arose in Albi that Pope Clement actually intervened and bade the prelate moderate his holy zeal. Bernard then made a grand gesture. He taxed his canons one-twentieth of their incomes and even assumed the same burden himself for the building of a new church which should be a lasting monument to the destruction of heresy and to himself as one of the most illustrious destroyers. The cathedral we see today was born under the shadow of violence and was a perpetual reminder to the now shrinking and hunted heretics that the church was impregnable.

To us this massive church would scarcely prove *troublant* for its size and grimness alone. We can survey an equally large warehouse in London or New York without a quiver. But in some way that is not easy to define, beauty lurks in every line of Ste.Cécile. The brick itself is of a peculiarly warm pink-red that is effective in almost any light. It was made by hand from the red alluvial clay created by the Tarn, and fired by wood fires, a material and a process as superior, from a purely artistic consideration, as the materials and processes of the old glassmakers.

To create for this wondrous cathedral a portal worthy of it would seem to present a problem. The west front is not a front at all, as we have seen, but a dungeon, and the main street which flanks the cathedral on its townward side is thirty feet below the floor level of Ste.Cécile. A bishop and a cathedral gloriously solved the problem or at least gave their names to the solution. A ramp now leads to the Avant-Porte named for Bishop Dominique, the Florentine, and thence fifty steps mount to the baldaquined porch and entrance created by Cardinal Louis d'Amboise, nephew of the famous George, Minister of Louis XII, whose tomb is in Rouen, and built, it is said, by a company of wandering masons from Strasbourg. The whole effect is one of such dazzling beauty that it cannot be set down in words. Prosper Mérimée tried to and though he piled adjective on adjective I think he failed lamentably. The gate of the Florentine wedged between the giant church and a fat round tower of the old city ramparts is charming and a bit astonishing but the porch itself—I shall dust off a phrase which has been in the attic for many years—beggars description.

Have you ever seen a birch tree at Chamonix when every twig was thick with rime, against the background of the Alpengluh on Mont Blanc? Have you ever been close enough to a cardinal to examine the bits of lace upon the rich red ensemble of his eucharistic vestments? (I have at Mechlin, where lace is made.) If so you have seen something very beautiful and faintly like the white stone tracery of the porch of Ste.Cécile with its Flamboyant baldaquin against the ancient pinky brick.

The interior of the cathedral is as surprising as everything else about it. It is a very wide, high room with no aisles, no transepts, no soaring pillars. It merely goes up and up for a hundred feet to terminate in fine frescoed vaulting, of clever construction. The whole effect is one of extreme simplicity in construction and extreme gorgeousness in decoration. An army of Italian painters was imported in the early sixteenth century and they made the mural decorations in a period of about six years, leaving their names all over the walls—Doneja of Carpa, Antonio of Lodi, Lorenzo of Modena and so forth.

In the very center of this "room," really dividing it into two, is a piece of stone furniture so huge, so inappropriate and so utterly gorgeous that it insistently monopolizes the attention: the jube or rood screen which separates the nave from the choir. For this, at any rate, Mérimée has words that satisfy. "*On a honte d'être raisonnable,*" he says, "*en présence de cette magnifique folie.*" Rood screens in general are a nuisance, a distraction, a belittling and cluttering of what could be noble. I can think of a great many of them that I dislike and only two that are able to annihilate my querulous objections—the one by Giovanni Gualdo in the little Madeleine church of Troyes and this one by unknown artists in Ste.Cécile. For more than four hundred years the incredible delicacy and richness of this one at Albi has excited all those who have gazed upon it. Richelieu is said to have mounted a ladder to examine the work closely, being suspicious that it was merely painted plaster, and almost in our own day a French scholar has thought it necessary to have the material chemically analyzed to establish the fact that there is no *trompe-d'oeil*. The secret of its delicacy appears to have quite escaped the guide-books, but Jean Laran in his monograph on Ste.Cécile makes it clear that the stone used in this jube is of a type almost as soft as chalk when quarried but hardening quickly when exposed to the air.

Fully half of the giant church is shut off or partly shut off by this screen. One has to be let in by a sacristan with a pleasant voice and an itching palm, but the concealed portion is a veritable cave of treasure. The intricacies of carving both in stone and wood can scarcely be matched in France. The choir screen is perhaps as fine as that of Chartres, though very different. The stalls rival those of Auch and Amiens. Repeatedly this church within a church has escaped destruction. A single engineer named Maries saved it in 1792 by an impassioned letter to Louis XVI's minister Roland, that "rhinocerous," that "Quaker *endimanché*" who is known to posterity principally as the husband of Madame Roland. Two years later, the Revolution now in full swing, Ste.Cécile was made a Temple of Reason and local devotees of the new cult set themselves to make the edifice "worthy of the name." They had got no farther than to remove seventy objectionable statues from the jube (we see the empty niches today) when the Convention was persuaded to halt the sacrilege. As in the case of Chartres the escape seems almost miraculous. The Virgin and gentle Cecilia must have intervened.

This saint lies in effigy under the *maître autel* oddly erected at the *west* end of the nave in the public portion of the cathedral. Her actual body, the sacristan told me, is in Rome—and he believed it. She looks passing sweet and mild and easy to worship here in her grim fortress of Albi, but actually her presence in this particular spot is the result of a rather horrible crime against art. Most of the great cathedrals in France tell the story of the Last Judgment in sculpture on the west front, but Ste.Cécile of Albi, having no west front, told the story in a great painting on the *inside* of the western end of the structure. It was of colossal dimensions, measuring sixteen yards by twenty-two, covering the inner surface of two of the great brick piers of the tower and the ample space between. For its size alone it was one of the wonders of the world and critics agreed that its technique and coloring were worthy of its size. But two of those "business bishops," hard-headed practical men who liked to get things done, slaughtered this famous art work. One cut a door directly through the center of the picture to connect the church with the tower guard-room which had been converted into a chapel. The other appropriated all that remained of the central portion as a base for the new organ. They got what they wanted, a fine organ with forty-three stops and five manuals, and a thirtieth chapel to add to the twenty-nine already in use. St. Cecilia's effigy under the *maître autel* occupies the central part of the arched door knocked out of this picture.

Even the pitiful remains of Albi's Last Judgment, seen on the rounded piers, are interesting. The painting was laid upon a thin glazed surface spread over the bricks, whose geometric outlines are plainly visible. The rich but sober coloring on a soft background of green mark this as a distinctive work of the fifteenth-century French school very different in spirit from the bright aggressive frescoes left by the invading army of Italian painters a few decades later.

Every visitor to Ste.Cécile unless actually infirm mounts the magnificent tower. One is permitted to walk completely around the military parapet at a height of one hundred and thirty feet and then continue the climb to the tower's lofty summit, whence the old heretic city and the River Tarn and many miles of hilly country are visible. The dominant color in this picture is *red*. Never have I seen anything quite like it. Not only is the cathedral beneath us red but the whole town is red—the red of brick and tile. The earth wherever scratched is red and the Tarn is reddest of all. This river gets its color from the Permian or red sandstone rocks through which it flows. To the people of the Midi in the spring of 1930, it seemed a snarling red devil straight from the jaws of hell; for it led its destructive cohorts in the worst flood France has ever experienced. Albi itself, perched on a rock, could laugh at danger but the city of Montauban a few leagues downstream was cruelly devastated. In passing through the town three months after the disaster I was horrified even then at the appearance of the place. It was like a city drowned in mud, trying to struggle back into life and tear off its clammy shrouds.

I could not get over the redness of Albi as seen from its cathedral tower. Not long before that trip I had been reading Thomas Hardy's *Return of the Native* and I could only think of the reddleman he so clearly pictured. A particular sentence lingered in my mind: "Reddle spreads its lively hues over everything it lights on, stamping unmistakably, as with the mark of Cain, any person who has handled it for half an hour." There was my picture of the Tarn. Albi has "handled" the river for some centuries and is stamped forever with its ruddy mark.

I became conscious of a French girl close beside me as I continued to gaze at the scene below. She was neatly inscribing her name on the parapet of carved stone which forms the topmost stage of the brick tower. She was very attractive and her name, as I discovered, was Emilie Escudigne. You will find the name when you climb the tower of Ste.Cécile and if by chance you ever find Emilie you may remind her that fools' names and fools' faces always appear in public places. My French was not quite equal to such an effort—and besides she was so pretty. Then, too, she was young—in 1930.

Albi is not an accessible town, especially by train. Those who go there go because they will not be denied. It is not in the least tourist-conscious like Carcassonne, but its image will never fade from the mind of one who has seen it. They say that sin and sorrow are far greater themes than virtue and happiness, that the greater beauties of art spring from uglier ground, like lilies from a compost heap. Chartres would seem to deny this but Albi shouts assent. The emotions evoked by these two master works of architecture are very different and each beholder must decide for himself which reactions are the more profound. For myself I would rather *live* with Chartres, far rather, and yet tranquillity would follow such companionship. Life would lack that disturbing, faintly terrifying sense of the unknown induced by Albi's *cathédrale troublante*.

## CHAPTER XXII

# A Bow to Conscience:
# Clermont-Ferrand et al.

I FIND myself smitten quite suddenly by pangs of conscience for my thoughts and my pen appear to be knocking about unconcernedly in southern France in disregard of my implied promise to limit our consideration of French cathedral towns to some five and twenty specimens. Lest I betray you too grossly I will heed forthwith the still small voice. Clermont-Ferrand, the lava city, home of Vercingetorix and Blaise Pascal, is worth unhurried attention, as is, of course, magnificent Bourges. Others, though in many cases noble or appealing, shall receive merely a friendly nod.

Auvergne, of which Clermont was the old capital, is a land of Puys or extinct volcanoes, there being no less than sixty of them, some of which have very distinct craters. Scientists say that this whole area is probably not dead volcanically but merely sleeping for a few hundred centuries. At Royat, a mile or two from Clermont, carbonic acid gas escapes from the ground in many places, a clear proof that there is activity not far beneath the earth's crust, but all the volcanoes, including the greatest of them all, Le Puy-de-Dome, appear to be as dead as stone. Clermont, which is the old Roman Clarus Mons (Clear Mountain) is at the base of this largest volcano and takes its true tone from the lava which once poured freely from the crater. The whole town is quite as lava-gray as Albi is Tarn-red. The streets and houses and public buildings are gray and even the Gothic cathedral, Notre-Dame-de-Grace, is built of the same Auvergne lava.

My first evening in Clermont was made memorable by a brilliant display of fireworks by man and God, and I more than half expected to see the Puy-de-Dome join in and belch forth a pillar of fire. In a café on the Place de Jaude I sat and watched incessant sharp lightning, unaccompanied by rain, play around the volcanic peaks while from the casino of fashionable Royat on the lower slope of the *puy*, elaborate fireworks offered their puny competition to the electric storm. Showy rockets and heavy bombs were often utterly "put out" and silenced by the blinding flashes of lightning and the crashes of thunder. It was a weird and fascinating sight and no one gave a moment's attention to the indomitable café orchestra which played on for dear life.

The whole scene seemed to me like a stage setting designed to bring into prominence the two great heroes of Clermont's past. In the square before my eyes was the brightly illuminated equestrian statue of Vercingetorix, hero of the Gauls, valiant foe of Caesar, and there in dark majesty, unperturbed by nature's bombardment or man's, rose the striking Puy-de-Dome on whose top Pascal conducted the experiments that made him immortal.

Vercingetorix was a man of noble lineage, character and stature, self-constituted leader of the comparatively civilized Gauls who bitterly resented the Roman yoke. He was a genuine patriot, and was able to organize a formidable resistance to the legions of Rome. At Gergovie, a stronghold six miles from Clermont, he inflicted upon Caesar a severe and humiliating defeat (a lava monument now marks the spot) and Caesar could never forgive him for this. When the inevitable Roman victory finally came Ceasar should have had the greatness of spirit to honor a defeated rebel who had so highly distinguished himself, but the actual events show Vercingetorix as a far nobler individual than Caesar.

The Gallic chieftain could easily have fled to safety but he offered himself in expiation of Gaul's rebellion. Donning his finest robes and mounting his horse he rode to Caesar's camp and flung at the Roman commander's feet his sword and helmet. Caesar surveyed him impassively, and had him thrown into prison, and after *six years* exhibited him to the Roman populace in one of those degrading triumphal processions which the people loved. The day's festivities were concluded when the triumvirs put the famous captive to death in the Tullianum. So died Vercingetorix, but to an extraordinary degree he still lives in the hearts of the Auvergnats. Boulevards, cafés and cinemas bear his proud name and in 1954 the people will celebrate the two thousandth anniversary of his vain sacrificial death.

To Blaise Pascal the whole city of Clermont seems to bear tribute. The Puy-de-Dome witnesses his power. The local

Lycée bears his name, statues of course are everywhere and his birthplace is pointed out in the cathedral square at the corner of the Street of the Hosiers. Pascal's genius was one of the most profound and comprehensive ever vouchsafed to a human being and this prompts all who think of him to ask the Creator an old question. Why is it that supreme power of the brain is so often linked with wretched physical health? Why should Blaise Pascal, who might have done monumental things in almost any line to which he turned his attention, have died at thirty-nine, his body so frightfully ravaged by disease that it sickened those who performed a post-mortem examination?

As a child he was an *enfant prodigue*, writing at sixteen a work of immense importance on conic sections. Later he laid the foundations for differential calculus. His "mystic hexagram" with its four hundred corollaries, his solution of the problem of the "general quadrature of the cycloid," delicious phrases which mean nothing at all to my inconsequent mind, were of genuine importance to the development of mathematical science, but he considered mathematics an unworthy pastime suitable only for a sick man who must beguile the weary hours.

In physics his work was even greater and comes nearer to us in Clermont. The experiments on the Puy-de-Dome, carried out under his direction, proved what one or two others had merely asserted, that air exerted a pressure which could be weighed and that the pressure differed at different heights. He also invented the hydraulic press and numerous other practical appliances.

As a man of letters (literally), a writer of ironic controversial epistles of deep power and flawless form he has been unequaled in the two and a half centuries since his death.

As a religious philosopher he was greatest of all, but here he was hampered by an extraordinary conflict which he was never able fully to wear down. His reason demanded proof—clear incontrovertible proof—of anything which he made his own. But in his thirty-second year (he records the exact date, Nov. 22, 1654) he experienced the phenomenon of religious conversion as definitely as Saul of Tarsus experienced it on the road to Damascus. He could not account for it, nor could he wave it aside. It was as real as anything which had ever occurred in his whole life. The conflict went on until the last year of his life when he wearily laid aside his doubts and prepared to die with all the simplicity of a peasant who has never dreamed of questioning the dogmas taught by the village priest. His *Pensées*, posthumously edited and garbled by the Jansenists, were published to prove the philosopher's orthodoxy, and by Condorcet from the identical material to prove his unorthodoxy.

One further achievement of Pascal's titanic intellect I cannot resist recording here for it shows the immense range of his interest. He established the first *omnibus line* for the transportation of passengers.

From his home at the corner of the Hosiers' Street Pascal as a boy could look across the square at the gray-black cathedral. It lacked then the façade and Gothic towers which Viollet-le-Duc added and must have seemed very austere in its huge somber bulk. One lava cathedral is enough, I think, for this small world of ours. Notre-Dame-de-Grace is very striking as it looms up against the blue skies of Auvergne but it is vaguely depressing too. It hints of the religion of the undertaker's chapel. Possibly I am not fair in this. One writer has likened the interior to "a grove of silver poplars on a cloudy day" but I confess that I tried in vain to capture the feeling which could evoke that beautiful simile. The great blue rose of the north transept and the red rose opposite are perhaps more brilliant for their dusky setting but even these did not quite dispel my vague sensation of being in a Stygian cave. To climb the Tour de la Bayette and emerge above the cathedral into the clear sun-washed air restores one's naturalness and zest. The view is magnificent if one can overlook the extensive Michelin tire works in the middle distance.

The cathedral square below us contains a Crusaders' Monument, which commemorates the celebrated council of 1095 when the papacy reached, at Clermont, its absolute zenith of glory and power. In this city Urban II, supported by Peter the Hermit, preached the first crusade and the multitudes shouted in a frenzy of religious excitement, *"Dieu li volt! Dieu li volt!"*

Clermont-Ferrand is a double town, as its name implies, the syllable *mont* being called upon for double service—Clermont and Montferrand. The second partner was once a center of aristocratic culture but was absorbed by the more vigorous and businesslike Clermont. The minor partner has been likened to an embalmed seventeenth-century town, its sleepy streets being full of beautiful old mansions of that period. It has steadily lapsed into genteel obscurity while its energetic partner has gone on to large achievement. Clermont has become, in short, the Akron of France.

I enjoyed many things about this ancient ecclesiastical city, from its ugly *église ouvrière* perpetrated by Michelin and its lovely old Notre-Dame-du-Port where white carved stone contrasts with black lava, to its *fontaines pétrifiantes* where anything from a deceased canary to a plush sofa can be petrified to order and brought to the hardness of marble in twenty-five days. Two associations, however, have fixed themselves above all else in my mind—roses and children. In the Jardin Lecoq I saw both in perfection. The roses were very profuse and varied. I wandered in and out freely among them and felt that I was in a sort of floral congress of nations. A lovely tea rose labeled La Tosca caught my eye and this operatic beauty was flanked by Jonkheer J. C. Moock and Lady Hillingdon. In the next path were Madame Ravary and Georg Arends and Red Letter Day, which last, a hybrid, seemed to sum up my feelings. I recalled a similar rose-wandering I had enjoyed on the Island of Mainau in Lake Constance. On both occasions I regretted my ignorance of rose culture and rose nomenclature almost enough to do something about it, but upon learning that there exist some three thousand species of *Rosaceae* and that one hundred and fifty new species, on the average, are catalogued each year I allowed my desire for comprehensive rose knowledge to languish.

The roses of the Jardin Lecoq were extremely beautiful but the children outshone them. How is it—I believe I have asked this question in an earlier chapter—that the French are able to produce such gloriously pretty children? The parents are not so very marvelous, in my candid opinion. There are stout ones and thin ones and plain ones and plainer ones with a few beautiful or handsome as with us and all races, yet the young children seem to be nearly always little beauties. The phenomenon has been noticed by many tourists in many parts of France where it is not to be discounted as in the Parc Monceau and Avenue Foch of the capital on the ground of rich clothes. Of course, French parents, even those of modest means, do very often burden their budgets by an excessive outlay for children's clothing, but clothes cannot altogether make the child. I think there is something about the Gallic cast of countenance that lends itself to juvenile beauty. It is an indefinable quality of physiognomy which we can only call by the lame adjective Frenchy.

The cathedral towns within easy reach of Clermont-Ferrand are very numerous. Five of them we shall select arbitrarily for a paragraph apiece.

Firstly there is Le Puy to the south. A more astonishing town does not exist in France and it is amazing that so few tourists make their way thither. Needle peaks, crowned by religious shrines, give an air of fantastic unreality to the scene as though some eccentric god of the Victorian era had planned it all for the garden of his country estate. The Romanesque cathedral, a motley of white sandstone, is as bizarre as the town, and it contains as one of its greatest treasures a Black Virgin and Child. An Ethiopian princess in gorgeous brocaded satin holds her little black baby, who peeps out of a round hole in the middle of her rich robe. Faithful worshipers come in thousands every year to kneel before this statue.

To the west of Clermont lies Limoges, which vies with Sèvres as the chief center of the French porcelain industry. Limoges is, as a matter of fact, much more important than Sèvres, boasting no less than forty factories and ten thousand operatives. Foregoing the opportunity of seeing one of these factories and foregoing also the attractions of a local musical show, *La Madonna des Sandwichs,* whose posters were all over the town, I made my way straight to the cathedral which is dedicated to St. Stephen. It is a noble Gothic structure nobly placed on a hill above the Vienne, but the main approach to it gives an impression of incredible severity for the west front is blocked by a bleak stone tower-base with one little slit of a door and over this base rises a tall bare tower of four stages which, one learns, gave birth to the Limousin school of architecture. The interior of the church entered from the north side warms one's spirit by its Gothic aisles, its rich blue glass and its half pagan rood screen in which, oddly enough, the labors of Hercules form the conspicuous theme.

To the north of Clermont lie Moulins, Nevers and Auxerre. Moulins is the sleepy old city of mills owned by the Bourbon dukes, who made it their capital. On a broiling summer day the cellar-like coolness of its large Gothic cathedral was very grateful to me. Being a mere man I entered unperturbed, but had I been a lady tourist I should have looked carefully to the length of my sleeves and skirt, for a severe sign, drawn up by the Bishop of Moulins, called down the *terribles châtiments de Dieu* upon her who should have the *impudeur et impudence* to enter without being what the bishop should judge "properly dressed." Tourists were especially warned that French law gave the canons full police power within the sacred edifice. In spite of this dubious welcome to tourists as a class I wandered comfortably about the cool cathedral in which, as often happens, priests were droning through the *office* without one single worshiper present—unless they counted me. A marvelous triptych of the Virgin and Child, variously attributed to Jean Perreal, to Ghirlandajo and to a vague *Maître de Moulins*, is by far the greatest treasure of this church and one of its donors was Anne de Beaujeu, Louis XI's eldest daughter, whose hand was offered by that monarch five times before a taker was found.

Nevers, a few miles north of Moulins, is of no great importance yet it is one of those towns which seems to linger unaccountably in the mind. It is on the Loire, a great and yellow stream even here, though much "younger" than at Orléans or Blois. Nevers was the home of two princesses who became Polish queens and laid the foundations for the Franco-Polish friendship which was strong for nearly three centuries. It was the home of Mazarin and is the burial place of Bernadette Soubirous, that strange girl (so ably pictured by Franz Werfel) who saw the Virgin eighteen times in a grotto at Lourdes and was thus the instrument for the development of the greatest miracle-working shrine in Christendom. One of the very saddest spectacles in this sad world is the sight of a train full of *grands malades* rolling into the station of Lourdes, and no one who has witnessed it can gaze without queer emotions at the tomb of Bernadette Soubirous in Nevers.

The Gothic cathedral, dedicated to St. Cyr, is rather a freak of architecture and all the more interesting on that account. Like the cathedral of Besançon it possesses two apses, one at the east end and one at the west. The latter was built first and the high altar set up, but the Nivernais conscience rebelled at what seemed almost a sacrilege—for true Christians prayed toward the *east*—so another apse was built and another altar erected. Nowadays, when the direction toward which prayer is propelled seems of slight importance even to Catholics, both apses and both altars are in good standing.

At Auxerre we are again in the heart of the Great Decades for its cathedral was substantially completed in twenty years from its commencement in 1215. There is a refreshing grandeur and harmony about it, and one feels that the Virgin of the twelve-hundreds could have taken up her abode here with genuine pleasure. Freaks and fancies are left behind us. The recessed portals, rich in sculpture, the sharp gables and little

Gothic pinnacles, the rose window and the Last Judgment of the main portal, all proclaim at first sight the date of birth of St. Etienne-d'Auxerre, which is often called the leader of the old Gothic cathedrals of the second rank. Its interior is not disappointing. All that one expects is there and in addition to the glories of glass and stone there is the tomb of Jacques Amyot, plebeian, struggling scholar, tutor, grand almoner, Bishop of Auxerre. By his translation of Plutarch's Lives he may be said to have set in imperishable colors the modern French language. Further, this work, translated into English, gave Shakespeare the setting for at least four of his plays, and Shakespeare's copy of Amyot's *Plutarch* is still extant, one of three existing books believed with reasonable certainty to have actually belonged to the bard.

Auxerre is for our purpose a logical introduction to the last cathedral town we shall consider, the last of the Big Six, one of the most significant manifestations of the Miracle. Without further trumpeting I present Bourges.

## CHAPTER XXIII

## *Bourges, the Heart of France*

MY EARLY "initiation" to Bourges was made memorable by one of those tragedies which turn to comedy when seen through the mellowing lens of retrospect. I had overnighted at Nevers and got myself up at six for an early start by train via the junction of Saincaize. My timetable indicated perfect connections and the impersonal being back of the ticket *guichet* seemed to confirm the timetable's findings. I rode the six miles to Saincaize, disembarked and looked for the train to Bourges. A guard looked meanwhile at me with a queer expression on his countenance.

"Did monsieur wish to go somewhere?" he ventured politely. (Saincaize was not "somewhere." It was nothing at all but a station.)

"But yes. I wish to go to Bourges."

Then the crash came. "Ah, how unfortunate," he sighed, "The next train will not go for six hours and that is a *rapide*, with a heavy extra fare for so short a distance."

I whipped out my little *horaire*. "How about this?" I demanded sternly as though he had written the thing. "It says here 7.16. Doesn't it?"

"Certainly it does," he admitted, "but that train has been removed."

"Removed?" and I am afraid I shouted the word. "But isn't this the latest *horaire?* Look at the date of it."

"Yes, monsieur, it is the latest; but mistakes sometimes occur in those books. In fact they often occur."

With that he smiled deprecatingly and swung aboard the south-bound train which I had quitted, leaving me to read with rage and despair a printed *Nota* on the cover of my time-table. This notice is familiar in all languages and was originally devised by one of Beelzebub's smart lawyers. "We believe the information herein contained to be correct but we do not guarantee its accuracy." I lived to reach Bourges and the softening influences of the old Berry capital actually convinced me that there were elements of humor in the morning's tragedy.

Bourges is in the exact geographical center of France as Madrid is in the center of Spain. For a brief period it was the capital of France and thereby hangs a drama of ingratitude as moving, I think, as anything in history. The personages of the drama are a king, his mistress, a commoner and a lady of the court.

The king was Charles VII, that listless worthless lump of a king whose face was all nose and no chin. The English called him derisively "King of Bourges" because he had installed himself in that city and watched France crumble away before his eyes. Things were in a desperate state but Joan came along, bolstered him up and won his crown for him. Charles must have been born under a lucky star, for there seemed always to be somebody ready to do for him what he could not do for himself. He could not have held what the Maid won for him, had not a great financial wizard come to his aid. The man was Jacques Coeur of Bourges, humble son of a furrier.

Coeur was a merchant-prince of the very first rank. By his personal genius he built up an immense trade with the Levant and his ships, literally fleets of them, sailed all the known oceans. His fortune became by a wide margin the greatest that had ever been built up in France. By the tactful gift of a loin of mutton to the king, who was actually too poor to buy such luxuries, he had early won Charles's favor. After Joan's martyrdom he pushed and prodded the monarch onward and upward to something of the dignity that was rightfully his. He literally carried the monarchy on his strong shoulders, advancing twenty-four million francs to finance the wars against England and fighting by the king's side until Rouen was finally taken. He was made master of the mint and king's steward and was able to effect drastic and sorely needed reforms. To Charles he was absolutely loyal. "Sire, all that I have is yours," he said and in a sense he meant just what he said. He was far too keen not to know that extensive loans to a weak monarch have a habit of never being paid back.

His fortunes after the capture of Rouen were at their zenith. He was the best-known personage in France. The volume of his business, it is said, exceeded that of all other merchants in the country combined. He had also successfully concluded three important diplomatic missions. But of course, since humanity is what it is, trouble was brewing. Many resented his meteoric rise to political importance. Many more were heavily in his debt. "Loan oft loses both itself and friend"

was just as true then as when Shakespeare wrote it a century
and a half later.

It happened that Agnès Sorel was then the king's mistress.
A kinder woman and one more unselfishly devoted to her
country never entered into that left-handed relationship with
a king. Her beauty and graciousness and, one is tempted to
say, her virtue have become legendary. She shares with the
Maid and the Merchant-Prince the honor of having made
Charles amount to something. Perhaps she deserves even more
credit than the other two, for she quietly steered the ship of
state by gathering about her king a group of able unselfish
councilors of whom Jacques Coeur was the greatest. But alas
she died in 1450 at the birth of her fourth child. Then jealousy
and greed reared their vile heads, at first timidly, then with
sickening boldness. The king without Agnès was his old chin-
less self again.

A lady of the court named Jeanne de Vendôme, who was
heavily indebted to Jacques Coeur, brought a charge against
him so absurd and so monstrous that the master of the mint
took it as a harmless display of the old viper's fangs. She said
he had poisoned the fair Agnès. But the king allowed the matter to come to a head and Coeur was arrested. Without waiting
for the trial his gloating enemies secured the king's order for
the seizure of the merchant's goods and much of his money.
The king himself reserved a large sum of money for his own
use. Then the trial took place, twenty-two months of it, and
never was remorseless cruelty and fierce greed more thinly
cloaked by legal forms. The judges were chosen from Coeur's
avowed enemies, his debtors and those who had already been
awarded portions of his forfeited estate. The poisoning charge
was so ridiculous (for Agnès had been the bulwark between

him and his enemies) that it was dropped, but innumerable other petty charges were trumped up and rolled into a formidable mass.

Jacques Coeur was put to the torture but refused to "confess," nor could any of the charges be proved, so he was baldly convicted anyway since a conviction was necessary. He was required to do public penance; to pay the king a sum of money equal to five million dollars; to surrender all his property; to remain in prison until "satisfaction" had been obtained. For five years in all he languished in various jails and it is as melancholy as it is true that his colossal estate, despite every element of justice, was dealt out to his enemies and debtors, to the favorites of the king and to the new mistress, Antoinette de Maignelais. He was not allowed to communicate even with his sons, one of whom was Archbishop of Bourges.

He finally escaped to Rome, was welcomed by the pope and given command of a papal fleet which was to be sent against the Turks. Perhaps he would have built up his fortunes anew, but alas death overtook him in the island of Chios, "one of the birthplaces of Homer."

Jacques Coeur is the heart of the heart of France and I permit myself this play on words because he himself could not resist it. His official motto in its quaint medieval spelling was:

*A Vaillans Cuers Riens Impossible.*

He is great enough in the accumulated glamor of centuries to pervade a great town and a wonderful cathedral. His *palais* in the town is one of the outstanding medieval palaces of France and in the cathedral itself one is shown the chapel he built with the small oratory where he and his wife could kneel in obscurity and watch their son, the archbishop, celebrating mass.

I forced myself to practice a certain deliberation in approaching the cathedral of Bourges. Having been fuming in the desolate junction of Saincaize all the morning, I wanted to let the atmosphere of old Bourges soak into my spirit and dispel any murky thoughts that might be lingering there. Then and not till then I would give myself over to that "dark leviathan" St.Etienne, which loomed so hugely from the midst of the city. Several of the old palaces I visited, including, of course, that of the Mint Master and that of Jacques Cujas, most eminent of early French jurists. He was born at Toulouse and his first important teaching post was at Cahors, but Bourges was his chosen home. Three times he was professor here only to be driven away by enemies or called away by the king, but a fourth time he returned to Bourges to spend his last years. His great mansion, *ravissant édifice de la Renaissance,* is now the Museum of Berry and offers a grand opportunity even to the casual tourist to introduce himself to the Bourges that Coeur and Cujas knew. For my part I confess that even to the neglect of some of the treasures connected with these two men, I devoted my attention especially to the death masks of two women. One was of Agnès Sorel, the other of Jeanne de France, a granddaughter of Agnès' royal lover. The contrast of their actual features was of immense interest to me. Agnès was beyond question very sweet and lovely and even with the shining eyes closed in death there was character in her face. One could understand Charles's infatuation.

Poor Jeanne had character too if ever a woman did, but I am afraid she needs her eyes. It is hard to look at her gaunt bony face, all out of gear, with a nose far too ponderous for

the other features, like Grandfather Charles's nose, and feel
any emotion other than that which her husband felt, repug-
nance. Jeanne carried a heavy load of evil inheritance. Grandfather Charles, deprived by death of fair Agnès, sank gradually down to his natural level of inertia and stupidity. He
finally died of starvation in a castle just outside of Bourges,
having eaten almost nothing for weeks because of an obsession
that his son was trying to poison him. His son was that Louis
XI whom we have met so often and none of us would put
patricide beyond him. He was born in Bourges and a striking
statue of him with his disagreeable clotted face, his queer hat
adorned with its fringe of little tin saints, disfigures the park
in front of the post office.

Louis was a great man and a very evil one. Jeanne was his
youngest daughter and he imposed her upon the Duke of Orléans, first prince of the blood, who was filled with wrath and
disgust. She was twelve and the prince fourteen when they
were married. Louis's only son, Charles VIII, had a short reign.
He it was whose two sons by Anne of Brittany are buried in
the beautiful white sarcophagus at Tours. Upon his death
Jeanne's husband became king as Louis XII. Almost his first
royal act was to induce Pope Alexander VI to annul his marriage on the old threadbare theory that it was illegal because
of consanguinity. He quickly made eyes at the widowed Anne
of Brittany and took her (and Brittany) to his arms.

Jeanne's heroism then came to the fore. She had always been
unfailingly devoted to her husband but when he cast her off
she uttered no word of complaint or of disparagement of Anne.
Quietly she withdrew to Bourges and devoted the rest of her
life to good works. The thirty-third successor of that pope
who had authorized her casting-off declared her "blessed." A

look at her death mask does not reveal the fact that she was lame and *bossue,* but shows only the ugly Valois features in a peculiarly unhappy combination. We would like to see the eyes and through them one of the most beautiful characters in the annals of French royalty. How did that intricate monster of craftiness and suspicion, Louis XI, beget a daughter so simple and saintly? *Ah, Voilà la problème,* as the French Hamlet said.

The first close approach to Saint-Etienne-de-Bourges should be circumspect for it is great in majesty and the first full photograph of it upon the mind is likely to linger through life. Without knowing what approach is architecturally orthodox I cast my vote for that roundabout way which leads through the beautiful public garden laid out by Le Nôtre. From this delightful park the giant cathedral looms up like a mountain, whose foothills are tiered chapels, flying buttresses and an enormous circular crypt which Viollet-le-Duc called "a subterranean church which is actually above ground." Nothing interrupts the awe-inspiring sweep of the church as thus seen from the south a little back of the apse. The towers, called "Butter" and "Deaf," are stumpy affairs, unworthy and half hidden from view. They do not distract us. And there are no transepts. This I suppose is the chief secret of St. Etienne's appearance of unequaled bulk, for one is quite ready to assert that it is the hugest cathedral in the world, not barring St. Peter's in Rome or Seville's Santa Maria de la Sede. Its actual area is exactly the same as that of Notre Dame of Paris, being thus exceeded by Amiens, Reims and Chartres, but it looks far larger than any of them. In height it is less than Beauvais and Amiens and a little less than Reims but the ground falls away sharply at the eastern end and, as in the case of Le Mans, contributes vastly to the effect of soaring height. Its width, on the other hand, is actually eight feet greater than that of any other French cathedral.

The interior does not in the slightest diminish one's sense of the incredible hugeness of the structure. Double aisles sweep clear around the ambulatory and form in the main body of the church five separate vistas of majesty, while the central nave, by a familiar trick of architecture, is made to seem much larger than it is. The main flanking pillars "separate" progressively as they approach the choir so that the last ones are nearly a yard more distant from each other, axis to axis than the first. This corrects the ordinary optical illusion of two rows of parallel columns drawing together in the distance and gives an almost weird effect of limitless space.

The details of the interior are full of interest, and first of all there is *glass*, which is superb both in general and in particular. It dates mostly from the thirteenth century and ranks higher than that of any other French cathedral save perhaps Chartres; but its show piece, the *grand housteau* of the western end, was constructed much later by the celebrated Guy de Dammartin. This, as we saw in imitation at Tours and Le Mans (here at Bourges it is original), is a four-sided central window with curved, bulging sides supported by tall lancets. As designed by the genius of Dammartin it is extremely effective here but it would certainly be a dangerous thing for small-caliber architects to play with. We may be glad that Dammartin came late and that the *grands housteaux* of France are few.

The Joseph window and the very famous *vitrail de la Nouvelle Allaince* which undertakes to link the Old and New Testaments are of absorbing interest, as are many others; but since we cannot consider them all let us select the quaintest of all, that which tells the story of an Alexandrian courtesan who became a saint. I first met this saint in the sculpture of the *Portail des Librairies* of the Rouen Cathedral, where her hand was placed on the head of a gentle lion; but here in the glass of Ste.Etienne her whole story is portrayed in twelve sections, starting with her professional solicitation of men before her Alexandrian house and concluding with her triumphant entry into heaven.

The interval was a severe one for Mary the Egyptian. She went to Jerusalem out of curiosity to see the Holy Cross, was thoroughly abased and thenceforward devoted forty years to penance in the desert, where she wore for covering only the long tresses which had once beguiled her Alexandrian clients. Her skin grew quite black under the sun's fierce rays. In this condition she became a friend of lions, but what lions! They remind one, whether in glass or stone, of Bottom's ideal lion, as gentle as any sucking dove, with the roar of a nightingale. Mary in her wild and penitent state was found by the Abbot Zozime, who threw a cloak about her and listened to her amazing story. He was deeply touched and promised to come to her again at Easter to administer the holy sacrament. When he did return, alas, he found poor Mary Penitent dead on the sands. A lion approached, looked at the abbot through streaming eyes and helped him dig a grave into which lion and abbot gently laid the dead woman.

This story from the Golden Legend has a considerable hold on the sensitive feelings of the faithful even today. They call the saint *Marie la Jussienne*, which is a corruption of l'Egyptienne. There is a tiny street in Paris near St. Eustache called rue de la Jussienne, for there once stood at the corner of this street and rue Montmartre a church dedicated to the Alexandrian saint. In the apsidal chapel at Bourges which contains the story of her life, I once saw a moving vignette of life, one person only, a woman dressed in black kneeling in fervent devotion. It was impossible to avoid wondering whether she had once devoted herself to the early profession of the Alexandrian.

The most astonishing, though not the most beautiful or impressive aspect of the cathedral is the west façade with its five porches. I have deliberately entered by the old Romanesque portal at the south in order to save what to me is climactic. To emerge to the little square before the west front and gaze at the awe-inspiring mass of Dammartin's façade is perhaps the pinnacle of sensation. The external width of the cathedral is 180 feet and its five portals lead directly to the five divisions of the nave. The effect of so huge a façade flanked by squat towers, one of which leans for support on a massive and ugly *pilier butant* is rather overpowering in its suggestion of weight, but the entire central portion from the lavishly decorated portal to the tip of the gable is an artistic delight and its detail is worth hours of study. Here better than anywhere else one can examine the thirteenth-century idea of the Last Judgment, that portentous theme which takes the place of honor, the tympanum of the central door, in nearly all of the great cathedrals. Let it not be thought that this sculpture is of interest only to the very learned who are determined to push scholarship to its limits. On the contrary it will capture the attention of the most casual beholder. I can think of nothing more absorbingly quaint, humorous, charming and ghastly.

Certain basic elements of the thirteenth-century conception of the Last Judgment must be understood before one can fully grasp such sculpture as this at Bourges. Firstly, age disappears in the resurrection. Everyone is thirty years old, *tam infans unius noctis quam aliquis nongentorum annorum* (whether an infant of one night or a person of nine hundred years [like Methuselah]). This belief was based on the theory of Vincent de Beauvais that Christ's age was thirty at His crucifixion and resurrection. Most churchmen placed the period of Christ's stay on earth at thirty-three years but Vincent was given the preference. Sex survives in the resurrection for no very clear reason since it is of no value and no interest to anyone. The dead, when summoned by the last trump, come forth out of the earth nude. This, according to Mâle, was contrary to the tastes of the medieval sculptors who disliked to portray the nude and always tried to avoid it, but felt that in this case it was scriptural. Bishops only come forth fully clad. I suppose the idea of presenting a venerated bishop without his vestments was too repugnant (at least to living bishops) to be endured.

Michael, the Archangel, always holds the scales, and the emphasis placed on him seems to have been an effort to make him the Christian successor to the pagan Mercury whom the people of Gaul still venerated. He took on nearly all the attributes and duties of Mercury, including that of conducting the dead to their final home.

At Bourges we see St. Michael in the very center of the picture benignly weighing the souls of the aspirants for paradise. Those at his right obviously are the saved. Their complacent grins stretch from ear to ear and would put a Cheshire cat to shame. Those at his left are being hustled, prodded and thrown into the cauldron by as lurid a company of devils as human imagination could devise. The candidate whose soul is being weighed does not come up to the specified age of thirty, but is a child unquestionably, a boy child, though Henry James, whose spectacles may have been a little blurred, calls it a girl. The test seems to have been successfully passed for the scales tip to the good side and the "chessy cat" smirk of delight is already on the child's face. The object in the good side of the scales, representing the candidate's good qualities, is probably a Wise Virgin's lamp and that in the bad side is a grotesque head with huge repulsive ears. Satan cannot reach the scales here, as in so many cases, to give sly pressure with his hand to the bad side but his eager leer is horrible.

The picture on either side of the archangel is rich in detail. The damned at Michael's left are having a very frightful time of it. Serpents and toads attack them even as they are thrown into the cauldron, which is planted in the upturned jaws of the flaming Leviathan. The devils, besides being hideous, are gross and indecent. Wings sprout from their buttocks and grinning human faces are on their stomachs or breasts or groins or the ends of their tails. Two particularly loathsome devils are pumping bellows in the flame-breathing jaws of the monster and others are stirring the damned in the cauldron as though they were soiled clothes in a wash-boiler. One is forced to believe that there was a latent touch of sadism in these medieval sculptors. They must have thought of their earthly enemies, those who owed them money and would not pay, or those who had sneaked in ahead of them to secure a coveted job. The schoolmen had a famous couplet which is said to have been the cruel inspiration for much of the sculptured horror in these Last Judgment scenes.

*Nix, nox, vox, lachrymae, sulphur, sitis, aestus;*
*Malleus et stridor, spes perdita, vincula, vermes.*

(Snow, night, a cry, tears, sulphur, thirst, boiling;
A mallet and hissing, hope lost, chains, worms.)

It is a relief to turn one's eyes again to that quaint smug group at the archangel's right hand. A king, presumably Saint Louis, is one of the lucky ones and is being presented by a rope-girdled Franciscan monk, presumably St. Francis of Assisi, to St. Peter, whose great key is in his hand. The little angels have golden crowns ready and the napkin held by Abraham, though already full to repletion with the souls of the elect, will always hold one more. This symbol of Abraham with a napkinful of saved souls is a familiar hieroglyph in the sculpture of many churches. It was the best the artist could do to picture paradise, but in the happy smirks of those on the Bourges tympanum, who have passed the examination and are on their way to the bosom of the patriarch, we are supposed to see a reflection of eternal blessedness. This is the solitary church in France, according to Mâle, where this type of eternal smile occurs and I can well believe it, for I am sure I should remember it had I ever seen it elsewhere.

St. Etienne of Bourges is not a cathedral to be seen, admired, and left. It is one like Chartres and Reims which must be seen repeatedly before even a tenth of its grandeur can be grasped. The mere size of it makes a minority of critics dubious about its artistic merit. They exhibit a desire to assert their independence and disparage this cathedral whose colossal bulk is not enough to fool *them*. But I like to agree and do agree with those who find it great enough to ignore its detractors and live down its admitted faults. It takes many faults and grave ones to destroy such grandeur.

The tiny street which leads directly to the cathedral's main portal is beautifully named *rue du Guichet*. I do not know the actual significance of this name but the street's effect is certainly that of a wicket in a great stone door. Through vines and tree branches which lean over a lichened wall one sees the *grand housteau* of Dammartin above the Judgment portal. All that is heavy or dull is shut out by the narrowness of the street. I am inclined to think that if I were to choose any one spot in which to say my adieux to the miracle of Cathedral France it would be exactly here. Bourges is Gothic grown mature but not Flamboyant, mellow but not overripe. It is the miracle at full tide.

# DATE DUE

| DEC 1 5 1964 | | |
|---|---|---|
| APR 3 0 '68 | | |
| MAR 21 '69 | | |
| APR 22 '69 | | |
| MAY 15 70 | | |
| | | |
| | | |
| | | |
| | | |
| | | |
| | | |
| | | |
| | | |
| | | |
| | | |
| | | |
| | | |
| GAYLORD | | PRINTED IN U.S.A. |